*Mrs. Murray's Strategy*

# THE WOMEN OF '76

# THE
# WOMEN
# OF '76

*by SALLY SMITH BOOTH*

*Hastings House · Publishers*
*New York* 10016

For Jim
"Dearest Friend"

Copyright © 1973 by Sally Smith Booth

*Library of Congress Cataloging in Publication Data*

Booth, Sally Smith. The women of '76.
   1. United States—History—Revolution—Women's work.  2. United States—History—Revolution—Biography.  I. Title.
E276.B66     973.3′15′042     73-13922
ISBN 0-8038-8066-9

Published simultaneously in Canada by
Saunders of Toronto, Ltd., Don Mills, Ontario

*Printed in the United States of America*

# Contents

| | | |
|---|---|---|
| I | *The First Shot* | 7 |
| II | *A Spreading Fire* | 25 |
| III | *Choosing Up Sides* | 59 |
| IV | *Christmas at Trenton* | 83 |
| V | *Armies on the March* | 121 |
| VI | *Women Take to the Road* | 171 |
| VII | *War Leaves the North* | 202 |
| VIII | *Secrecy Behind the Scenes* | 238 |
| IX | *Independence at Last* | 271 |
| | *Epilogue* | 284 |
| | *Acknowledgments* | 306 |
| | *Bibliography* | 309 |
| | *Index* | 323 |

*Mrs. James Warren* (Mercy Otis), painting by John Singleton
Copley. Courtesy of Museum of Fine Arts, Boston; bequest of
Winslow Warren.

# CHAPTER ONE

# The First Shot

Should I attempt to describe to you the complicated miseries and distresses brought upon us by the late inhumane acts of the British parliament my pen would fail me. Suffice it to say, that we are invaded with fleets and Armies, our commerce not only obstructed, but totally ruined, the courts of Justice shut, many driven out from the Metropolis, thousands reduced to want, or dependant upon the charity of their neighbours for a daily supply of food, all the Horrours of a civil war threatning us on one hand, and the chains of Slavery ready forged for us on the other.

Abigail Adams to Catharine Macaulay, 1774

AMERICA was tense in 1774, but for Mercy Warren, tension was not enough.

For nearly a decade, the Massachusetts housewife had watched while resentments built against the crown's colonial policies. Now firebrand radicals were haranguing mobs in city streets throughout the country, while the Continental Congress clashed in discord of a higher level in Philadelphia.

But Mercy was interested in more than speech making or debates. Her goal was complete independence for the colonies. Her way was revolution.

Mercy Otis Warren seemed an unlikely fomenter of violence. To most she appeared as the gentle and uncomplicated wife of a Plymouth farmer. Only a few, high-placed rebel leaders knew that the unassuming woman was one of the most important

figures in the drive for liberty. For two years she had been working behind the scenes to kindle the rebellion. Secretly, she was
one of the most influential propagandists in America.

Thousands of citizens had been swayed by Mercy's inflam-
matory tracts which attacked British policies and representatives.
The material, however, had been printed anonymously, for sedi-
tion and treason were grave offenses under common law. Mod-
esty may have been a second reason for the tactic, because in Pu-
ritanical Boston sections of her writings were considered obscene.

Mercy's deep committment to revolution stemmed in part
from her close friendship with John Adams, but her dedication
was also based on strong emotional grounds. Each day she
watched as her brother James drew closer to complete insanity.
Many attributed the failing directly to his treatment at the hands
of Boston's tories.

James Otis had once been considered the most promising and
intelligent man in Massachusetts. Ten years before the war, he
had predicted that a massive rebellion would break out in the colonies and had begun to dedicate his total efforts to assuring that
the conflict came as quickly as possible. Otis, once described as a
"plump, round-faced, smooth-skinned, short-necked, eagle-eyed,
politician," became one of the best known advocates of independence and a major target of British wrath.

In early 1770, however, the radical's career was effectively
ended when he was severely beaten in a Boston coffeehouse by a
band of offended loyalists. Soon after the attack, Otis' actions became more erratic and unstable. The condition grew progres-
sively worse until at last he experienced long periods of complete
irrationality.

As her brother's condition deteriorated, Mercy grew more
committed to war. In 1772, the first Committee of Correspondence, an organization created to publicize liberal ideas, was
formed in her house. Within a year, 75 similar committees had
been established in other communities. Her husband James became
a prominent whig leader as a result of his work with the groups,
but Mercy's private accomplishments soon eclipsed his public
ones.

In 1772 her first play, a pointed satire which ridiculed British

*Mrs. John Adams* (Abigail Smith), painting by Gilbert Stuart. Courtesy of the National Gallery of Art, Washington, D.C. Gift of Mrs. Robert Homans.

authorities for their corrupt and inept administration was published anonymously in a radical Boston newspaper. The work was an immediate sensation and although government censorship forbade its performance on the stage, the play was soon widely distributed in pamphlet form. A second play, entitled *The Defeat*, soon followed and also met with overwhelming enthusiasm. Mercy continued her propaganda barrage by producing a series of poems and broadsides aimed at policies she considered to be abusive or oppressive.

Few of his majesty's loyal servants were immune to the writer's sharp pen. Major characters in her works were prominent members of the ruling tory government in Massachusetts, all lampooned under easily penetrated aliases, such as Brigadier Hateall, Dupe, Simple Sapling, Crusty Crowbar, Hector Mushroom, Sir Sparrow Spendall and Hum Humbug. Women were not exempt from her scorn and one female loyalist appeared in Mercy's writings under the name of Mrs. Flourish, a common slang term for sexual intercourse.

In addition to her published writings, Mercy carried on a massive correspondence with leading figures of the day such as

George Washington, Sam Adams, Henry Knox and Thomas Jefferson. But most important were the sensitive letters she exchanged with John and Abigail Adams.

For Abigail, perhaps the only colonial woman who matched Mercy's intellectual capacity, the exchange provided a vitally important outlet for thought during the long war years when the future first lady lived in isolated Braintree. For John, Mercy Warren represented a great talent which could be exploited as a weapon to oppose the British crown.

Soon after the Boston tea party, Adams sought to capitalize on his friend's growing popularity and requested that she compose a piece to commemorate the event. Adams was delighted with the witty parody which she forwarded to him for publication and may have told others of his part in "commissioning" the work, for soon other friends were suggesting ideas for the Plymouth writer.

Adams quickly became Mercy's most ardent supporter. In periods of discouragement, he wrote her soothing consolation and urged her to continue. When she doubted the propriety of her writings, Adams praised her "genius" and told her again of her great worth. In one letter he confided to James Warren: ". . . God Almighty has entrusted her with Powers for the good of the World, which, in the Cause of his Providence, he bestows on few of the human race. That instead of being a fault to use them, it would be criminal to neglect them."

Mercy, born in 1728 and one of thirteen children, had developed her writing talents early in life. Unlike all but a handful of colonial women, she had been exposed in childhood to the great works of classical writers. Both her father, a local judge, and her mother, a descendant of a signer of the Mayflower Compact, believed in a liberal education for children of both sexes.

Thus instead of receiving the usual female instruction in sewing, cooking and etiquette, young Mercy joined her brother James in the classroom to learn history, literature and politics. She read Raleigh's history of the world, Alexander Pope's works and translations of Homer and Virgil. After her marriage to Warren in 1754, Mercy continued to educate herself, and as the revolution neared, she concentrated upon political theory.

Writing assumed an almost total place in her life and her vision centered prominently on revolution. Only rarely did her personal correspondence mention the domestic activities which consumed most women of her generation. Instead her letters are filled with discussions of politics, military strategy, the government of the new nation she hoped to help create and the basic philosophies under which laws should be formulated. While the wives of other patriot leaders successfully ran farms and businesses in the absences of their mates, the Warren land left under Mercy's care fell into almost complete ruin.

But Mercy was not entirely without familial emotions. Particularly difficult for her were the long periods of separation from her husband, which grew more frequent as the Plymouth farmer and his writer wife grew in importance. During one long absence she wrote him: "My heart has just leaped in my bosom and I ran to the stairs imagining I heard both your voice and your footsteps in the entry."

The pair's sacrifices in working for independence were accepted unhesitatingly, for Mercy had developed a sense of inevitability concerning the war which loomed so threateningly. Only rarely did she express hope that widespread violence could be averted. Peace was most desirable, she believed, but only if all the demands of the colonies could be met with no compromise by the Americans. To Adams she wrote: "I will breathe one wish more; and that is for the restoration of peace—peace I mean, on equitable terms; for pusillanimous and feeble as I am, I cannot wish to see the sword quietly put up in the scabbard until justice is done in America."

In her public writings, Mercy gradually relaxed her formal, precise style and substituted instead the everyday language of the common colonial. No longer did she seek to influence only the well-educated few, but directed her material to the average man and woman who were constantly confronted with the problems of British government. These were the people who would begin the revolution.

Avenues for agitation were also opening up for women less gifted than writer Warren. Among the most accessible were various groups called the Daughters of Liberty. These organizations, which had become popular along the eastern seaboard, were composed of women from all stations in life who met periodically to discuss the political scene and plan ways in which they could assist in opposing English rule.

One of the most effective means was through numerous boycotts of British goods and supplies. By this action, rebels hoped to severely hamper British merchant shippping, thus prompting powerful English commercial interests to exert pressure on the crown for a more lenient colonial policy. Although the boycotts were often ill-organized and ineffective they did create widespread attention.

Perhaps the most famous of these campaigns was undertaken by fifty-one women in Edenton, North Carolina, who announced that they would refuse to buy both tea and English-made clothing. Leading the group was Penelope Barker, a woman who would outlast three husbands and later gain fame as a sword-wielding folk heroine who warded off maurauding horse thieves.

The Edenton women's proclamation declared:

> As we cannot be indifferent on any occasion that appears to affect the peace and happiness of our country, and as it has been thought necessary for the publick good to enter into several particular resolves, by meeting of Members of Deputies from the whole Province, it is a duty that we owe not only to our near and dear relations and connections, but to ourselves who are essentially interested in their welfare, to do everything as far as lies in our power to testify our sincere adherence to the same, and we do therefore accordingly subscribe this paper as a witness of our fixed intentions and solemn determination to do so.

The Edenton compact immediately gained attention on both sides of the Atlantic. The news spread to London where Arthur Iredell discussed the incident in a letter to his brother James living in North Carolina. Although the letter is humorous on the surface, its undertones warn of a basic conflict in the allegiances of the two brothers. Such inter-family differences would soon divide many kinsfolk:

*A Society of Patriotic Ladies,* mezzotint by Philip Dawe. A 1775 cartoon lampooning the women of Edenton, North Carolina. Photo courtesy of the Library of Congress.

I see by the newspapers the Edenton ladies have signal-
ized themselves by the protest against tea drinking. . . . Is
there a female Congress at Edenton too? I hope not, for we
Englishmen are afraid of the male Congress, but if the ladies
who have ever, since the Amazonian era, been esteemed the
most formidable enemies, if they, I say, should attack us, the
most fatal consequence is to be dreaded. So dextrous in the
handling of a dart, each wound they give is mortal; whilst
we, so unhappily formed by Nature, the more we strive to
conquer them the more are conquered! The Edenton ladies,
conscious I suppose of this superiority on their side, by
former experience, are willing, I imagine, to crush us to
atoms by their omnipotency; the only security on our side
to prevent the impending ruin that I can perceive is the
probability that there are few places in America which pos-
sess so much female artillery as in Edenton.

Just 120 miles away at Bath, England, Catharine Sawbridge
Macaulay was preparing her own artillery against British policies.

Most physical descriptions of Catharine are not flattering.
"Painted up to the eyes," suggested John Wilkes, the lecherous
English whig, "and looking as rotten as an old Catherine Pear."

Catharine was born in 1731, the daughter of a London heiress and a country squire. Until she was married at twenty-nine to
Dr. George Macaulay, her life was undistinguished, but by the
eve of the revolution she was at the peak of a brilliant literary career. Her multi-volume *The History of England from the Acces-
sion of James I to the Elevation of the Brunswick Line*, had
pushed her into prominence as England's first major woman historian.

Catharine specialized in despots, and George III she feared
would become the worst of the lot. Together with her brother,
the Lord Mayor of London and a Member of Parliament, the historian had built a widespread reputation as a champion of unpopular causes. This identification as a defender of the powerless
had grown with her public pronouncements urging equality of
the sexes, abolishment of the peerage, correction of primitive conditions in prisons and prohibitions on the unlimited acquisition of
wealth by the aristocrats. It had also gained her numerous enemies in the English establishment.

For some time, Catharine corresponded with Mercy Warren and Abigail Adams, decidedly biased writers who kept her informed on the growing difficulties in the colonies. In 1775, Catharine issued a major treatise on the conflict entitled: *An Address to the People of England, Scotland and Ireland on the Present Important Crisis of Affairs.* Although the historian was a staunch advocate of individual liberties, her opposition to British policies was based not on terms of infringements on the rights of the provincials, but rather on the possible detrimental effect that an American war might have on England.

Instead of suggesting that the colonials were entitled to more liberal treatment, she warned that an English victory in the new world would concentrate such power in the hands of the crown, that the King could become a tyrant at home. A war with America could not only result in enslavement of the British in Britain, she claimed, but could also weaken the nation's world-wide power and expose the country to the expansionist desires of other great countries. In addressing the common people in the British Isles, Catharine wrote:

> If a civil war commences between Great Britain and her Colonies, either the Mother Country, by one great exertion, may ruin both herself and America, or the Americans, by a lingering contest, will gain an independency; and in this case, all those advantages which you for some time have enjoyed by your Colonies, and advantages which have hitherto preserved you from a national bankruptcy, must for ever have an end; and whilst a new, a flourishing, and an extensive empire of freemen is established on the other side the Atlantic, you, with the loss of all those blessings you have received by the unrivalled state of your commerce, will be left to the bare possession of your foggy islands, and this under the sway of a domestic despot, or you will become the provinces of some powerful European state.
>
> Suffer me again to remind you of the imminent danger of your situation: Your Ministers, by attacking the rights of all America, have effected that which the malicious policy of more judicious minds would have avoided. Your colonists, convinced that their safety depends on their harmony, are now united in one strong bond of union. . . . Your ministers

also, deceived by present appearances, vainly imagine, because our rivals in Europe are encouraging us to engage beyond the possibility of a retreat, that they will reject the opportunity when it offers of putting a final end to the greatness and the glory of our empire. . . .

Catharine's private behavior was as disdainful of conservative sentiments as her public philosophies. Soon after she arrived at Bath for relief of a "bilious complaint," Catharine moved into the house of Dr. Thomas Wilson, rector of London's St. Stephen's Church. Wilson would become almost as controversial as the woman he loved, by placing a life-sized marble statue of her in his church.

The prominent objet d'art, depicting Catharine as the muse of history, was removed only after offended vestrymen created a public outcry. Although the Doctor would later make a bitter break with the writer and sell the elaborate funeral vault he had provided for her remains, the statue would remain in the Wilson family for generations.

As the possibility of war grew hotter, Catharine's reaction became stronger. A popular rumor printed in the *Morning Post*, revealed that the historian planned to leave England and head for Philadelphia "to take command of a large corps of American amazons, who are to be called the Hancock volunteers."

Instead Catharine sailed for France. For a time she corresponded with Paris-based Benjamin Franklin, but the exchange was ended because of her fear that she would be castigated in England for consorting with the enemy. On her trip abroad, Catharine adopted several sophisticated customs which were not calculated to endear her to conservatives at home. One new mode was the liberal use of rouge, another was frequent and vocal swearing. Despite the mounting criticism, Catharine continued her diatribes against the colonial war. Several years later in another action which scandalized England, she would figure again in the revolution.

In the colonies, things were heating up between the bloody-backs and the mohairs, the nicknames given to the British troops and the rebels. Most of the population sensed that war was imminent and that only a spark was needed to set off the conflict. On April 19, 1775, the tenuous peace was at last broken.

The catalyst was General Thomas Gage, military governor of Massachusetts, who suddenly ordered 700 troops from the Boston garrison into the countryside. Their objective was to capture a supply of rebel gunpowder stored at Concord. Paul Revere, head of a local spy ring, rode out on April 18 to warn defenders at the arsenal, stopping along the way at Lexington to alert John Hancock and Sam Adams who had been marked by the British for arrest. Revere did not complete his journey, but was captured soon after midnight by an enemy patrol. But a travelling companion, Dr. Samuel Prescott who was returning from a late hour visit with his girlfriend Miss Mulliken, managed to escape and alert the townspeople at Concord.

Minutemen alarmed by Revere gathered quickly on the Lexington green, but their defiance only temporarily halted the British column. After a slight skirmish, the rebels were severely routed and the King's troops marched on to Concord. On arriving, the men halted near the center of town at the home of widow Martha Moulton.

Martha, at age seventy-one, was defended only by an eighty-five-year-old friend, for all the young men in the village had vanished, planning to regroup and confront the invaders en masse. Martha was not delighted at the prospect of entertaining a major contingent of the British army in America, according to her later account:

> [The English] in a hostile manner, entered the town and drawed up in form before the door of the house where I live; and there they continued on the green, feeding their horses within five feet of the door; and about fifty or sixty of them was in and out of the house; calling for water and what they wanted. . . .

As several units of the troops made themselves comfortable at widow Moulton's, other companies marched on in an attempt to locate the contraband gunpowder. At the North Bridge, the redcoats encountered the main body of townsmen. Here the Minutemen fared better than at Lexington, and after a short series of volleys, Gage's troops retreated back into town. In the confusion, a massive fire broke out, reportedly set by the British and threatening to destroy the entire settlement. Martha Moulton begged her unwanted guests to fight the blaze, but "they took no notice, only sneered." Martha believed that she showed incredible bravery in the face of such trying circumstances and later applied for a financial reward based on her actions. Her petition maintained:

> . . . knowing that all the row of four or five houses, as well as the school house, was in certain danger, your petitioner (not knowing but she might provoke them by her insufficient pleading) yet ventured to put as much strength to her arguments as an unfortunate widow could think of; and so your petitioner can safely say that, under Divine Providence, she was an instrument of saving the Court House, and how many more is not certain, from being consumed, with a great deal of valuable furniture, at at great risk of her life. At last, by one pail of water after another, they sent and did extinguish the fire.

About 1,000 reinforcements joined the expeditionary force for the march back to Boston. Throughout the retreat, rebel snipers hidden behind fences and trees blasted away at the redcoats. The regulars were hampered not only by fatigue from the outward march, but by their heavy packs which often weighed up to 125 pounds.

British officers would later recall the almost complete absence of women along the line of march. Most had hidden in their shuttered houses or taken refuge in large colonies away from the road. One exception was at Jewett's Bridge near Groton.

Although they were not in direct danger, the men of Groton like those in Pepperell and neighboring communities had left for the scene of action as soon as the alert was received. Their women were not idle. Prudence Wright and the wife of Job Shaddock were also rallying their friends to battle.

After donning their husband's clothing, the women of Groton and nearby villages armed themselves with muskets and pitchforks. Prudence was elected leader and the band moved out of town, intending to defend the local bridge against encroaching tories. According to a report by Col. William Prescott, a commander at Bunker Hill, the ambush soon produced results. The first enemy to approach was hapless Leonard Whiting of Hollis, New Hampshire. Whiting, carrying secret dispatches from the British in Canada, was arrested by the Minutewomen and his messages forwarded to friendly rebel officers.

Other women involved in the day's activities were not so fortunate. The wife of Capt. Isaac Davis, an Acton gunsmith, saw her husband leave for battle early in the morning. All day she nursed her four children, several of whom were ill with "canker rash." After the battle, Isaac came back to his wife. "In the afternoon he was brought home a corpse," she wrote. "He was placed in my bedroom till the funeral."

The British, continuing their retreat toward sanctuary, stopped periodically to loot and plunder roadside homes and villages such as Menotomy. When the redcoats finally reached Cambridge, their casualties totaled 250, but some critics suggest that the figure should have been much higher. Thousands of defenders had sniped at the troops for many hours, but the relatively low casualty rate may have been due not to poor marksmanship of the whigs, but because of the heavy arms which were used. Unlike the long rifles of the frontier, the New England musket was not a particularly accurate weapon.

As dusk fell on April 19, the battle was over, but the war had begun. Many Americans were concerned about the future, but in the Massachusetts countryside, others were picking up the pieces of the afternoon's violence. Cambridge's Hannah Winthrop described her experiences that day, in a letter to Mercy Warren:

> . . . we were roused from the benign slumbers of the season, by beat of drum & ringing of Bell, with the dire alarm That a thousand of the Troops of George the third were gone forth to murder the peaceful inhabitants of the surrounding villages. A few hours with the dawning day Convinced us the bloody purpose was executing . . . it seemed necessary to retire to some place of safety till the calamity was passed. . . . After dinner we set out not knowing whither

we went, we were directed to a place calld fresh pond about a
mile from the town but what a destressed house did we find
there, filld with women whose husbands were gone forth to
meet the Assailants, 70 or 80 of these with numbers of infant
children crying and agonizing for the Fate of their husbands.
In addition to this scene of distress, we were for some time
in sight of the Battle, the glistening instruments of death
proclaiming by an incessant fire, that much blood must be
shed, that many widowd & orphand ones by left as monuments of that persecuting Barbarity of the British Tyranny.

After the battle, Hannah received word that it was unsafe to
return to her home. The British were progressing up river and
setting fires along the way. Again she fled:

> Thus we began our passage alternately walking and rid-
> ing, the roads filld with frighted women & children. Some in
> carts with their tatterd furniture, others on foot fleeing into
> the woods. But what added greatly to the horror of the
> scene was our passing thro the Bloody field at Menotomy
> which was strewd with the mangled Bodies. We met one af-
> fectionate Father with a Cart looking for his murdered son
> & picking up his Neighbors who had fallen in Battle, in
> order for their Burial.

As news of the engagement spread throughout the colonies,
other groups began to take up arms. A force headed by Ethan
Allen and his Green Mountain Boys, joined with troops under
Benedict Arnold and headed north to Fort Ticonderoga, a major
British installation guarding Lake Champlain. In a bloodless victory on May 10, the rebels captured Ft. Tie along with artillery
and ammunition sorely needed by the whig army.

Historians have long singled out brave and eloquent statements made by Americans in the height of battle. At Bunker
Hill, Israel Putnam poetically ordered: "Don't fire until you see
the whites of their eyes." James Lawrence, captain of the ship
*Chesapeake* reportedly called out: "Don't give up the ship!" just
moments before it was given up to the *Shannon*. John Paul Jones
made literary history on the *Bonhomme Richard* when he supposedly cried: "I have not yet begun to fight!" But Ethan Allen

was not in the elegant mode. Although the exact words he chose to use in demanding the surrender of Ticonderoga were not inscribed on the spot, one observer later claimed that Allen simply yelled: "Come out you damned old rat!"

In Philadelphia, the Congress, seemingly less enthused than the remainder of the colonies, had not yet elected a commander to lead the troops rallying around Boston. The situation was chaotic for the citizen soldiers flocking to the bay area were led by a mass of various generals and colonels from state militias.

Inside the city, the British were retrenching. New blood arrived from England in the persons of Generals Howe, Clinton and Burgoyne who brought reinforcements to quell the colonial discontent. Curiously, the vessel on which the triumvirate of generals arrived was named the *Cerberus*. In Greek mythology, Cerberus was the name of a three-headed dog condemned to guard the gates of hell.

Loyalists from towns surrounding Boston began fleeing into the city for refuge from the excesses of their whig neighbors. One onlooker was Margaret Kemble Gage, the American wife of General Thomas Gage. The New Jersey native was a curious looking woman, according to contemporary accounts. Although Lady Gage's life was rooted in the colonies, her lineage was one-fourth Greek, one-fourth Dutch, one-fourth French and one-fourth English. Peggy Gage was not particularly popular in her native land, primarily because many citizens thought she nagged her hen-pecked husband into providing important positions for her not so competent relatives.

But the general's wife was a puzzle to some war observers and the rumor was spread that she was actually a rebel spy who revealed to Paul Revere the British plan to march on Concord. Documentary support for the tale was non-existent, and the legend seems to have stemmed from a set of circumstances which were not particularly incriminating.

First, General Gage was credited with announcing that he had told only one person of his marching plans, but that the entire countryside knew of them by the time he informed his assistant Hugh, Earl Percy. Advocates of the Margaret Gage spy theory claim that the "one person" privy to the secret was the general's wife. However, the individual may have been another officer. Gage may have actually told two people, or ten or a hundred.

Second, at the time of the incident, it was alleged that the plans were revealed by "a daughter of liberty." In April of 1775, there were approximately 7,500 women in Boston, all daughters and all just as likely of passing intelligence to the rebels as the wife of the British commander. The "daughter of liberty" may have referred to a member of the radical organization of the same name. Or she may have been the wife of John Stedman who lived on Winter Street. Mrs. Stedman reported that on the eve of the march, a British officer came to her house and left a message for a campfollower lodged there. The order was that the army woman was to have her husband present on Boston Common at 8:00 a.m. with thirty-six rounds of ammunition and a full day's provision. Mrs. Stedman may have passed the information along and the actual destination of the troops was actually deduced by members of Revere's spy ring.

A final claim made by those who suggested that Lady Gage was a traitor to her husband, was the contention that Peggy's father Peter Kemble was given favorable treatment as a result of her sabotage.

Actually Kemble was an intimate of George Washington and other patriot notables. His farm property near Morristown, New Jersey, was once used as Washington's headquarters and there is little evidence that he at any time vigorously opposed the American cause.

There are no indications that Lady Gage became estranged from her husband over the issue of the rebellion. Her return to England in August of 1775 was not because of the general's dissatisfaction with her activities, but probably stemmed from pressure from London officials who did not relish the concept that the commander's wife was an American.

For nearly two months after the Concord fiasco, Gage waited in Boston as the rebel army gathered nearby. Finally in mid-June he made plans to station some of his troops on two unoccupied rises overlooking the city. The Americans, learning of the plan, quickly moved up to fortify the points, known as

Breed's Hill and Bunker's Hill. On June 17 a bloody engagement was fought for control of the rises and although the whigs ultimately retreated, the victory was a questionable one for Gage.

During the contest, the redcoats repeatedly charged directly into the fire of the defenders. British losses in this frontal attack were devastating, for nearly one-half of the 2,300 regulars were casualties. For the Americans the number was about 440. Clinton remarked that the battle was "a dear-bought victory," and claimed that another such success would have ruined the entire British army.

The debilitating losses at Bunker Hill would affect the battle plans of British commanders for the remainder of the war. In almost every later confrontation, officers who had witnessed the slaughter at the June battle would reject any plan which included a frontal assault. In some cases, this refusal meant defeat.

Bunker Hill also left scars on women who witnessed the event. Faith Trumbull Huntington, daughter of Connecticut Governor Jonathan Trumbull, was on the scene that day. Her brother John Trumbull would later become a great painter, but on June 17, he was serving as a rebel volunteer. In his autobiography, John sadly recalled Faith's visit:

> About noon of that day, I had a momentary interview with my favorite sister, the wife of Colonel, afterwards General Huntington, whose regiment was on its march to join the army. The novelty of military scenes excited great curiosity through the country, and my sister was one of a party of young friends who were attracted to visit the army before Boston. She was a woman of deep and affectionate sensibility, and the moment of her visit was most unfortunate. She found herself surrounded, not by the "pomp and circumstances of glorious war," but in the midst of all its horrible realities. She saw too clearly the life of danger and hardship upon which her husband and her favorite brother had entered, and it overcame her strong, but too sensitive mind. She became deranged, and died the following November in Dedham.

Swift reaction came from other quarters. Cambridge was burned. The city of Boston turned into a giant hospital for great numbers of desperately wounded King's men. Some did not survive.

In August, 60 widows and orphans sailed for England aboard the *Charming Nancy*, a brig which also carried 170 debilitated soldiers. With them was Peggy Gage, whose husband had already come under fire in England for his handling of the colonial situation.

The *St. James's Chronicle* reported that the Gage on board ship was not Margaret, but was actually the general in disguise as his wife. The paper applauded the switch, suggesting that if Lady Gage had indeed assumed command of the army, she would prove significantly more capable than her husband.

But the general had fought his last battle on American soil. In October he was relieved of command and replaced by William Howe.

When Margaret landed at Plymouth, many Britishers received their first glimpse of the colonial conflict. It was not pleasant. The *Annual Register* noted that the ship's party "exhibited a most shocking spectacle; and even the vessel itself was almost intolerable from the stench arising from the sick and wounded." Bystanders immediately collected £100 for the ragged women and children.

The war had come home to England.

# CHAPTER TWO

# *A Spreading Fire*

. . . I see the inhabitants of our plundered cities quitting
the elegancies of life, possessing nothing but their freedom
—taking refuge in the forests—I behold faction & discord
tearing up an Island we once held dear as our own inheritance and a mighty Empire long the dread of distant nations,
tott'ring to the very foundation.

Mercy Warren to Catharine Macaulay

ANTIWAR PROPAGANDA by whigs such as Catharine Macaulay
had not been ignored in England. Opposition to the war
was being voiced not only by wealthy lords in Parliament, but
by those farther down the economic ladder in the working class
groups who were dependent upon American trade for their liveli-
hood. Liberal organizations not only condemned British prosecu-
tion of the war, but actively supported the rebel cause. In one
such act, members of the Constitutional Society meeting at the
King's Arms Tavern in London collected a special fund to assist
the survivors of Americans killed at Lexington and Concord.

London newspapers were particularly critical of the colonial
situation. While conservative publications described the rebelling
colonists as "ungrateful monsters" and "detested homicides," the
opposition press took every opportunity to ridicule crown policies. The *Evening Post* called the war "unnatural, unconstitu-
tional, unnecessary, unjust, dangerous, hazardous and unprofit-
able." Some sources predicted that the rebels would win. Others

*Lady Sarah Lennox*, painting
by Richard Cosway. Courtesy
of Victoria and Albert Museum, London.

estimated that as many as 165,000 men would be needed to subdue the colonies and that as a result the economy of the mother
country would be ruined.

Later, George Washington would be praised by these
friendly papers and occasionally congratulated for his victories.
But almost every move of the British government was criticized.
The King's domino theory received particular scorn. This rationale for pressing the conflict contended that if the Americans were
successful in their secession, the West Indies, Ireland and other
overseas possessions would soon fall.

One aristocrat who voiced doubt about the struggle was
young Lady Sarah Lennox, the intimate companion of George III
before his marriage. Lady Sarah was the daughter of the Second
Duke of Richmond, a government power who had served as Regent of England during the absences of George II. Like her father, Lady Sarah was a high ranking figure in the English court
and was of royal blood, for her grandfather was the illegitimate
son of King Charles II and his mistress Louise de Quérouaille.

Sarah Lennox was a striking woman. Horace Walpole wrote
that she "was more beautiful than you can conceive. No Magda-

lene by Correggio was half so lovely and expressive." At age fifteen, Sarah had attracted the attention of George III, then Prince of Wales. Ambitious relatives, led by her uncle Lord Holland, had hoped that the result of the romance would be a royal marriage. Many of her kin had diligently promoted the affair.

The Prince seemed willing to commit himself and informed his adviser the Earl of Bute: "I was struck with her first appearance at St. James, my passion has been increased every time I have since beheld her; her voice is sweet, she seems sensible, has a thorough sense of her obligations . . . in short, she is everything I can form to myself lovely."

The liaison, opposed by Bute, George's mother Princess Augusta and some members of Lady Sarah's own family, lasted less than two years. Finally the stronger faction triumphed and suddenly an engagement was announced between George and Charlotte, princess of Mecklenburg-Strelitz. The basis of the match was the strengthening of bonds between Britain and the German states east of France, thus providing a counterbalance to the power of the Bourbon nations.

Although the union was met with consternation in some quarters, Lady Sarah was not particularly sorrowed. Her son would later note: "When the King's marriage with Princess Charlotte of Mecklenburg became public, Lord Holland's indignation and astonishment were unbounded; my mother would probably have been vexed, but her favourite squirrel happened to die at the same time, and his loss was more felt than that of a Crown."

The shunned sweetheart was a bridesmaid at the royal wedding and several months later, Sarah married Thomas Bunbury, a noted horseman whose chief claim to fame was his ownership of the first Derby winner at Newmarket. Sir Thomas may have neglected his wife in favor of his horses, for during the first years of their marriage her name was linked with numerous suitors.

Soon after the birth of her first child in 1769, Sarah left Bunbury to live with Lord William Gordon, reportedly the father of the infant. After a brief affair strongly criticized by her family, she left Gordon and moved to her brother's estate. Here she began to live a reclusive life.

Sarah was troubled by the American war which was being

*Queen Charlotte of England*, painting by Benjamin West.
Courtesy of The Historical Society of Pennsylvania.

contemplated by her former admirer, the King. Her brother was a leader of the opposition forces in Parliament, and one of the strongest opponents to the crown's colonial policies. Her powerful nephew Charles James Fox, son of Lord Holland, joined with Richmond as an open advocate of the whig's liberal policies. Through relatives and friends, the secluded Sarah Lennox was kept well informed of events of the rebellion. Her correspondence was filled not only with social gossip, but with observations on the political workings of the conflict. Of particular interest to her were the actions of her cousin General Charles Lee, a retired British officer who was contriving with the Americans.

On July 29, 1775, Lady Sarah discussed the situation in a letter to her friend Lady Susan O'Brien:

> I think His Majesty and poor Mr. Lee are much upon a par; they are both vain and obstinate, the King has a bad cause, and Mr. Lee a good one, for the King wants to have it in his power to oppress, and my cousin Lee to put out of his power, but, in my mind, both their intentions will come to at last the same thing as far as concerns the Americans, for, if the King can oppress, I don't think it at all clear he will do it, and, if he does, his son may be a better man, and if he is not, it's still time for them to fight. Now if they free themselves from one King, they will only fall by the ears together and quarrel among themselves . . . tho' I certainly am no admirer of the King's character, you know I don't believe he is a bit more, nor so great a tyrant as my cousin Lee would be were he king himself, for he loves his own way as well as anybody. . . .

In the midst of writing her letter, Sarah received word of the battle at Bunker Hill. Her former intellectual analysis of the American situation quickly changed to an emotional one:

> Since I began this I've heard the news of the action near Boston. Oh Lord! how it makes one's blood run cold to think of *any action*, much more such a bloody one as that & among one's own people almost. Thank God our friends are safe . . . poor little Mrs. Howe fainted away with only the shock of the word *action*, and could not for a long time believe her husband was alive till luckily his letter came.

Another lady of quality was not as gracious in her estimation of the Americans. Scottish born Janet Schaw, a distant cousin of Sir Walter Scott, became intimately involved in the conflict when she landed in North Carolina after a journey to the West Indies.

Janet found American men to be crude and ignorant, but was delighted with the sophistication of their women. She wrote: "I have however, gained some most amiable and agreeable acquaintances amongst the Ladies; many of whom would make a figure in any part of the world. . . ."

By late 1775, the spirit of rebellion had moved south from Boston to the tidewater lands of Virginia, North Carolina and South Carolina. Countrypeople and farmers were arming themselves and forming militia groups. In perhaps an imitation of the British regulars, infantry drills were being attempted by men to whom ordered march was as alien as a minuet. Janet witnessed one such attempt at public parading and was not particularly impressed with the ill-clad group:

> Their exercise was that of bush-fighting, but it appeared so confused and so perfectly different from anything I ever saw, I cannot say whether they performed it well or not; but this I do know, that they were heated with rum till capable of committing the most shocking outrages. . . . They at last however assembled on the plain field, and I must really laugh while I recollect their figures: 2000 men in their shirts and trousers, preceded by a very ill-beat drum and a fiddler who was also in his shirt with a long sword and a cue at his hair, who played with all his might. They made indeed a most unmartial appearance. But the worst figure there can shoot from behind a bush and kill even a General Wolfe.

The review turned ugly when the English groom of one Mr. Neilson smiled at the motley assembly. He was dragged forth to the loud cries of "tar and feathers," according to Janet, but was pardoned when he made a full public apology. Afterwards the offender was duly "drummed and fiddled" out of town. Although Neilson's groom escaped the ordeal, others did not, for the practice of tarring and feathering tories was becoming widespread. Connoisseurs of the art devised exotic variations on the theme, such as substituting blubber oil, molasses and excrement for the tar, and flower down for the feathers.

The rebel persecution of those who would not speak out against the crown soon reached the Schaw family. Janet's brother Alexander, a searcher of customs at St. Kitts on leave in North Carolina, gained the locals' animosity by carrying an urgent message for aid from Governor Josiah Martin to the Earl of Dartmouth. Intense pressure was placed on another brother, wealthy colonial merchant Robert Schaw who had once served as Commissioner of Wilmington.

Yielding to threats, Robert agreed to join the revolting colonists, and was appointed First Quartermaster with the rank of a colonel. Secretly, however, he made plans to send his wife, sister and children to England. When they had reached safety, he would follow them himself.

The stakes were high for those refusing to swear allegiance to the new government. Personal danger and the loss of private property were the most immediate prospects. Loyalists of particular importance such as the Schaws were also forced to provide bonds which would be confiscated if they made any public disturbance or attempted to join the King's forces.

Physical force was regularly used to "convert" those who were undecided or lukewarm in the controversy. Rebel recruiting drives often allowed almost no choice of action for the prospective volunteer. Janet, in perhaps biased terms, described the situation as she saw it in North Carolina in 1775:

> At present the martial law stands thus: An officer or committeeman enters a plantation with his posse. The Alternative is proposed, Agree to join us, and your persons and properties are safe; you have a shilling sterling a day; your duty is no more than once a month appearing under Arms at Wilmingtown, which will prove only a merry-making, where you will have as much grog as you can drink. But if you refuse, we are directly to cut up your corn, shoot your pigs, burn your houses, seize your Negroes and perhaps tar and feather yourself.

In the fall as the situation became worse, Janet left the colony with other refugees and boarded the frigate *Cruizer*. She was delighted to leave the "tar pot" called America, and rejoiced when she was moved to the *George*, which was soon to weigh anchor. Janet sailed on November 10, bound for Glasgow via Lisbon. For her the war was over and she was going home.

In neighboring Virginia, Royal Governor John Murray, the Earl of Dunmore, was waging his own war against the whigs. After urging slaves to revolt against their rebelling whig masters, Dunmore took refuge on a British ship, from which he directed a bombardment of Norfolk. A fire resulting from the cannonade caused extensive damage to the city and contributed to the ill feelings between citizens of differing philosophies.

As a result of the British offensive, many whigs were leaving their homes. In Buckingham County, the local committee of safety invited the wives, children and slaves of displaced rebels to resettle in local communities. But the friends of Lord Dunmore did not receive such a welcome in Isle of Wight County near Norfolk. Citizen Mary Easson was one loyalist who discovered that the freedom guaranteed by liberal elements did not always extend to those who opposed the will of the majority.

Mary, accused of tory activities by an unknown informant, was called for questioning by the local committee on October 26, 1775. She was evidently an extremely uncooperative witness according to the official minutes of the gathering:

> *Mary Easson*, of the said County, (on a suspicion of her being privy to certain intelligence being conveyed to his Excellency Lord *Dunmore*—a charge exhibited against divers persons in this country, by some person unknown,) being summoned, appeared before the said Committee, but refused to be sworn, or answer such questions as the Committee might demand of her; and after behaving in a very insolent, scandalous, and indecent manner, departed without leave.
>
> It is therefore the opinion of this Committee, that the said *Mary Easson* holds principles inimical to the rights of liberties of *North-America*, and ought to be considered as an enemy of her Country, and that every person ought to break off all kinds of intercourse and connection with her.

Resolved, That the Clerk of the Committee send a copy
of the above to Messrs. *John Dixon* and *William Hunter*,
and they are requested to insert the same in the *Virginia
Gazette.*

Thus Mary received a particularly trying sentence from the
committee, that of being "published." Under this practice, an individual or family was both publicly and privately isolated from
any contact with other human beings. The ban on social and
business intercourse could, of course, be lifted if the offender
showed proper contriteness.

As the war percolated in the South, Congress finally appointed a commander-in-chief of the army besieging Boston. Although George Washington claimed he had not sought the post,
his martial presence in the council chamber was rather obvious.
Unlike other delegates who dressed in subdued civilian clothes,
Washington chose to wear a full dress military uniform during
the debates on the selection of a leader.

Charles Lee, Lady Sarah Lennox's cousin, was appointed second in command, primarily to satisfy the more conservative elements. To those who considered Washington more of a country
planter than a soldier, Lee's professional record in the British
Army assured that long-term military experience would be available to the troops.

When Washington arrived in Cambridge, he found a large,
unorganized group of citizen soldiers almost entirely unskilled in
warfare. For generations, military training in the colonies had
been haphazard and was traditionally limited to festive gatherings
held two or three times a year. Many of the men at Cambridge
came to the camp as part-time soldiers, who left at will to return
home for harvesting or other farm chores. The men often attached no significance or homage to those in command. Rank
had almost no privileges and even Israel Putnam, commander
of the Connecticut forces, stood in line with his men to receive
meals.

Security was practically non-existent. Women visited their
lovers and husbands at any time and great masses of townspeople
came simply to view the army. Always present was the danger

that loyalists or British agents were also moving about, recording the strength of the troops and the condition of supplies.

The senior general in the Massachusetts army, Artemas Ward, sought to halt at least one avenue of intelligence leakage by warning his men to be wary of "lewd women" who might pass through. His alert was not only an attempt to safeguard the morals of the soldiers, but an effort to limit spying by women coming out of Boston. Six months later, the prohibition was evidently still in effect for two prostitutes were ceremonially drummed out of camp.

Washington immediately began issuing more stringent rules in which severe punishments were prescribed for infractions. He also acted to improve the sanitary conditions, partially created by backwoodsmen and women who were unaccustomed to living in large groups. One order suggested frequent bathing for the continentals but not:

> . . . at or near the bridge at Cambridge, where it has been observed and complained of, that many men, lost to all sense of decency and common modesty, are running about naked on the bridge, whilst passengers, and even ladies of the first fashion in the neighborhood are passing over it, as if they meant to glory in their shame. . . .

The rebel ring around Boston was gradually pulled tighter as Washington attempted to make an army out of his rag tails. No longer could British commissaries come out of the city to forage for food. On the sea, privateers commissioned by the whigs began preying on enemy supply ships. Scurvy broke out in the port as the stores of fresh vegetables and fruits were exhausted.

In desperation, sauerkraut and spruce beer were used as curatives. Women volunteers were hired as nurses. Small pox grew into an epidemic and deaths became so numerous that a halt was ordered to the custom of ringing church bells during funerals. The rationale was that the bells would never stop tolling if the tradition were observed literally.

In his fury at the rapidly depleting army, the British commander blamed much of the smallpox epidemic on women, who he maintained were breaking into quarantine houses to loot, and were then bringing the disease back to the troops with their booty. The punishments for such thievery were severe. On January 3, 1776, a campfollower named Isabella MacMahan was sentenced to receive a hundred lashes on her bare back for "receiving sundry stolen goods, knowing them to be such."

Some women sought to escape into the country, but those leaving Boston were watched closely for any signs of treason or possible spy activities. Any suspicious characters were detained by whig committees for close examination. The Massachusetts assembly joined in the surveillance by appointing special boards to deal with possible traitors passing through the lines.

One such board, convened to investigate a trio of women apprehended while leaving Boston, found that two, a Mrs. Goldthwart and her companion Mrs. Chamberlain: "appear so friendly to the Country, your Committee think they may, without danger thereto, be freed from confinement."

But their colleague Hannah Goldwait was a more serious threat. The committee recommended that she be sent to Stafford: "to endeavor the recovery of her health," but while there she should be closely watched by the local rebels. However, Hannah protested the ruling and submitted a statement from her doctor, Marshall Spring, which claimed that she was ". . . too much indisposed by a paralytick disorder to undertake so distant a journey as the Town of *Stafford*." The committee relented and allowed Hannah to set out for Newtown, her preferred destination.

Even women friendly to the American side were drawn into the involved intricacies of cross accusations and anonymous information. Lydia Paddock of Middleborough, petitioned the Massachusetts House of Representatives for help in such a case. According to Lydia's petition, her husband Thomas had outfitted a ship bound for the West Indies. He received clearance for the voyage from his local committee:

> . . . but by some evil-minded person the vessel was stopped proceeding on her voyage, and the said *Thomas* is confined to his farm, as your petitioner supposeth, under an apprehension of being unfriendly to his country: but no evidence is produced by which he has justly forfeited the

esteem and favour of his countrymen. His vessel and cargo are spoiling, himself and family suffering, and he totally ignorant of anything he has done contrary to the safety of his Country, or the advice of the Continental or Provincial Congresses.

The assembly agreed with Lydia that her husband's punishment was unjust and cleared the vessel for sailing.

Other eyes were watching Boston. John Adams, isolated in Philadelphia, complained that his friends in Massachusetts were not writing him details of local happenings. Abigail was instructed to become his observer and the Congressional delegate clearly indicated that no matter was too trifling for her attention.

Despite the elaborate networks by which rebels sought to isolate the city, some intelligence did filter through the lines. One of the most startling information leaks involved Dr. Benjamin Church, the chief physician and director of the first continental military hospital.

For many months, Church, who had "dismissed" his wife in favor of another woman, had been a prominent member of Paul Revere's spy ring. The group, organized in 1774 to watch the British army was perhaps unique in the annals of espionage, for its members made no attempt to hide their identity. Instead, they met openly at the local Green Dragon Tavern. Church as a member of the Provincial Congress was in almost constant contact with important revolutionary figures and was trusted implicitly with the most secret information. Unfortunately for the Americans, the doctor was also a double agent in the pay of the British.

In mid-1775, Church passed along to his pregnant mistress a coded message giving intelligence on the strength of American troops and certain army movements. His girlfriend's task was to see that the information was received by British officers in Boston, a difficult assignment for the city was effectively sealed off from the rest of New England.

The woman first went to Newport, Rhode Island, a crown stronghold. Here she asked a former lover named Godfrey Wenwood to arrange a meeting with the commander of the H.M.S. Rose, anchored off the coast. If this clandestine rendezvous proved impossible, Church's mistress requested an interview with one of two prominent tories in the city. Her idea was to pass the dispatch to a third party who in turn would see that it was delivered to Boston.

Wenwood refused both requests, but the woman, perhaps misunderstanding his reluctance to become involved in the operation, left the coded letter from Church, assuming that it would be delivered to a go-between. Nothing was done. Several weeks later the doctor's "miss" wrote to Wenwood, inquiring if the message had been passed along. The result of the note was a disaster to the British.

Wenwood, at last becoming suspicious at the urgency of the request, opened the original document and finding the strangely coded dispatch, went immediately to Washington.

After the American commander secured a deciphered copy of the incriminating contents, Church's mistress was arrested and questioned for several hours before she finally revealed the name of the sender. Church was captured, but claimed that the letter was actually part of a private attempt to discourage the British from attacking the vulnerable continental line by grossly overestimating the rebel troops strength. The figures were indeed greatly exaggerated, but Church was immediately jailed.

According to Sarah Church, the doctor's English-born wife, a mob almost immediately looted her house, stealing almost every possession and leaving her not even a change of clothes or a bed on which to sleep. Sarah did manage to salvage some silver plate of sufficient value to pay for her passage to England. The rebels, however, refused to grant permission for the voyage so she sailed instead for France. Sarah Church would later claim a reward from the crown for her husband's services. Her contention that he had greatly aided the King's cause was confirmed by a Mr. Sparhawk and eventually she was granted a pension of £150 a year.

Church was jailed for a time in Norwich, Connecticut, but was ultimately returned to Boston for confinement. In 1780, he was paroled and immediately booked passage for British held islands in the Caribbean. Neither Church nor his ship ever reached their destination. Both were assumed to have been destroyed in an ocean storm.

The full extent of Church's involvement with the British was not discovered for 150 years, when documents revealed that for many months the physician had been in the service of Thomas Gage. The general's papers also included a letter from Rachel Revere to her husband Paul. More than a century earlier, Rachel had entrusted the note to Church along with £125 destined for her husband. Revere received neither.

The excitement caused by the Church controversy gradually lessened and life in the American lines returned to normal. Although the days of the average soldier were routinely dull and often uneventful, Washington filled his hours by dictating correspondence to hundreds of revolutionary figures. But perhaps none of his correspondents boasted a background as strange as that of Phillis Wheatley. Phillis, a black woman, was an ardent and influential spokesperson for the American cause.

In 1761, Phillis had been bought at a Boston slave auction by John Wheatley. At the time she was about seven, considered the prime age at which to begin training as a lady's maid. Her instruction was soon expanded from purely menial duties, for various members of the Wheatley family helped in educating the young girl. Within sixteen months, she had learned to read and was soon digesting classical materials. Five years later she was writing poetry which compared favorably with the best works of the day. Her first public poem was released in 1770 and went through at least six editions in the colonies within several months.

Phillis' fame spread quickly to England where her later writings received an overwhelming audience. In 1773, a complete book of her poetry was issued. In order to allay the suspicions of those who found it difficult to believe that the sophisticated poetry was actually written by a young, former slave from Africa, the volume contained affidavits from prominent Bostonians such as Thomas Hutchinson and John Hancock who swore that they "verily believe" she had written the material.

The ex-slave was a prominent personality not only in Britain. In rural Virginia, Philip Fithian read her poems just a few months after they were first published. Benjamin Rush, who

Published according to Act of Parliament, Sept.ᵗ 1, 1773 by Arch.ᵈ Bell, Bookseller Nº 8 near the Saracens Head Aldgate.

*Phillis Wheatley, Negro Servant to Mr. John Wheatley, of Boston*, engraving by Archibald Bell. Photo courtesy of the Library of Congress.

would later gain fame as a war leader, wrote: "There is now in the town of Boston a Free Negro Girl, about 18 years of age, who has been but 9 years in the country, whose singular genius and accomplishments are such as not only do honor to her sex, but to human nature."

The young poet's work was particularly appealing to those eighteenth century liberals, who, considering themselves oppressed, perhaps read their own ideas of individual liberty into the ex-slave's words. Although much of her poetry involves religious themes, some of Phillis' most famous and influential material deals with the American conflict.

As early as 1772, Phillis, like Mercy Warren, recognized that the policies of the King presented a great danger to the freedoms of the colonists. In probably what was her first politically-oriented poem, Phillis called upon the Earl of Dartmouth, the newly appointed Secretary for North America, to look with favor upon the requests of both black and white provincials. Thus long before the war erupted, the Massachusetts writer began to plead the whig cause with high level authorities.

The poem, commemorating Dartmouth's appointment, contains an optimistic note that the new Secretary would be a stronger friend to America than previous leaders had been:

No more, *America*, in mournful strain
Of wrongs, and grievance unredress'd complain,
No longer shalt thou dread the iron chain,
Which wanton *Tyranny* with lawless hand
Had made, and with it meant t' enslave the land.
Should you, my lord, while you peruse my song,
Wonder from whence my love of *Freedom* sprung,
Whence flow these wishes for the common good,
By feeling hearts alone best understood,
I, young in life, by seeming cruel fate
Was snatch'd from *Afric*'s fancy'd happy seat:
What pangs excruiating must molest,
What sorrows labour in my parent's breast?
Steel'd was that soul and by no misery mov'd
That from a father seiz'd his babe belov'd:
Such, such my case. And can I but pray
Others may never feel tyrannic sway?

One year later Phillis made a triumphal tour of England with Wheatley's son Nathaniel. During the visit she was entertained by Lord Dartmouth, who presented her with a copy of *Don Quixote*, and by other aristocrats such as the Countess of Huntingdon. Benjamin Franklin offered to aid her in any difficulties, but her visit was cut short when news arrived that Mrs. Wheatley was dying.

By the time Phillis returned home, most public attention was riveted on the coming war. The poet reached again into the political arena for inspiration and on October 26, 1775, forwarded a new poem to Washington at Cambridge. Her letter accompanying the piece reveals that Phillis was enthusiastically hopeful of the success of the rebellion. This support may have been based on the assumption that independence from Great Britain would help to accelerate the freeing of blacks in America.

Washington was delighted with the poem, but answered that he hesitated to have it published because his critics might declare it a vain gesture. He did, however, invite Phillis to meet with him at camp:

> I thank you most sincerely for your polite notice of me in the elegant lines you inclosed; and however undeserving I may be of such encomium and panegyric, the style and manner exhibit a striking proof of your poetical talents; in honor of which, and as a tribute justly due you, I would have published the poem, had I not been apprehensive that, while I only meant to give the world this new instance of your genius, I might have incurred the imputation of vanity. This, and nothing else, determined me not to give it a place in the public prints. If you should ever come to Cambridge, or near head-quarters, I shall be happy to see a person so favored by the Muses, and to whom nature has been so liberal and beneficent in her dispensations. I am, with great respect, your obedient, humble servant,
>
>                                    GEO. WASHINGTON

The poem was printed two months later in the *Pennsylvania Magazine*, an important publication edited by Thomas Paine. Phillis continued to produce material dealing with the revolution.

One piece commemorated the capture of Charles Lee, while another praised the virtues of peace and liberty. But, although her literary career was still successful, Phillis' personal life slowly began to crumble.

In 1778, John Wheatley died. His son Nathaniel took up permanent residence in London. Former friends who could have been in positions to financially assist the poet were occupied by the war. The situation did not improve in August of 1778 when Phillis was issued a license to marry one John Peters, also a free black.

Controversy surrounds the exact character of Peters. The French counsel in Boston reported that he was an admirable pleader for the cause of poor blacks. According to other accounts, however, he was an unsuccessful grocer with a great aversion to work of any type. Peters and Phillis left Boston after their marriage to take refuge in Wilmington, Massachusetts. A major incentive for the move may have been that her early opposition to the crown had made remaining on the coast a dangerous risk. In the relatively safe interior of the state, three children were born.

When the Peters family returned to the port city, they were in desperate financial condition. Some reports indicate that John Peters was jailed and that Phillis supported the children by working as a servant in a low-class rooming house. This report may not be entirely accurate, but the family was certainly near destitute at this time. Two of the children died during the winter of 1783–1784. The thirty-one-year-old poet and her one surviving daughter did not live another year.

Despite the large scale sales of her works, Phillis Wheatley died a pauper. A note accompanying a book donated to Harvard College in 1824, indicates that the volume had been sold soon after her death so that certain debts could be paid. The book was a copy of *Paradise Lost*, and was inscribed: "Mr. Brook Watson to Phillis Wheatley, London, July-1773." Watson, Lord Mayor of London, had made a gift of the epic to the young poet during her festive European tour.

Some literary critics have considered Phillis merely an anthropological oddity and suggested that her poetry gained attention not because of its quality, but because she was black, young and a woman. Thomas Jefferson scorned her efforts as being "below the dignity of criticism."

Originality is indeed lacking in much of her work. Phillis sometimes closely copied the popular styles of her day, yet the value of her poems from a historical viewpoint is singular. Unlike other writers of the period, Phillis wrote not from the fashionable world of the upper classes, but out of humble and sometimes tragic circumstances. She alone conveyed the intimate feelings of a black woman in America.

Phillis Wheatley lived just long enough to see and help establish independence for her white friends. Nearly a hundred years later, her poems would again become popular, this time in the struggle to free blacks in the South.

Phillis' trials were far in the future as the continentals dug in around Boston in early 1776. Inside the beleaguered city another woman was writing for the people. She was Margaret Green Draper, publisher of the *Massachusetts Gazette* and *Boston News Letter*. Margaret's readers were truly a captive audience, for all other newspapers in the city ceased publication after the siege began.

Margaret had assumed control of the loyal-leaning publication when her husband died in June of 1774. A brief partnership with John Boyle lasted less than two months, for on August 4, Boyle noted in his diary: "My partnership ceased with Mrs. Draper, on account of an unhappy Dispute which arose respecting the Contract entered into between her late husband and myself." The argument may have been partially political for Margaret, unlike Boyle, was strongly pro-British. She would later claim that he had attempted to convert her paper into a revolutionary organ.

Margaret Draper's editorship was not unusual, for printing was a long established profession for colonial women. The first press in the colonies was brought by Elizabeth Harris Glover in 1638. The tradition was continued by females such as Dinah Nuthead, who became government printer and Anna Zenger who published the *New York Weekly Journal* while her husband was jailed for libel. Anna's continuance of the paper was vital to the

Zenger case which ultimately established basic concepts of freedom of the press. By the time of the revolution, the prominent role of women in printing was well accepted.

One of the most famous pre-war printers was Annapolis' Anne Catherine Greene. At the death of her husband in 1767, Anne took control of the *Maryland Gazette* and was awarded the job of Printer to the Province. The mother of fourteen received $948½ for her work that year with the colonial government. Her contract stipulated that she would be paid 48,000 pounds of tobacco for printing jobs during the years in which the Assembly was meeting, and 36,109 pounds when they were not in session.

Like most printers of the day, Anne Greene had dissatisfied readers. Bennet Allen, a famous duelist, once threatened to knock up her press because of insulting articles she had published.

In neighboring Virginia, Clementine Bird Rind began to publish the *Virginia Gazette* in 1773, and was made public printer the following year. The paper had formerly been owned by loyalist Joseph Royle who refused to publish many of the anti-British debates in the House of Burgesses. Penelope Russell produced the *Boston Censor* in 1771 and in Hartford, Hannah Watson was chief of the *Connecticut Courant* from 1778–1779.

Yet none of these papers carried the distinguished history of Margaret Draper's publication. The *Boston News Letter* was the first paper founded in the colonies. Both her father and grandfather had been printers to the King. Although British authorities directly subsidized her paper during the siege, Margaret was not completely one-sided in her reporting of the political scene.

As Public Printer she was expected to publish all official declarations, documents and council proceedings. From England came royal decrees for inclusion along with parliamentary proclamations and government directives. But the *News Letter* also included much material from the rebel view. Discussions in the Congress were reported unaltered and without comment. Many of George Washington's statements from Cambridge were published and whig activities in other colonies were given extensive coverage.

Some of the most unusual pieces in the strong loyalist newspaper were advertisements placed by New Englanders to proclaim their unwavering allegiance to the aims of the rebellion. These public pronouncements may have been required by various committees of safety as evidence that suspected tories were willing to openly declare themselves friends of the new government in Philadelphia.

Another curious item appeared in the December 21, 1775, edition of Margaret's publication. The blurb was a public notice which advertised the sale of a bookshop owned by Henry Knox. Knox had left the city to become an important rebel partisan. His shop may have been confiscated as a result of the collaboration, but no mention was made in the *News Letter* that Knox was helping to lead the forces surrounding the city. The advertisement did go into great detail in describing the property to be sold which included mathematical instruments, kitchen furniture, books, prints, hunting whips, looking glasses, assorted paper hangings and fifes fit for the army.

But widow Draper was not always unbiased in her news reporting. In some cases, she added her own opinions to articles and the results were part-news, part-editorial stories usually favorable to crown policies:

> The continental congress have sent another address to the Canadians, in which, they are again trying by flattery and promises, to attach them to their interest; but it is most probable, it will, like the other, rather provoke their resentment than in any answer the end they have in view.

> General Lee has sent a Letter to Lord Barrington, dated 12 of June, renouncing his half pay from the date thereof. Quere, whether he might not have sav'd himself the Trouble.

Margaret may also have influenced her readers by the selection of material which was emphasized in the paper. Gradually the *News Letter* carried less correspondence from whigs and more from tory readers. One letter, printed during the siege and datelined London, was probably calculated to boost the sagging spirits of those in Boston. The letter reported that the boycotts and blockages which were so important to the American protests, were doing almost no damage to English manufacturers. The loyalist correspondent wrote:

> Since my departure from Salem last February, I have been in the principal manufacturing towns, and be assured the people are fully employed, goods high, and be assured government is firm and will apply its whole power to reduce the Americans to order. Soon after you receive this, the King's forces will be reinforced by 7,000 men. General Amherst will have the supreme command of the army . . . people here are greatly offended at the Americans refusing to pay for their protection. . . . be of good courage as all the foreign potentates have declared against aiding our provincial rebels. Success must attend the arms of George the Third, which is the sincere wish of every true britainer, and none more than me.

Margaret was able to produce one significant scoop for the citizens of the port city, when an American courier was captured by British troopers near Newport. Included in his parcel were letters written by John Adams, critical of other congressional delegates.

When the notes were reprinted in the *News Letter*, a major feud sprang up between the Massachusetts delegate and John Dickinson, a representative from Pennsylvania. Adams had described Dickinson as a "piddling Genius" and declared that he had "given a silly Cast to our whole Doings." The publication was disconcerting to Adams who was already wary of entrusting secrets to the mail. His earlier letters to Abigail had contained detailed descriptions of events in Philadelphia, estimates of military strategy and comments on the opinions of various prominent people. This openness ended for a short time and the future president explained that care should be taken with his earlier, more indiscreet notes. "Pray, bundle up every Paper, not already hid," he notified her, "and conceal them in impenetrable Darkness."

During the drab winter of 1775–1776, some cheerfulness did enlighten Boston with the opening of a new play entitled

*The Blockade of Boston.* The script was written by General John Burgoyne, a man about town who considered himself a particularly proficient playwright. *The Blockade* was a satire ridiculing American forces, but according to contemporary notes, the opening performance at Faneuil Hall was not a complete success. American artillery chose to bombard a distant section of the city during the show and when an actor rushed into the theater to spread the alarm, he was greeted with wild applause and cheers by the audience who thought the activity was an innovative part of the play.

Mercy Warren immediately countered with a production called *The Blockheads; or The Affrighted Officers: A Farce.* For the first time she used women as characters. Holding the starring roles were characters with names such as Captain Bashaw, Lord Dapper and Shallow, while Dupe, Judge Meagre and Simple, featured in earlier plays, made return performances. The language of Mercy's newest production was sometimes bawdy and captured the gross vernacular of British troops in the eighteenth century. Because of this reality and her custom of anonymous publishing, *The Blockheads* was not attributed to Mercy until the end of the nineteenth century.

One officer not parodied in the play was Captain David Johnston of the Royal Marines, a man who would later become an aide to Earl Percy. The young soldier's view of the siege was not particularly enthusiastic, for Johnston had been wounded in earlier fighting. He wrote: ". . . on the 17th of June, 1775, I was wounded at the attack on Bunkers Hill, and when brought over to Boston I must have died on the street had not the Memorialist and daughter taken me into their house. I therefore owe my life to their humanity."

The "Memorialist" to whom Johnston was indebted was Dorcas Pringle Griffiths. At the time of the officer's statement, Dorcas was applying for a British pension because of the great losses she had incurred in supporting the crown and the assistance she had provided to British troops during the siege.

The widow Griffiths may have been a famous Massachusetts prostitute. But more probably she was merely an indiscreet mistress who would have remained innocuous if her lover had not become a famous figure. For many years, Dorcas ostensively supported herself and her daughter Sarah Hinson, by operating a "huckster's shop" at the head of Hancock's Wharf. Here she sold tea, groceries and liquor. But a large part of her living probably came from John Hancock, the future governor of Massachusetts, president of the Continental Congress and one of the wealthiest men in New England.

Although Dorcas was about eighteen years older than Hancock, she was his close companion for some time before the war. It is not clear when the affair first began, but Hancock remained single at age thirty-eight despite the vigorous pursuits of Dorothy Quincy, a member of a prominent, but not so prosperous, Braintree family. Dorothy's unmarried status at twenty-eight was considered unusual, for most women her age had been married for at least ten years and produced numerous children. It was not until 1775, two months after the Battle of Bunker Hill, when Hancock and Dorcas had irrevocably chosen to support opposing sides in the revolutionary struggle that John Hancock finally married Dorothy Quincy.

Although Dorcas and her daughter lived well in their quarters at the shop, the women later claimed that they were subjected to "vindictive resentment," and "cruelties" from the rebels because of the welcome they gave to the King's friends. But whigs were not the only enemies made by Dorcas and Sarah in Boston. Years later, the animosity of Thomas Flucker, the last secretary of the province, would prove costly to them.

Lady Agnes Franklin, the widow of an English baronet, had also taken refuge in Boston. Despite her title, Lady Agnes was not a high-born aristocrat, but a former tavern maid who had attracted Sir Charles Henry Franklin when she was only sixteen years old. Franklin was collector of customs in Boston in 1741, when he first saw Agnes at an inn in Marblehead. He immediately became greatly attracted to the young girl and with parental approval, took her to Boston where she was educated and installed as his mistress in a large mansion at Hopkinson.

Agnes' "peasant" origins made marriage impossible, but she accompanied Sir Charles to Portugal when he was appointed as English counsel-general. Here, according to romantic legend,

Franklin was trapped underground in a violent earthquake and, repenting of his past sins, promised to marry his companion if he were saved. Surprisingly, Charles honored his vow even after he was rescued. The pair returned to Massachusetts where he was again appointed customs collector, but in 1759 he was removed from the post because of inattention to duty.

After the dismissal, the Franklins settled in England. However following the death of Sir Charles in 1765, Agnes returned to the land of her birth. When the war broke out, her loyalties were with England and during the siege, she requested permission to leave Hopkinson for Boston. The committee of safety approved the move, perhaps because of the influence of Benjamin Church who had not yet been revealed and who signed her pass.

Although Agnes had substantial wealth, she was allowed to take with her only six trunks, one chest, a small bag of pickled tongue, some hay, three bags of corn, three beds and bedding, six sheep, two pigs and other items which were absolutely necessary. The Provincial Congress was more generous than the local organization for it supplied her with an escort and allowed her to add a basket of chickens, two barrels, a hamper, some ham and veal to her luggage.

With the main elements of the King's army safely contained in Boston, American military figures were quick to shift their attention towards other areas. Rebel troops still held Ft. Tie, forestalling a British invasion into the colonies from Canada by way of Lake Champlain. Instead of maintaining this defensive position, provincial leaders began mapping plans for a northern offensive aimed at defeating the crown garrisons in Canada and adding that territory as a giant fourteenth colony.

Under the American scheme, a contingent of continental troops under General Philip Schuyler would move toward Montreal while a second force commanded by Benedict Arnold would attack the strong fortress at Quebec. This two-pronged invasion would supposedly divide the enemy manpower, allowing the continentals to ultimately join in a massive pincer movement.

On September 29, Arnold and about 1,000 rebels left Fort Western near the mouth of the Kennebec River in Maine. By following waterways, portaging around rapids and covering the last part of the journey on foot, the group planned to cover the estimated 185 miles to Quebec in about three weeks. Time was imperative, for soon the winter snows would complicate the journey and perhaps halt any attempt at storming the fortress on the St. Lawrence.

But many obstacles confronted the army. Beyond the southernmost settlements of the Kennebec, Arnold's march was primarily through territory that was uncharted and unexplored by continentals. In addition, the army was poorly equipped for the water voyage because, instead of canoes, the troops had been supplied with heavy wooden boats called bateaux. These sturdy vessels were primarily suited for ferrying cargo across smooth lakes or streams and were not designed for the quick maneuvers which would be required to traverse the rapids of the fierce Kennebec. Unknown to the planners, many boats would break up in the treacherous cascades. Others would become waterlogged and sink. Some would be simply abandoned by weary troops who were too weak to carry the heavy load on portages.

Several women had decided to accompany Arnold's men on the hazardous offensive. One was reported to be a half-French, half-Abnaki Indian named Jacataqua who joined the group near Fort Western. Approximately twenty braves from the tribe had left their settlement on Swan Island to guide the army and forage for food. Numerous legends grew up concerning the young Indian girl who supposedly took part in the march. Most suggest that she was a sachem or chieftress of the tribe who was noted as a great hunter and famed for her knowledge of the medicinal qualities of various roots and plants. Other stories suggest that Jacataqua became immediately attracted to Captain Aaron Burr and was almost inseparable from him for the remainder of the journey.

In addition to Jacataqua, the wives of two Pennsylvania soldiers were included in the entourage. Jemima Warner had earlier followed her husband James to Cambridge where he served as a private in the elite rifle corps led by Daniel Morgan. These buckskin clad frontiersmen were probably the most respected of the continental troops because of their strict discipline and their sharpshooting abilities with the Pennsylvania long rifle.

The wife of a Pennsylvania sergeant named Grier, completed the
female contingent.

Problems plagued the army from the first days of the march.
About two-thirds of the food supply was lost before October 15
as bateaux broke up and water flooded the supply parcels. Unex-
pectedly, the army ran into vast swamps where large numbers of
men contracted dysentery and pneumonia. As the march dragged
farther into the late fall, game disappeared in the forests and the
food problems became critical. Eating became almost an obses-
sion.

"Our bill of fare for last night and this morning consisted of
the jawbone of a swine destitute of any covering," wrote Dr.
Isaac Senter, a New Hampshire soldier on October 27. Five days
later the situation worsened:

> Our greatest luxuries now consisted in a little water,
> stiffened with flour, in imitation of a shoemaker's paste,
> which was christened with the name of Lillipu. . . . In com-
> pany was a poor dog hitherto lived through all the tribu-
> tions [which] became prey for the sustenance of the assassi-
> nators. This poor animal was instantly devoured, without
> leaving any vestige of the sacrifice. Nor did the shaving
> soap, pomatum, and even the lip salve, leather of their shoes,
> cartridge boxes, &c., share any better fate. . . .

Jemima Warner was meeting problems more severe than
hunger. One witness to her struggle was John Joseph Henry, a
sixteen-year-old Pennsylvanian. Thirty-six years later, the soldier
dictated to his daughter recollections of Jemima's hardships. Henry's company had halted at a great marsh so that stragglers could
catch up with the main force. The day was November 1, 1775,
the time was about 10:00 a.m.

> There were two women attached to those companies, who
> arrived before we commenced the march. One was the wife
> of Sergeant Grier, a large, virtuous and respectable woman.
> The other was the wife of a private of our company, a man
> who lagged on every occasion. These women having arrived,
> it was presumed that all our party were up. We were on the
> point of entering the marsh, when some one cried out,

"Warner is not here." Another said he had sat down, sick, under a tree a few miles back. His wife begged us to wait a short time, and with tears of affection in her eyes, ran back to her husband. We tarried an hour. They came not.

Abner Stocking of Connecticut was marching behind the Pennsylvania troops. Although he did not know the Warner couple, Stocking witnessed what happened when Jemima ran back to find her husband:

> My heart was ready to burst and my eyes to overflow with tears when I witnessed distress which I could not relieve. The circumstances of a young Dutchman, and his wife, who followed him through this fatiguing march, particularly excited my sensibility. They appeared to be much interested in each others welfare and unwilling to be separated, but the husband, exhausted with fatigue and hunger fell a victim to the King of terrors. His affectionate wife tarryed by him until he died, while the rest of the company proceeded on their way. Having no implements with which she could bury him she covered him with leaves, and then took his gun and other implements and left him with a heavy heart. After travelling 20 miles she came up with us.

Jemima's attempt to hide her husband's body with leaves was designed to keep maurauding wolves from following the main march and preying on those who fell out along the path. Meanwhile, Sgt. Grier's wife was doing better at the swamp. Henry's company had decided to leave Jemima behind and proceed forward. He reported:

> Entering the pond (Simpson foremost), and breaking the ice here and there with the butts of our guns and feet, as occasion required, we were soon waist deep in the mud and water. As is generally the case with youths, it came to my mind that a better path might be found than that of the more elderly guide. Attempting this, the water in a trice cooling my armpits, made me gladly return into the file. Now Mrs. Grier had got before me. My mind was humbled, yet astonished, at the exertions of this good woman. Her clothes more than waist high, she waded before me to firm

ground. No one, so long as she was known to us, dared intimate a disrespectable idea of her.

By this time the order had been given that each man was to
save himself. The sick, wounded and stragglers were left behind
to fend for themselves in the barren land. George Morison, a
Pennsylvanian, was appalled at the order and stunned by the faces
of those he was directed to bypass: "Their haggard looks, their
ghastly countenances, their emaciated bodies, and their struggles
to proceed with us, have left impressions on our minds which
nothing but death can erase."

Morison would be less solicitous of his fellow soldiers in the
war after he had been captured and exchanged. An argument
with a Maryland colonel finally ended his career for the discussion became so heated that the officer drew his sword. Morison
promptly broke his arm with a spade and received a court martial
punishment of 1,000 lashes. The sentence, which meant certain
death, was not carried out and instead the veteran left the service.

On November 9, after a march of 45 days and 350 miles, the
remnants of Arnold's force finally reached the banks of the St.
Lawrence. Here they camped near the towering walls of the fortress at Quebec. A large contingent under Lt. Col. Roger Enos of
Connecticut had given up the march on October 25, and returned home. Enos would later be court martialed for the action.
Others had died along the way, thus making the final number of
survivors about 600.

On the western campaign, General Schuyler had fallen ill
and had been replaced by General Richard Montgomery. Upon
reaching Montreal, American troops had easily taken the British
garrison, thus making Montgomery the hero of the hour. Arnold
now waited for the general to bring reinforcements down the St.
Lawrence for the storming of Québec.

Much of the lull was absorbed in planning various ways in
which the city could be taken. In one unsuccessful try, a woman
was sent into Québec from the American camp. She carried messages to merchants asking for their help in establishing a fifth column inside the walls and a formal ultimatum requesting that
Governor Guy Carleton surrender the fort. Carleton, who had

secretly slipped into the city while dressed as a peasant, notified
Howe that he had rejected the woman's proposal, jailed her for
several days and then drummed her out of Québec.

One not so genteel suggestion by American officers was to
herd a group of Canadian women, children and priests in front of
and amidst the attacking legions. The bodies of these unwilling
civilians would serve as shields for the advancing troops. This
idea was rejected and instead a direct assault using ladders to
scale the high walls was planned. On December 5, General Montgomery finally reached the bivouacked rebels of Arnold's march.
Under the cover of a blinding snowstorm, the combined units attacked Québec on New Year's Eve day, 1775.

Although some troops were able to breach the defenses and
enter the city, most contingents were held back by fierce fire
from the walls. Arnold was shot, Montgomery killed. Just sixteen
years before another hero, British General James Wolfe, had been
slain while leading a charge on the nearby Plains of Abraham.
Then the French defenders had come out of Québec to meet the
English attack in the open. Wolfe's offensive had been successful.
France was defeated and Canada was brought into the British do-
main. But in 1775, the British wisely remained inside their fortress. This day would not go to the Americans.

The rebels fell back under the intense fire and hundreds of
those fighting atop the parapets or inside the city were taken prisoner as the shattered infantry retreated. A second attack was ve-
toed. The fragmented rebels elected to begin a siege similar to
that which was proving so successful at Boston.

By spring, the army surrounding Québec had gained no advantage. According to some reports Jacataqua was pregnant,
probably with Burr's child. On April 18, Massachusetts private
Caleb Haskell noted:

> A woman of the Pennsylvania troops was killed today
> by accident—a soldier carelessly snapping his musket,
> which proved to be loaded.

The woman may have been Grier's wife or Jemima Warner,
but also, she could have been a follower of Montgomery's rein-

forcements or even a Canadian who had taken up with the invaders.

By May 1, an estimated 900 of the 1,900 troops before Québec were ill, chiefly from smallpox. Another 200 had recently been innoculated and undoubtedly would become immobile from the reaction. Ice had begun to break in the frozen St. Lawrence and soon ships of the British navy would be able to sail into Québec, challenging the besieging forces.

The American army reluctantly started back to New England. Never again would rebel troops pose a threat to the northern province. Canada would remain British and would not become the fourteenth colony.

While Arnold's troops were recovering from defeat at Québec, the fortunes of the Continental Army at Boston were rapidly improving. Although short-term enlistments of volunteers had expired on New Year's Day, Washington cajoled others into joining. The situation inside the city was growing more desperate each day. Food and fuel were almost exhausted. In the idle American camp, a rumor was spread that the British in desperation were using germ warfare by sending those exposed to smallpox out among the continental troops.

The American position was soon to be even further strengthened. Help was on the way in the form of Deborah Champion, the eighteenth century woman's answer to Paul Revere. Twenty-two-year-old Deborah was living with her parents in Connecticut during the siege, but like most other New Englanders, her life was altered by events around Boston.

In a letter to her friend Patience, Deborah described her war adventure, which had begun one morning, not significantly different from any other.

Soon after Deborah had settled herself for a long day of spinning, a horseman rode into her yard and quickly entered the house to speak with Deborah's father Colonel Henry Champion. Soon she was called inside and Champion requested that she undertake a two-day ride to Boston, to carry urgently needed dispatches to Washington. Champion warned "the way is long," but added that the importance of the mission outweighed the danger. It was agreed that Deborah would begin the ride the following

day, accompanied only by a trusted servant named Aristarchus, a
move calculated to lessen the suspicions of any British troops
who might be encountered. Deborah's chronicle of the journey
indicates that although the trip was a hard one, it was exciting:

> Early in the morning, before it was fairly light, mother
> called me, though I had seemed to have hardly slept at all.
> . . . Father told me again of the haste with which I must
> ride and the care to use for the safety of the dispatches, and
> I set forth on my journey with a light heart and my father's
> blessing.

> The British were at Providence, in Rhode Island, so it
> was thought best I should ride due north to the Massachu-
> setts line, and then east as best I could to Boston. The
> weather was perfect, but the roads none too good as there
> had been recent rains, but we made fairly good time going
> through Norwich, then up the Valley of the Quinebaug to
> Canterbury, where we rested our horses for an hour, then
> pushed on, hoping to get to Pomfret before dark. . . . All
> went as well as I could expect. We met few people on the
> road, almost all men being with the army and only the very
> old men and the women at work in the villages and farms.
> Dear heart, but war is a cruel thing!

Deborah rested for a while at the home of her uncle where
she secured fresh horses. Then she and Aristarchus continued on
their way:

> I heard that it would be almost impossible to avoid the
> British unless by going so far out of the way that too much
> time would be lost, so I plucked up what courage I could
> and secreting my papers in a small pocket in the saddlebags,
> under all the eatables mother had filled them with, I rode on,
> determined to ride all night. It was late at night, or rather
> very early in the morning, that I heard the call of the sentry
> and knew that now, if at all, the danger point was reached,
> but pulling my calash still farther over my face, I went on
> with what boldness I could muster. Suddenly I was ordered
> to halt; as I couldn't help myself, I did so. I could almost
> hear Aristarchus' teeth rattle in his mouth, but I knew he

would obey my instructions and if I was detained would try
to find the way alone. A soldier in a red coat proceeded to
take me to headquarters, but I told him it was early to wake
the captain, and to please to let me pass for I had been sent
in urgent haste to see a friend in need, which was true if
ambiguous. To my joy, he let me go, saying: "Well, you are
only an old woman anyway," evidently as glad to get rid of
me as I of him.

Deborah contined on her ride and ultimately reached Washington. Unlike Paul Revere, she had successfully completed her
ride.

Henry Knox was also on the road to Cambridge. Now a
general, Knox had been sent to Fort Ticonderoga to bring back
the heavy siege guns which had been captured when the installation was taken from the British. Now the arms were slated to be
used against their former owners.

Knox, who weighed more than 260 pounds, was in constant
action during the war. Despite the rigors of eight years of campaigning, the deprivations of Valley Forge and the constant
travel, the soldier managed to gain an additional 20 pounds. Knox
was completely untrained as a soldier, and had learned his military strategies solely from old books. It was ironic that he could
come through the war relatively unscathed, but die prematurely
by choking to death on a chicken bone.

The general encountered certain difficulties on the road from
Fort Tie. Moving the heavy guns with oxen proved impossible
after the train encountered snow drifts of more than three feet.
General Schuyler searched the Hudson Valley area and managed
to locate 124 pairs of horses with sleighs to pull the load. Some
friends of the cause gladly donated their animals, but others with
an eye toward profit charged exorbitant rates.

Several of the cannon fell through the ice while being
dragged across the Hudson and precious time was lost as they
were retrieved. On the far bank, additional hazards were discovered. Citizens packed the roadsides to view and touch the ma-
chines. Most countrypeople had never seen even a sketch of such
large artillery and their experience with guns had been limited to

the family musket. Teamsters had to be constantly alert to keep
their animals from trampling over the enthusiastic farm folk who
clambered aboard the cannon for a ride.

Despite the difficulties, the arms finally arrived at Cambridge
and were readied for action. On the eve of the sixth anniversary
of the Boston Massacre, a band of continentals secretly climbed
to the top of Dorchester Heights overlooking Boston. Here,
working through the night in almost complete silence, the soldiers managed to construct elaborate fortifications. By dawn, the
formerly deserted hill was fully equipped with the threatening
cannon.

Howe, realizing that his position had been made untenable,
gave orders for his troops to evacuate the city. Approximately
1,100 loyalists prepared to depart with the forces. The worth of
these refugees, in land, securities and personal property was stag-
gering, but for the seaborne retreat, each was allowed to carry
only the most personal necessities.

On March 13, the general ordered shipboard provisions cut
to the basic minimum so that the meager supplies would be sufficient for the journey to Halifax:

> The QrMasters of Corps to subsist their Women and
> Children on board Ship, with Flour and Rice only, till fur-
> ther Orders, and that it be issued to them with Economy. A
> small Quantity of Fish may be given to them with it. Each
> Corps to apply immediately at No. 16 on long Wharf for a
> Barrel of Salt Fish, to be divided among the Men and
> Women.

The retreat was orderly. Howe refrained from burning Boston and Washington did not direct artillery fire on the departing
fleet. On March 17, 1776, the sails were set and the British vessels
weighed anchor. Many of the tories saw their city for the last
time, for most would never return. Instead they would start new
lives in primitive settlements in Nova Scotia or would continue
on to England. Howe and his troops, however, would soon return.

# CHAPTER THREE

# *Choosing Up Sides*

A tory is a thing whose head is in England, and its body
in America, and its neck ought to be stretched.

The tories with their brats and wives,
Have fled to save their wretched lives.

*Two revolutionary doggerels*

M OST OF THE LOYALISTS sailing toward Halifax with Howe
were facing a long and difficult future. The way was particularly bleak for William McKinstry's wife from Taunton, who
had already experienced persecution. Earlier in the war, the ". . .
finely educated and high spirited woman, of elegant manners, was
compelled, by a large collection of females, to march around the
Liberty Pole."

The McKinstry family left home for the safety of Boston
where Dr. McKinstry was appointed Surgeon-General of the
city's hospitals. But the war was soon over for the physician. He
died on board the hospital ship *Dutton* as it lay in the harbor and
his widow sailed on to start her new life alone.

Many of her sailing companions would settle in the town of
Shelburne, a small village in Nova Scotia. Some would die of
starvation when the supply ships from England failed to arrive on
schedule. Others would live rugged lives in the wilderness interior. This pioneer existence in Canada was particularly difficult

for expatriots from the higher economic levels of society who were formerly dependent upon servants and entirely unaccustomed to manual labor. Some like Dorcas Griffiths found that the outlands held none of the exciting advantages of city living and left the province to resettle in England.

The British government, assuming a responsibility to assist those who had given up their wealth to support the crown, attempted to provide aid for the refugees. A special commission on loyalist claims was established. Under this panel, those leaving the colonies could present petitions, outlining the losses they had sustained and detailing any help that they had given to the British. If properly documented and supported by testimonials of reliable witnesses, the commission could award gratuities in the form of pensions or flat sums of compensation.

Although the system was reasonable on the surface, its operation was often complicated by bureaucratic regulations. Rarely did the commission act quickly. Even when the petitioner was in dire need of funds, the board's processes were unhurried. The case of Dorcas Griffiths ranks as one of the most complicated and lengthy in the history of the program.

Dorcas' first petition was filed soon after she and her daughter Sarah arrived in London. In the document she maintained that they had been forced to flee for the "preservation of their lives," and that they were ". . . compelled to leave all their industriously acquired property behind. . . ." This move, she suggested, had reduced them from ". . . affluence and comfort to poverty and misery."

Dorcas' petition was rejected because of insufficient supporting evidence, but she soon filed a second motion stressing that she was in "extreme distress." This time Dorcas sought aid from the highest level. Attached to her memorial were affidavits from General Howe and Sir William Pepperell. In addition, Thomas Gage filed a statement on her behalf swearing: "I certify that I have been informed the Petitioners humanely assisted the Sick and wounded Officers of the King's Army at Boston; which drew the Resentment of the Rebels upon them, and obliged them to leave their Country."

A pension of £50 a year was finally granted to the women,

but the situation was not settled. Now, Thomas Flucker came
into the picture. Flucker had also fled Boston, but had suffered
less than most refugees, for he had been maintained on government payrolls as Secretary of the Province of Massachusetts *in
absentia* with a salary of £300 a year. His appointment was probably made in anticipation that the war would be quickly over and
British officials would return to their former positions in the defeated colony.

As a member of the influential Brompton Row Tory Club,
an organization of prominent loyalists, Flucker was constantly
delving into the affairs of those who had left Massachusetts. The
Secretary also served as an anonymous informer and relayed to
the commission the story of Dorcas' past association with John
Hancock. Flucker also reported that Dorcas was actually a ". . .
Common prostitute and bred her daughter in the same way. . . ."
As a result, the commission immediately cancelled the women's
pensions.

Dorcas was left without any means of support, yet she was
not deterred and filed still another petition. The widow was evidently ignorant of Flucker's specific accusations and contended
that the commission had been swayed ". . . by persons who must
have deviated from the truth. . . ." She further plead that ". . .
the discontinuance of the Treasury allowance has brought on
your Memorialists such distress as to compel them to dispose of
the little Furniture they had left for the support of their existence." The Bostonian may have thought that the pensions had
been withdrawn because of irregularities in the financial loss she
had earlier claimed, for she carefully outlined her property holdings in America.

Although this petition was supported by two men who had
known Dorcas in Boston, the opinion of the commission remained
unchanged and the pension was not restored. A plea by daughter
Sarah did no good and the decision of the board stood final. The
commissioners hesitated, however, to put into writing any evidence that Flucker had informed or the specific allegations he
had lodged against the women. Although the Secretary had died
while the controversy still raged, the commission merely noted
for the record:

The History of Mrs. Griffiths and Mrs. Hinson was given to those Gentlemen by one of the most respectable Gentlemen of the province (who is now dead) in a Confidential Conversation who convinced them that they were not proper Objects of the Bounty of Government.

If the Lords of the Treasury wish to know all the Circumstances of this Case we shall be ready at any time to communicate them to their Lordships which we should prefer to giving them on Paper.

Margaret Draper was more successful in obtaining funds. Her house in America had been confiscated and sold. The remainder of her property and printing equipment had also been seized and was a total loss to her. As a result, Margaret, who the commissioners noted was "in a bad state of health," was awarded an annual pension of £100 and a flat settlement of £929.

Boston loyalists such as Dorcas and Margaret were soon joined by thousands of tories who had left the colonies for refuge in British-held areas. Some estimate that as many as 100,000 provincials chose to leave the country as a result of the revolution. Many more conservatives remained in the colonies to fight the rebels in an attempt to restore the King's authority.

The loyalist controversy aroused even the most temperate whigs. John Adams, a fiery but usually gentle man, said: "I would have hanged my own brother if he took part with our enemy in this contest." Adams estimated that of the total population in America, one-third were rebels, one-third loyalists and one-third uncommitted. The delegate's estimate of tory strength was probably unrealistically high, but allegiances were constantly shifting according to the fortunes of war. When American victories were on the rise, the number of loyalists decreased. When Britain seemed in control of the situation, the tories became more numerous.

The decision to support England was a difficult one for many. Some residents had not expected the war to come at all and had delayed committing themselves until the last possible moment. Even Thomas Jefferson, who was greatly knowledgeable with the political situation, noted as late as August of 1775 that he was ". . . looking with fondness toward a reconciliation with Great Britain. . . ."

Many of those departing during the early days of the war did not realize that the move would be permanent, but merely viewed the resettlement as a temporary inconvenience until a British victory would enable them to return home.

While some loyalists were farmers and workers, a great number were wealthy, upper economic class citizens. Perhaps more important, many were highly educated and skilled in government, finance or trade. Such education was rare and valuable in the colonies and later this "brain drain" was severely felt in day to day economic operations of the new government.

Another important contingent of loyalists was composed of black slaves who had been offered their freedom by the British. Most of the Negro tories held no particular allegiance in the political realm, but were attracted to that side which promised the quickest avenue to liberty.

Few geographical areas could be classified as being entirely devoted to one side of the rebellion, for most communities housed adherents of both combatants. However, there was some pattern to the destination of the fleeing loyalists. Those from northern colonies tended to go to England, Nova Scotia, settlements on the coast of Maine or in the interior of Canada. In the South, tories were usually slave owners and chose to resettle in British held islands in the Caribbean where human bondage was acceptable.

Many were disappointed with their new lives. The resumption of a stable pattern of living was not easy and the psychological displacement was difficult to accept. Samuel Curwen, a Judge of Admiralty who left Boston soon after the battles at Lexington and Concord, led the life of a typical escaped tory. On May 4, 1775, Curwen made the first entry in a journal he would keep throughout his sojurn in England:

> Having in vain endeavoured to persuade my wife to accompany me, her apprehensions of danger from an incensed soldiery, a people licentious and enthusiastically mad and broken loose from all the restraints of law or religion, being less terrible to her than a short passage on the ocean; and

being moreover encouraged by her, I left my late peaceful home (in my sixtieth year) in search of personal security and those rights which by the laws of God I ought to have enjoyed undisturbed there, and embarked at Beverly on board the schooner *Lively*. . . .

Curwen's wife was Abigail Russell, a member of a prominent New England family. The judge may have been mistaken in his description of her as a loyalist supporter, for Abigail chose to remain in America throughout the entire war, evidently undisturbed by the rebels. But Curwen's existence was not as pleasant as his wife's.

Like many other colonials, the judge felt out of place in London, where tories were often treated as outsiders. Here suicides were high and economic deprivation was common. The conditions and confinement of the heavily populated English cities affected many ex-Americans such as Eleanor Addison, the wife of Maryland clergyman Jonathan Boucher. Reverend Boucher, who kept a pair of loaded pistols on his pulpit as he sermonized against the rebellion, left the colonies for England in 1775. The crossing was not luxurious for the minister and his wife, who used a canvas sail as a blanket and a bag of grits for a pillow. Upon arriving, plantation-bred Eleanor was greatly frightened by London's mobs. Perhaps even worse, the Bouchers' financial situation was near desperate and the daughter of a wealthy American planter was forced to take in boarders to survive.

Curwen was not reduced to such severe circumstances, for his hardships were primarily mental ones. He associated much of the time with other homeless Americans and most of his writings involve the land which he had left. In April, 1780, Curwen voiced the feelings of melancholy which many of his colleagues may have felt:

This day, five years are complete since I abandoned my house, estate, effects and friends. God only knows whether I shall ever be restored to them, or they to me. Party rage, like jealousy and superstition, is cruel as the grave;—that moderation is a crime in times of civil confusions, many

good, virtuous and peaceable persons, now suffering banishment from America, are the wretched proofs and instances.
—May it please God to inspire with wisdom and true policy the principal conductors in this truly lamentable war on
both sides the Atlantic, and give peace in our time. Did I
know how to emancipate myself from this constrained, use-
less, uniform blank of life, and enter on an active course, I
would joyfully seize the occasion.

The occasion would not come until after the war when Curwen, seventy years old and absent for a decade, returned home.
His marriage as well as the country he had known was destroyed.
Upon his arrival, Abigail had a "hysterick fit," and the marital
situation went downhill from that point. One of his last wishes
was that he was not to be buried alongside his wife. His reason-
ing was that on the morning of the judgement day, he did not
want to be immediately confronted by a resurrected Abigail.
    Other families found parting less easy to endure. William
Franklin, Benjamin's illegitimate son, was separated from his wife
Elizabeth Downes early in the conflict. William, probably the
country's most famous loyalist and the Royal Governor of New
Jersey, was placed under virtual house arrest in January of 1776.
A midnight confrontation between Franklin and a band of rebels
terrified Elizabeth, according to the deposed governor and
"nearly deprived her of her life."
    In June, Franklin was taken for close confinement in Con-
necticut. Elizabeth was urged to return to her family in Barbados,
but she chose to remain in New Jersey even though she claimed
she was mistreated by radicals who were "rude, insolent and abusive." Elizabeth Franklin at last joined the growing numbers of
loyalists flocking to New York City, but suffered a mental breakdown and became severely ill. Franklin's pleas that he be allowed
to join his ailing wife were refused and she died alone. A plaque
placed in New York City's St. Paul's Church commemorated her
miseries with the words: "Compelled to part from the husband
she loved, and at length despairing of the soothing hope of his
speedy return, she sunk under accumulated distresses. . . ."
    Benjamin Pickman of Salem, Massachusetts, was also sepa-
rated from his wife and family, but his absence was probably a

calculated financial maneuver rather than a political one. Several prosperous families such as the Pickmans chose to separate during the conflict in order to play both sides of the military fence. A supporter in each camp meant that regardless of which side lost the war, the family property would be saved by the member who supported the winner.

Pickman added a new dimension, for not only did his wife, who remained at Salem, retain possession of their property as a rebel supporter, but Pickman attempted to be reimbursed by the claims commission for his supposed backing of the King. As in the case of Dorcas Griffiths, the decision of the commissioners on Pickman's plea was influenced by an informant. An agent notified the court that the Salem loyalist had not lost one shilling as a result of the war. The commissioners agreed and cancelled even the temporary pension which had been awarded to the refugee.

For loyalists who decided to remain in America the situation was much different than for those who chose to flee.

Banishment was the simplest punishment. Margaret Inglis, Susannah Robinson and Mary Morris were cited in the 1779 New York Act of Attainder which not only confiscated their estates, but also declared that their adherence to the enemies of the state was a felony. The three women were warned that if they were "found in any part" of the state, all three would be liable to the death penalty.

Those refusing to swear allegiance to the rebel government often could not vote, hold office or appeal to the courts in any legal matter. This suspension of legal protection was particularly perilous to tradespeople such as Susannah Marshall of Baltimore.

Susannah, a native of Wales, came to America in 1774 with £500 to set up a lodging house. One year later her husband was forced to leave the city for the West Indies, because of his refusal to support a rebel instigated arms raid. Susannah was required against her will to house several whig soldiers, a British tradition which had earlier caused resentment to the radicals.

In 1776, she refused to take in additional fighting men and was threatened with tarring and feathering. More important, debts of about £100 which were owed to her by customers were cancelled and about £50 of her shop goods stolen. As a loyalist,

Susannah had no means by which to compel payment of the debts or punish the looters.

Often crown supporters were prohibited from practicing certain professions or were restricted to house arrest. The wife and daughter of John Stuart, superintendent of Indian affairs for the southern district, received such a punishment when the South Carolina provincial congress decreed that the Stuart women were to ". . . be restrained from absenting themselves from his house in *Charlestown*." A guard was placed at the residence to assure that the female hostages would not slip away.

Employment was often difficult for the anti-Americans. Well educated Elizabeth Dumaresq found that jobs were so scarce that she was forced to serve as a maid on a ship bound for Granada.

One of the most popular penalties was to increase taxes on the possessions and land held by those not committed to the whig cause. In many cases, loyalists were assessed fees far above those of their rebel neighbors in similar circumstances. This technique was partially a move to gain badly needed revenue from sources with little political power, but was also a not so subtle method of ridding communities of disruptive influences. Sometimes the high taxation was a device for satisfying the desires of local whigs who coveted land held by tories.

The story of Elizabeth Belcher of Milton, Massachusetts, is typical of this indirect confiscation. Elizabeth's husband Andrew, a registrar of admiralty, died in 1771 leaving her to supervise the family interests. Elizabeth was plagued with difficulties from the beginning of the conflict and claimed that on the day after the battle at Lexington, a unit of American soldiers broke into her house and:

> . . . plundered [it] of plate, Linnen, Furniture, and Horses, to the value of £1000, and that at the time of the Blockade of Boston, her said house having by Accident Caught Fire, her Goods, and Effects were Carried away by the Americans, who in Consequence of her Attachment to His Majesty's Government refused to Use any Endeavors Whatever to Extinguish the Flames, which might have been with great Ease effected; the House being situated Close to two Springs and a Large Pond of Water.

Elizabeth remained on her property despite the fire and looting. But in 1781, the annual tax bill was raised to £1,500, about one-third of the value of her entire estate. Unable to meet the increased fee, she was finally driven from her home.

As the war progressed, the treatment of tories changed from harrassment to physical punishment. In some areas committees of safety turned into vigilante groups. George Chalmers of Baltimore slept with side arms by his bedside after he learned of a plot to throw him out of the window of the local courthouse.

Charleston's George Walker refused to drink a toast against the King and was thus stripped, tarred, feathered and stoned for five hours. The mob then "pumped upon him for an hour," and he was thrown into a river. Two of Walker's ribs were broken and his house was burned. For these and other inconveniences, George claimed the loss of his watch, clothes, £39 16s, five hogsheads of rum, a large quantity of cheshire cheese, biscuits, sugar and other articles totaling £593 12s.

Polly Jarvis Dibblee found that women were not exempt from the wrath of the mob. The first time her house was plundered, the rebels ". . . took even the children's Hats from their Heads and shoes from their feet," she claimed. In later strikes she and her five children were turned into the street naked. After four incidents of looting, Polly and her family left the colonies for New Brunswick where life was no easier. Her cabin burned to the ground, was rebuilt and burned again. Her husband committed suicide and she was left to support the family.

The father of Barbara Frietchie paid the ultimate price for supporting the King. Frietchie, found guilty of plotting against the rebels, was sentenced to be hanged, cut down while still alive, his entrails removed and then burned. His head was then to be cut off, his body quartered and then all the different parts of his body were to be dispersed where the Governor suggested. The grisly sentence was not carried out, however, and instead Frietchie was simply hanged.

As many as 50,000 tories were sufficiently opposed to the rebel cause that they joined the British army or navy. The effect of these enlistments was largely negligible. Major conflicts arose when loyalists, many of whom were former leaders in their communities, were placed under the command of young, inexperienced officers from England. The resentment was somewhat lessened when special loyalist regiments, led by Americans, were organized, but these units were effective primarily on the frontier where they served as guerrillas and raiders.

When fighting on their home ground, tory legions proved particularly vindictive. The most severe fighting of the war did not involve formal British troops or Indians, but loyal forces who plundered and burned the homes of whigs in retribution for rebel persecution. As a result, the hatred of continental forces for loyalist troops was usually far greater than the dislike of professional British or German soldiers. The tories who sometimes wore red or white cockades on their hats became favored targets in battle. Many of the collaborators were assigned to foraging details, possibly because of their personal knowledge of the local agricultural picture. Eventually these units became known as "cowboys" because of their talents for stealing food animals from farms.

The first major battle between loyalist elements and American whigs took place less than a month before Howe evacuated Boston. The scene was Widow Moore's Creek Bridge near the Cape Fear River in North Carolina. Here, loyalists, mostly Scottish highlanders, met rebels in a savage battle that lasted only three minutes.

For several years, North Carolina had been the destination for masses of Scottish immigrants. Unemployment, high rents, crop failures and a generally depressed economy forced thousands of Scots from their homes in the old world. The early months of 1771 were so severe that they became known as the "Black Spring" because of the great numbers of cattle which died of starvation.

By 1774, an estimated 10,000 Scots had settled around Campbellton, North Carolina. Most were intensely loyal to the English crown. Soon to join them was the family of Flora MacDonald, an 18th century woman who had already become one of the greatest heroines of the British Empire.

Born on the isolated Hebrides Islands in 1722, Flora's life was not particularly different from other farmwomen until 1746. That year she was catapulted into fame as a companion and guide to

"Bonnie Prince Charlie," less well known as The Young Pretender.

Prince Charles' father, James, was the most authentic claimant to the English throne from the Catholic Stuart line which had been expelled from Britain when William and Mary assumed control in 1688. Charles' 1745 mission in Scotland was to raise a mighty army, invade England and thus capture the throne for his aged father.

The move was based on the assumption that the Scots would rally to his cause in droves, but the great legions of followers failed to materialize. The Prince's small band of supporters was defeated by English troops at Culloden Moor and afterwards subjected to a reign of terror which crushed any overt opposition to rule from London.

Charles managed to escape, but a £30,000 price was put on his head. With the help of a few friends, the Pretender managed to make his way to the northern islands to await a French rescue ship dispatched to take him back to the continent.

Here Charles met Flora MacDonald, a shepherdess who escorted him through enemy territory, once transporting him across the Sea of the Hebrides in an open boat while he was disguised as her maid Betty Burke. The plan was discovered and although the Prince once again managed to flee, his companion was captured.

Although Flora was held under arrest on various British prison ships, she soon became a national heroine to those who stood against the English government and abhorred the excesses committed after Culloden. Her confinement may not have been extremely discomforting, for much of the time she was allowed a personal servant. Wealthy ladies often visited her aboard ship, bringing gifts and arranging dances in her honor.

After several months, Flora was taken to London and placed in a messenger house. These confines were comfortable places of internment operated by messengers of the courts for the convenience of prominently placed offenders who had found disfavor with the regime. Because the environment was more pleasant than the cold cells of London's grimy prisons, the lodging was expensive. But Flora's public raised £1,500 for her maintenance and in July 1747, after one year's confinement, she was released.

Flora was wined and dined by nobility, but finally she returned to Scotland and married Allan MacDonald of Kingsburgh. Conditions became hard, the heroine was not exempt from the economic catastrophes which affected all rural Scots. Dr. Samuel Johnson visited her in September of 1773, with his friend James Boswell, who observed that the fortunes of the family had fallen considerably: "My heart was sore to recollect that Kingsburgh had fallen sorely back in his affairs, was under a load of debt, and intended to go to America. However, nothing but what was good was present, and I pleased myself in thinking that so fine a fellow would be well everywhere."

Within a year, the MacDonalds sailed for North Carolina and soon after arriving bought a farm in Anson County. From the beginning, the MacDonalds were influential with other Scots in the areas, primarily because of Flora's reputation. Allan became one of the first supporters of the crown as the revolution neared. After a meeting with Governor Martin, Allan recruited an entire battalion of loyalists to fight the rebelling whigs and much of his success in attracting men to the cause was attributed to Flora, who spoke frequently at recruiting rallies.

But the Scotswoman expected that things would not be easy for the tory brigade. In February of 1776, the troops raised by Allan were preparing to march toward the coast, confronting whigs along the way and ultimately joining with formal elements of the British army. Just before their departure, Flora wrote to a friend:

> Dear Maggie: Allan leaves tomorrow to join Donald's standard at Cross Creek, and I shall be alone, wi' my three bairns. Canna ye come and stay wi' me awhile? There are troublous times ahead I ween. God will keep the right. I hope all our ain are in the right, prays your good friend,
>
> Flory McDonald

Unfortunately for the MacDonalds, the King's flag did not survive the battle at Widow Moore's Creek Bridge. Rebel militia arrived before the Scots, partially dismantled the bridge and then greased the rails which remained. As the unsuspecting loyalists slipped and slid across the supports, the rebels opened fire from ambush on the far bank. Within minutes the rout was over. The 1,100 whigs counted one of their men dead and one wounded. The Scots' casualties were thirty times as great.

Highland officers, their general ill and their next in command dead, voted to disband and the men scattered in retreat. Some escaped into the swamp, but 850 including Allan MacDonald were taken prisoner. The loyalist threat to whig domination in North Carolina was over.

According to various legends, the aftermath of the skirmish was severe to those who had lost. Duncan MacNabb's wife was robbed and pillaged while her husband hid in a North Carolina swamp to avoid capture. Finally, wearying of waiting for the British rescuers, MacNabb walked to New York to join the King's army. Mrs. Norman MacLeod, who sought protection in Charleston, returned home, but was captured and imprisoned for seven weeks. To add additional insult, her husband was billed for the confinement expenses.

Flora was also facing problems. In the absence of her captured husband, her house was looted, her servants ran away, her plantation fell into disuse, she became ill and finally broke her arm in a fall from a horse. Neighbors were of little help for many blamed Flora as well as Allan for the defeat at Moore's Creek. The shepherdess of the Hebrides finally left North Carolina about 1777 and made her way to Manhattan where Allan was exchanged and given the rank of Lieutenant Colonel.

Together they sailed for Halifax and ultimately home to Scotland. Allan would later claim that he had lost the use of both legs as a result of mistreatment in rebel jails. The family was offered 3,000 acres of land near Windsor, Canada, in compensation for their services, but the pair decided against making another start.

After the Moore's Creek defeat, many of the North Carolina loyalists dispersed to other sections of the colonies such as Charleston where five hundred Scots participated in the later British defense of the town. Others sailed for Europe. Some returned to their homes on parole and took no further part in the conflict. But a new avenue was opening up for both loyalists and rebels. The frontier by 1776 had become a hotbed of activity.

Since the end of the French and Indian War, British representatives had attempted to promote peace on the frontier and to subdue the more warlike tribes. The effort was a constant struggle, for the expansion of the colonial population along the Atlantic seaboard produced increasing pressures in the Indian territories.

The British found their pacification program growing more difficult as Euro-American settlers pushed farther into the frontier seeking farm land. Although early colonists had lived in relative peace with the Indians, the bloody wars of the mid-eighteenth century created animosities which were fed by atrocities on both sides.

Justice for the Indian became almost non-existent. Pioneers who used violence against the red people were often glorified rather than punished. A mob of Irish settlers in Lancaster County, Pennsylvania, slaughtered fourteen men, women and children of the Conestoga Tribe. Ironically, these peaceful families were the last surviving members of a band which lived by selling their hand-made baskets and brooms to the newcomers and had never used violence in defense of their land.

At a Moravian mission in western Virginia, ninety Indians who had been given sanctuary in order to harvest their corn, were attacked by vengeful whites. In one afternoon's work, the pioneers dispatched the entire party by crushing their skulls with a cooper's mallet. The death toll was twenty-nine men, twenty-seven women and thirty-four children.

With the coming of the Revolutionary War, Britain seized on the growing hatred of the Indian for the encroaching whites. The English strategy was to encourage Indians in ravaging the frontier by a series of constant raids. In this manner, many of the western whigs who would otherwise turn east to fight against the formal British armies, would be forced to remain at home to protect their own settlements.

In addition, great numbers of militia from seaboard areas would have to be detailed to prevent the Indians from swooping down upon the populated areas of the coast. Few British regulars would be sent to the frontier. Instead, the King's forces would be represented by loyalists who planned the campaigns and accompanied the Indians on their missions.

On the eve of the war, a native population of more than 100,000 ringed the colonial settlements in a crescent curving from Canada west and south to Georgia and then east along the Florida border. In the north, the most powerful tribes were members of the Iroquois confederation or Six Nations which included the Seneca, Mohawk, Oneida, Tuscarora, Onondaga and Cayuga. In the middle colonies, the Shawnee, Potawatamie, Miami and Delaware were forceful as were the Cherokee whose land extended as far north as the Ohio River. To the south, the Creek, Choctaw, and Chickasaw, though not as populous as the Cherokee, were important elements.

Indian support of the British was not based on the politics of the war, but instead stemmed from personal experience. Sir William Johnson, Indian superintendent for the crown in the north, was held in great esteem and revered as dearly as many full-blooded chiefs. Johnson had sired an estimated hundred children by various Indian women, perhaps qualifying him for the title of Great White Father. But the most important woman in his life was Molly Brant, his housekeeper for twenty-one years and the mother of eight of his children.

The liaison between Molly and Johnson would have great influence on the revolution. Molly's brother Joseph Brant was raised by the British official as a son. With Sir William's aid Brant was sent east to Indian school, educated by Eleazar Wheelock, founder of Dartmouth College, and converted to Christianity. Although Brant married the daughter of an Oneida chief, he was a true Britisher in outlook and life style.

In 1775, Brant was sent to London on a grand tour where he was befriended by Boswell and other leading figures. His portrait was painted by Romney. The purpose of the visit was to reinforce the Indian's allegiance to England and the trip was completely successful. Brant in fashionable London, however, presented a different picture than the renegade of later years who would personally lead his mighty Mohawk into the war on the side of the British.

The Americans were also wooing the Indians. A special department had been created to work ostensively for neutrality, but it was actually an instrument to secure the services of all those who would fight for the whig cause. For a time the effort seemed successful. The peaceful Abnaki served as guides on Arnold's march to Quebec. Several Penobscot Indians enlisted in the Massachusetts militia. Members of the Stockbridge Tribe rallied as Minutemen at the Battle of Bunker Hill. More important, the Stockbridge offered to mediate with western tribes on behalf of the Americans. Their suggestion read:

> Brothers, whenever I see your blood running, you will soon find me about you to revenge my brothers' blood. Although I am low and very small, I will grip hold of your enemy's heel, that he cannot run so fast and so light, as if he had nothing at his heels. So then, if you please, I will take a run to the westward and feel the minds of the Six Nations, who have always looked this way for advice concerning all important news that comes from the rising sun. . . . If I find they are against you, I will try to turn their minds.

The mission to the west was partially successful, for the Oneida pledged to remain neutral in the conflict. A message forwarded from the tribe to Governor Jonathan Trumbull soon after the arrival of the Stockbridge emissaries pledged the love of the Oneida warriors and female governesses. Other powerful Iroquois, feeling pressure from the Americans, also agreed to remain neutral despite a concerted recruitment drive by the British.

In the fall of 1775, the rebel policy produced other results. In a meeting at Pittsburg, several Indian groups consented to free all white women and children who had been taken captive. Runaway slaves were also to be returned to their masters. But the Indians vehemently refused to release the offspring of blacks and Indians, for the chiefs felt it immoral to send children who were one-half Indian into slavery.

Charles Lee who had lived for a time among the Iroquois was of additional benefit to the Americans in their western operations. While stationed with the Mohawk, Lee had married the daughter of Seneca Chief White Thunder. The Britisher was inducted into the tribe and given the name Ounewaterika or Boiling Water. Lee was proud of his Indian wife: "She is a very great beauty." He informed his sister Sidney, "I shall say nothing of her accomplishments, for you must be certain that a woman of her fashion cannot be without many." Twins were born of the union, and some sources suggest that the male child later lost his nose as a result of syphilis.

By 1776, American attempts to hold back the Indian tide were beginning to fall apart. To the Indians, the people who were constantly pushing into their lands were the enemy. Most of the encroachers were whigs, therefore, the whigs were the enemy. While the British did provide food and supplies, their recruiting successes among the tribes were not based primarily upon material considerations. If the pioneer situation had been reversed, and most of those pushing west had been loyalists, the red people undoubtedly would have chosen to side with the whigs.

Soon all vestiges of neutrality had vanished. Congress authorized the recruitment of 2,000 Indian mercenaries, but the program did not succeed.

In the north, Joseph Brant and his Mohawk went on the war path with John Johnson, Sir William's son. In retaliation, American forces under Colonel Elias Dayton captured the family estate Johnson Hall on May 25, 1776. Lady Mary Watts Johnson, a twenty-three-year-old New Yorker and the wife of Sir John, was taken prisoner in the skirmish, and sent to Albany as a hostage to assure that her husband would keep Brant under control.

Lady Johnson's cousin General Schuyler was pleased with the situation and wrote: "It is the general opinion of people in Tryon County, that whilst Lady Johnson is kept a kind of hostage, Sir John will not carry matters to excess, and I have been entreated to keep her here." Although Mary's brother appealed personally to Washington for her release, Schuyler refused to consider the possibility. After six months of confinement, she was allowed to move to a friend's mansion near the Hudson. Despite constant surveillance, Lady Johnson finally managed to slip away and join her husband in British-held territory.

Attention was given to other women connected with the Johnsons. Margaret Francis Hill, housekeeper to Sir Guy Johnson, William's nephew and son-in-law, was "stripped naked of all her cloaths, confined to a cold room in Bedford, New England," for three wintry months. Margaret maintained that the action was taken because she was a loyal tory and had refused to secretly poison her employer.

The British also held prestige in the tribes of the South, where a counterpart to Sir William Johnson had been appointed. Lower level field representatives, designated to live with the powerful Cherokee, soon became deeply involved in the tribe's life. Alexander Cameron, who lived with the Over Hill clan, married an Indian woman and established a large estate named Lochabor on the Indians' land. John McDonald, who was detailed to Chickamauga Creek, wed a mixed-blooded woman named Anne Storey and became an intimate of the tribe.

Because of strong ties such as these intermarriages, the Cherokee, supplied by the British, were laying plans in 1776 to war on outlying whig communities. Alarmed governments in Georgia, South Carolina, North Carolina and Virginia, detailed 5,000 militia troops into the troubled area. The aid was urgently needed for the Cherokee were already on the move.

Near Boonesboro in the Kentucky territory, Jemina Boone, daughter of explorer Daniel Boone, was kidnapped by Cherokee returning from a war council. Boone tracked his daughter and her companions Elizabeth and Frances Calloway for three days before rescuing the girls from their captors.

Because the Choctaw and Creek were battling among themselves, no help was available for the Cherokee warriors in their battle against the whites. Militia men moved west, zealously burning native villages and spurred on by a bounty offered by the South Carolina Assembly for Indian scalps. Other bounties would be set on red peoples by the rebels, but the British never offered similar payments for the scalps of their enemies. The King's troops, however, did encourage scalping by giving guns, ammunition and supplies as rewards for particularly successful campaigns. For the Indians, who often worked alone, scalps were the most concrete evidence of military victory.

During their advance into the Cherokee lands, the North Carolina militia under Griffith Rutherford, claimed to have found a dead Indian woman, dressed in men's clothing and painted as a warrior. Cherokee women did not usually participate in actual fighting, but their influence was strong in many areas concerning the war.

The place of women in Cherokee society was often misunderstood by casual observers who did not comprehend the basic democracy which governed the tribe. Instead, the few travelers into Indian lands usually judged sexual roles by white standards. For example, traders seeing Indian women toiling in the fields while men lounged in front of huts, usually assumed that the females were held in chattel-like status.

Actually women worked the fields because they usually owned the land. In addition, male Cherokee spent long hours hunting and tracking in the woods and were often too fatigued for efficient farm labor. One eighteenth century writer was not misled and noted: ". . . the women rules the rost and weres the britches and sometimes will beat thire husbands within an inch of thire life."

William Bartram closely observed the Cherokee society during a visit to their country in 1776. Of the women he wrote: "They are tall, slender, erect and of a delicate frame: their features formed with perfect symmetry, their countenances cheerful and friendly, and they move with a becoming grace and dignity."

Equality among the sexes was a natural way of life for the Cherokee. There were no degrees of status or respect automatically allocated for any particular characteristics. The oldest woman and the most feeble farmer were thought equal to the bravest warrior. All voices were even in power at councils. But the society did vest ownership of property, children and land in the female heads of families. Because the society was matrilineal, men lived in the houses of their wives after marriage. Often the stay was brief, for Cherokee women entered into wedlock lightly according to some accounts and frequently committed adultery. Divorce was extremely common.

Women were also given special responsibility as guardians of the land and were thus considered peacemakers in situations which could endanger the property of the tribe. Women rarely served on town councils, but male members of these groups were probably chosen primarily by the female clan leaders. From each local community or from each clan in the seven "Mother Towns," or major settlements, representatives were selected for a national council. This body discussed war and peace, and made general suggestions concerning overall policies.

A companion to the central body was the Women's Council, composed of powerful females. According to some authorities, the Women's Council could overrule decisions of the male groups. Women accompanied men to peace conferences with the enemy and although they rarely spoke publicly, the females were always consulted concerning the terms.

Although the Cherokee were loosely connected by the overall council into a unified "nation," there was no machinery for compelling compliance to any "law" or policy which the group recommended. The ideal was that adherence to a council decision would be unanimous. If a tribal member refused to abide with a recommendation, the tribe made no move. Damaging acts were privately controlled and parties who were wronged took personal revenge against the offender. Sanctions were thus private, between one individual and another, or between one clan and another.

Since the Cherokee lacked any understanding of allegiance to a legal authority, it may have been difficult for many to accept the British contention that the colonists were obligated to obey the crown or that the whigs should be punished for disagreeing with the policies of the King. The decision of the Cherokee to battle against the rebels, was based primarily upon everyday experience and not upon political concepts which were completely alien to the philosophy of the tribe.

The most honored office in the Cherokee nation was that of Ghigan, meaning "Beloved Woman" or "War Woman." Nancy Ward held the influential post during the revolutionary war years and was an active participant in the conflict.

Nancy had earned the high position for her actions at the 1755 Battle of Taliwa during the Cherokee-Creek War. Here, when her husband Kingfisher was killed, Nancy stepped into his place as a war chief. At the time she was about fifteen years old. The Ghigan was closely connected with the white community through various friendships, and she was rumored to be the daughter of a British Army officer and an Indian woman. Another tie was her relationship with Brian Ward, a white trader who lived with her several years before settling in South Carolina with a white woman.

Nancy worked for peace throughout the duration of the war. Her actions were probably not the result of any sympathy she felt for the whigs, but because she feared that the Cherokee would be greatly harmed by undertaking a full-scale rebellion against the populous settlers.

Her first revolutionary activity may have been the freeing of three captives held by the tribe while debate was underway on the advisability of an eastward attack. Some stories indicate that she informed one Isaac Thomas of the Cherokee's plan to begin a series of raids, then arranged his escape with two other prisoners and assured that the trio made their way safely to warn outlying frontier settlements of the impending forays. The tale may be partially true for John Sevier, a frontier leader, did send messages to various villages that three escaped captives had brought news revealing that Indian uprisings were imminent.

Some communities were unprepared for the emergency, but improvised stockades were constructed in populated areas within the danger zone. Here families from the woodlands took refuge. One large concentration was gathered about Eaton's Station, the outermost door leading from Indian territory to the farms of the east.

In a confused battle near Island Flats, a force under Dragging Canoe was turned back by militia men in an ambush. The same day, other Indian elements attacked Fort Lee, a stockade at Watagua. After two weeks of siege, the Indians retreated when Virginia reinforcements approached.

During the siege at Fort Lee, a Mrs. William Bean was captured outside the stockade and taken to a Cherokee camp on the Nolichucky River. Romantic legends evolved concerning her rescue by Nancy Ward, who supposedly in a moment of great kindness and charity, ordered the woman to be freed just as she was about to be burned at the stake. Nancy Ward probably did rescue the woman, but for reasons completely unconnected with kindness, for a young boy captured the same day was not spared.

Nancy, who owned one of the first cattle herds in the Cherokee nation, was constantly seeking methods to improve the life of her people. The rationale for her action in saving Mrs. Bean, seems to be that the Ghigan was convinced that the prisoner was worth far more alive than dead. Mrs. Bean was not released, but was kept in captivity to instruct the squaws in the most efficient methods of spinning and making cheese and butter.

The contention that the office of Ghigan included the power to pardon prisoners such as Mrs. Bean, is completely inconsistent with the basic Cherokee doctrine against arbitrary power. Actually, Nancy, lacking coercive authority, directed Cherokee activities because of her effective powers of persuasion and leadership. Her great influence stemmed not from official power, but from the ability to convince others of the correctness of her viewpoints.

Nancy's position continued to rise. For many years she served as the public voice not only of Cherokee women, but of the entire tribe. She would be sent to make peace at the end of the war, and her counsel was sought even when she was too old and feeble to attend the great councils.

But in 1776, Nancy's opposition failed to stem the violence. The Cherokee War against which she had counseled was soon over. Indian raiding parties were no match for the overwhelming power of the southern militia. In October, 1776, militia troops swept through the lands of the Holston to victory. Under a treaty partially dictated by white settlers, the defeated tribe deeded away much of their land and dropped their claims to territory which involved more than one-half of the state of South Carolina. Large tracts in North Carolina and the Tennessee territory were also lost.

The settlement was a bitter one to many young braves. Dissident elements loyal to Nancy's cousin Dragging Canoe left their old towns and formed a new tribe which would be known as the Chickamauga. While some Cherokee would continue to make hit and run raids throughout the Revolutionary War, the nation itself would never again take united action against the colonists.

# CHAPTER FOUR

# *Christmas at Trenton*

—God only knows what will be the End of these troubles. . . .

Margaret Beekman Livingston, July 6, 1776

FOR THE FIRST TIME in almost a decade, Boston was free of British troops and in the spring of 1776, the city was relatively peaceful. High ranking officers of the Continental Army, however, believed that the lull following Howe's evacuation would be brief. Already Sir William had deposited his loyalist passengers in Halifax and was regrouping his regiments for an invasion somewhere in the colonies.

To Washington, the logical place for such a landing was in the New York area where tory support for the King was strong and neutrals controlled much of the territory. In April, the American army moved from Boston to Manhattan. The long wait began.

For about three months all was quiet on the war front. During Washington's New York campaign numerous rumors sprang up, primarily concerning the commander's private life. One tale reported that Martha Washington, actually a strong tory, had left her husband because of his participation with the rebels.

Throughout the war, conservative British papers paid special attention to printing any gossip relating to the general, who had replaced John Hancock as the most prominent revolutionary figure.

*Town and Country Magazine* reported that Washington had forced a New Jersey loyalist named Mary Gibbons to receive him at night. Supposedly Mary had designs of her own. Unknown to her guest she was reportedly searching the Virginian's pockets for secret information which could be passed along to Howe. *Rivington's Gazette* in New York maintained that Washington kept a soldier's girl named Betsy Sidman at his headquarters and fathered a son named Hebaccue by her. Later, Betsy was supposedly drummed out of camp in disgrace. A corporal's wife was also reported to be Washington's mistress. As a reward for his silence, the husband was promoted to sergeant.

One of the most popular rumors was that Washington's housekeeper Lorenda Holmes planned to poison him with tainted green peas. The scheme aborted, but, according to gossips, was confirmed when several chickens died after eating the vegetables. Lorenda later claimed she was apprehended by vindictive whig partisans and her right foot severely burned with live coals as a punishment for her complicity.

Many of the unsubstantiated tales concerning the general's safety may have been prompted by an actual plot on his life. Sgt. Thomas Hickey, a disgruntled American soldier, was convicted in a conspiracy involving mutiny, treason and plotting against Washington's life. Hickey was hanged on June 28, 1776, in front of 20,000 spectators in a festival-like atmosphere that was reported to have been a major social outing for New Yorkers of the time.

Hickey claimed that he had not intended to kill Washington, but insinuated that he had been led astray by "lewd" women. One of the lewd women may have been Phoebe Fraunces, the daughter of a tavern keeper who managed an inn often visited by Washington.

One of the most popular stories concerning the commander stemmed from the publication of a letter supposedly written to him by Virginia politician Benjamin Harrison, ancestor of two presidents. Harrison had more than the health and welfare of

Washington at heart according to the incriminating note. If authentic, the letter indicates that Harrison was actually the future President's panderer. The controversial dispatch read:

> As I was in the pleasing task of writing to you a little noise occasioned to turn my head around, and who should appear but pretty little Kate, the Washerwoman's daughter, over the way, clean, trim, and rosey as the Morning; I snatched the golden glorious Opportunity and but for that cursed Antidote to Love, Sukey [Mrs. Harrison], I had fitted her for my General against his return. We were obliged to part, but not till we had contrived to meet again; if she keeps the Appointment I shall relish a week's longer stay-I give you now and then some of these adventures to amuse you, and unbend your mind from the Cares of War.

Pro-Washington forces immediately branded the letter a forgery and an attempt on the part of the British to discredit the integrity of the American leader. Anti-Washington parties accepted the note as genuine and an illustration of the corruptness of the rebel commander.

Not all the rumors concerning Washington dealt with his relations with women. He was often reported dead or captured. One story claimed that the American situation was so desperate that Washington was forced to hold his pants up with a string because he had sold his trouser buttons to pay for food. The Virginian may have participated in spreading tales himself. Reportedly he personally instigated the rumor that Americans who deserted to the enemy were being sold as slaves to the British East India Company.

As the wait for the British stretched into weeks, new problems confronted the army in New York. Prostitutes were flocking in droves to ply their trade with the occupying troops. The main meeting place was an area formerly owned by a church and aptly named "the holy ground." The territory was one of the roughest in the city for one man observed: "Several limbs and heads of men were found at the holy ground which was supposed to be killed by the whores. . . . No man is suffered to be there after nine o'clock at night."

Colonel Loammi Baldwin detested the women of the night. In a letter to his wife, Baldwin outlined the difficult situation and underscored his own innocence:

> The inhabitants of the holy ground has brought some of the officers and numbers of the soldiers into difficulty. The whores (by information) continue their imploy which is become very lucrative. Their unparalleled conduct is sufficient antidote against any desires that a person can have that has one spark of modesty or virtue left in him and the last attum must certainly be lost before he can associate himself with those bitchfoxy jades, jills, haggs, strums, prostitutes and these multiplyed into one another and then their full character not displayed.

> Perhaps you will call me censorious and exclaim too much upon bare reports when I say that I was never within doors of nor 'changed a word with any of them except in the execution of my duty as officer of the day, in going round with my guard of escort, have broken up the knots of men and women fighting, pulling caps, swearing, crying "Murder" etc., hurried them off to the Provost dungeon by half dozens—Hell's work.

The inactivity of the army in Manhattan was matched by the lethargy of various colonial assemblies who were hesitant to take firm action toward permanent separation from England until a more favorable military situation was reached. The Massachusetts Provincial Congress was one body which seemed paralyzed with indecisiveness. In writing to her delegate husband James, Mercy Warren not so subtly suggested that the assembly should make some move or the group should disband and go home.

Abigail Adams in Braintree, was also urging her husband to act. John, still in Philadelphia with the Congress, was bombarded with suggestions from his wife that the delegates should get on with the business of declaring independence.

Abigail Smith was eighteen years old when she married John Adams in 1764. Her mother, a proud Quincy, objected to the union because of Adams' humble origins. The groom was considered by his contemporaries to be somber, intellectual, almost devoid of humor. But Abigail brought out a private man who even attempted levity.

Before their marriage, Abigail requested that John send word to her listing the personal faults he felt she should remedy. Adams complied and among the most glaring handicaps he noted was that she carried her head like a bullrush, sat with her legs across and could not carry a tune. Perhaps the most blatant blemish, he suggested, was ". . . that of Walking, with the Toes bending inward. This Imperfection is commonly called Parrot-toed, I think, I know not for what Reason. But it gives an Idea, the reverse of a bold and noble Air, the Reverse of the stately strutt, and the sublime Deportment."

Before the war, the Adams' moved frequently as John's political maneuvering propelled him ahead in Massachusetts politics. But throughout the rebellion, Abigail remained at the family farm in Braintree, singlehandedly managing their modest holdings. In 1776, she despaired that she was incapable of the task and not so meekly ordered John to leave Congress so that he could attend to his own business:

> I cannot consent to your tarrying much longer. . . . I shall send you word by and by as Regulus'es steward did that whilst you are engaged in the Senate your own domestick affairs require your presence at Home, and that your wife and children are in Danger of wanting Bread. If the Senate of America will take care of us, as the Senate of Rome did of the family of Regulus, you may serve them again, but unless you return that little property you possess will be lost. In the first place the House at Boston is going to ruin. When I was there I hired a Girl to clean it, it had a cart load of Dirt in it. I speak within Bounds. One of the chambers was used to keep poultry in, an other sea coal, and an other salt. You may conceive How it look'd. The House is so exceeding damp being shut up, that the floors are mildewd, the sealing falling down, and the paper mouldy and falling from the walls. I took care to have it often opened and aird whilst I tarried in Town. . . .
>
> In the next place, the Lighter of which you are or should be part owner is lying rotting at the wharf. One year more without any care and she is worth nothing. You have

no Bill of Sale, no right to convey any part of her should
any person appear to purchase her. The Pew I let, after having paid a tax for the repairs of the meeting House.

Despite Abigail's ultimatum, John remained at Philadelphia.
Eventually she proved a much more capable financial manager
than he, and her secret investments later supported the family
when his own ventures failed.

Adams maintained that Abigail's letters were far superior to
his own in value as chronicles of the era. His prediction proved
true, for Abigail Adams and Benjamin Franklin are often considered the foremost writers of letters of the eighteenth century.

The voluminous revolutionary correspondence between Abigail and John shows not only the deep love affair which bound
the pair, but reveals the significant impact of her libertarian philosophy on his actions. Abigail, like her friend Mercy Warren,
was strongly opposed to the establishment of a strong central
government. She suggested to John:

> I am more and more convinced that Man is a dangerous
> creature, and that power whether vested in many or a few is
> ever grasping, and like the grave cries give, give. The great
> fish swallow up the small, and he who is most strenuous for
> the Rights of the people, when vested with power, is as
> eager after the perogatives of Government. . . .

As a perceptive observer of events, Abigail also predicted
how various actions taken in Philadelphia would be accepted by
the population as a whole. She commented on revolutionary leaders and military strategies, but she did not completely fill her letters with news of national importance. On August 14, 1776, she
wrote:

> I expected Mr. Gerry would have set off before now,
> but he finds it perhaps very hard to leave his Mistress—I
> wont say harder than some do to leave their wives. Mr.
> Gerry stood very high in my Esteem—what is meat for
> one is not for an other—no accounting for fancy. She is a
> queer dame and leads people in wild dances.

Elbridge Gerry, a wealthy merchant and close friend of John Adams, had long supported the revolution. In 1775 he had narrowly escaped in his bed clothes from an inn in Menotomy, Massachusetts, which was being searched by a band of redcoats. Gerry hid from the party in a cornfield and barely managed to avoid capture. His "queer dame" mentioned in Abigail's letter was Catherine Hunt, the daughter of another merchant. Unfortunately for the romance, the older Hunt did not believe that education was needed by women. Thus illiterate Catherine could not read or answer Gerry's love letters. He, finally tiring of the situation, married Ann Thompson.

Abigail detested the British traditions which relegated women to inferior positions in fields such as education and legal rights. Many of her contemporaries in England were working through the Bluestocking movement to bring about social reform. Abigail was outspoken in her belief that the revolution, with its emphasis upon freedom and justice for all, should not result in liberty reserved for men alone.

In one restless letter to John, she suggested that if the Congress did not act to improve the lot of America's women, then the deliberative body could be faced with a mass revolt. She announced:

> I long to hear that you have declared an independence— and by the way in the new code of laws which I suppose it will be necessary for you to make I desire you would remember the ladies, and be more generous and favorable to them than your ancestors. Do not put such unlimited power into the hands of the husbands. Remember all men would be tyrants if they could. If particuliar care and attention is not paid to the ladies we are determine to foment a rebelion, and will not hold ourselves bound by any law in which we have had no voice, or representation.
>
> That your sex are naturally tyrannical is a truth so thoroughly established as to admit of no dispute, but such of you as wish to be happy willingly give up the harsh title of Master for the more tender and endearing one of Friend. Why then, not put it out of the power of the vicious and the lawless to use us with cruelty and indignity with impu-

nity. Men of sense in all ages abhor those customs which treat
us only as the vassals of your sex. Regard us as beings. . . .

Despite Abigail's urgings, politicians in Congress continued
to haggle over the future course of action. Although American
armies had been in the field for more than a year, the delegates
had spent much of their time in non-productive debate. Finally,
despite opposition from conservatives and moderates, a committee
composed of Robert Livingston, Benjamin Franklin, John Adams,
Thomas Jefferson and Roger Sherman was appointed to draw up
a document relating to the independence of the colonies.

Many of the committeemen's colleagues still believed that
reconciliation could be reached with Great Britain. Delegates
from New York, Pennsylvania and Georgia argued that the dras-
tic step of actually declaring independence would create unnecessary bloodshed and that additional attempts should be made at
seeking a compromise.

But the radical elements were at last able to muster the votes
needed and on June 2, Congress passed a resolution declaring independence from England. John Adams was jubilant and immediately wrote Abigail:

> The Second Day of July 1776, will be the most memora-
> ble Epocha, in the History of America.—I am apt to
> believe that it will be celebrated, by succeeding Generations,
> as the Greatest anniversary Festival. It ought to be com-
> memorated, as the Day of Deliverance by solemn Acts of
> Devotion to God Almighty. It ought to be solemnized with
> Pomp and Parade, with Shews, Games, Sports, Guns, Bells,
> Bonfires and Illuminations from one End of this Continent to
> the other from this Time forward forever more.

On July 4, the final draft of the Declaration was adopted and
several days later the document was made public. The July 4 date
was ultimately chosen as the officially commemorated date only
after years of argument. Finally Adams, a strong supporter of the
second, relented.

Most delegates signed the Declaration on August 2, but although the final lines maintain that the signers pledged their

"lives," "fortunes," and "sacred honor," the names of all but President John Hancock and Secretary Charles Thomson were kept secret in 1776. The military situation was not promising and if the rebellion was to be crushed, the signatories did not want to be jeopardized.

General reaction among the population to the Declaration ranged from exuberence to anger and fear. From New York came a message from Margaret Beekman, mother of delegate Robert Livingston, warning of possible danger: "—God only knows what will be the End of these Troubles, I fear much for your safety—I Beg and Entreat you for my, and my Children's sake, that you do not cross at Powlas Hook Ferry—the Enemy may have you before you are aware & we shall be miserable. . . . We are here I fear in some danger from the Tories."

In England the reaction was terse. *Gentleman's Magazine* announced: "The sword is drawn, and the slaughter of the people is begun."

On July 9th at 6:00 p.m., the Declaration was publicly read in New York City. During the ensuing gaiety, a gold plated statue of King George was pulled down, taken to Connecticut and moulded into bullets.

But there was little time for rejoicing in the city. Howe's ships suddenly appeared offshore. The British were back from Halifax to strike at New York as Washington had predicted.

The bay was soon filled with a mighty armada. One observer remarked that the collection of bare masts at anchor looked like ". . . a wood of pine trees trimmed. . . ." Within weeks, the initial fleet was joined by new vessels carrying troops under Clinton who had made an abortive attempt to land in Charleston, thus rallying southern loyalists in a second front war.

The result of Clinton's exercise had been remarkably unsuccessful. His vessels ran aground in Charleston harbor, fired upon each other and showed unusually poor marksmanship. Of 7,000 cannon balls fired into the palmetto lined Ft. Sullivan, only thirty-six American casualties were recorded.

By August 27, a total of more than 30,000 British and German troops were massed in the Manhattan area, the largest English expeditionary force ever assembled in the new world.

American forces numbered about 20,000, but were split into garrisons in New Jersey, Manhattan and on the west side of Long Island at Brooklyn Heights.

General Howe, supported by the ships of his brother Admiral Richard, Lord Howe, chose to attack on Long Island. After a bombardment by gunships, the British landed upward from the heights. Unfavorable winds and water currents prevented a simultaneous attack from the rear. The resulting Battle of Long Island was a complete rout. The defeated Americans were pushed to the edge of the heights with their backs to the water and no quick means of retreat. Approximately 9,000 continental soldiers were suddenly quartered in an area about two miles long and a mile and one half wide at the western end of the island.

Washington's position became more desperate by the hour. A direct charge by Howe would mean certain defeat, the capture of one-half of the entire Continental Army and almost every high-ranking officer in the service. The revolution would be thus ended less than two months after independence had been declared.

But the British, remembering the heavy losses sustained in the frontal charge at Bunker Hill, chose to remain in their waiting position. Their major hope was that the prevailing winds would change directions, enabling Admiral Howe to sail up the East River and shell the Americans from their rear.

Washington at last chose to retreat back to Manhattan. Under the cover of darkness, John Glover and his Marblehead Mariners ferried the survivors and much of the army's equipment across the choppy channel. The task took just thirteen hours and was completed just after dawn in a thick fog.

Glover's men were particularly qualified for handling the open boats, for most were seamen and dockworkers who formerly sailed out of Massachusetts ports. The evacuation was so silent and successful that the British, camped just 600 yards away from the American outposts, did not realize until dawn that the enemy had escaped.

Reverend John Woodhill was among those who arrived safely in Manhattan. On August 30, he wrote news of the defeat to his wife:

My dear Sally:—Thro' divine goodness I am very well
as are our congregation in general that are here. Adam
Woods has the ague. General Washington has thought
proper to draw his men from Long Island, this was done last
night.

The enemy are now firing upon New York, from Long
Island; our men here are drawing up (to be) in readiness, in
case we are needed.

How many were lost upon the Island is yet uncertain,
some say we have 700 missing and that we have killed twice
as many of the enemy, tho I believe it is but guess work as
yet.

Generals Sullivan and Stirling who are missing are
said to be prisoners, it is also said General Grant on the other
side is killed, they talk of another General of theirs killed.

It is reported that Col. Atly is wounded and a prisoner.
Think it likely that our people will burn New York and retreat into the chain of Forts which are above it-when that is
done am in hopes our Enemies will get no farther. Poor
Long Island! I know not what will become of my Relations
there. May God help them. They are left to the mercy of
our Cruel Enemy.

Our men are in high spirits and I trust we shall, thro' ye
help of God soon break the power of our Foes.

Help did not come. The Americans were soon forced to pull
back from their bases and retreat to the upper forts. In the order
of march, soldiers under General Israel Putnam were scheduled
to be the last to leave the city, but the forces delayed too long.
Soon they were in danger of being isolated by British troops who
had landed between them and the main rebel force. A series of
fortuitous events again saved a major element of the whig army.
The 3,500 desperate rebels under the leadership of Putnam's
aide Aaron Burr, began marching north by an obscure route. At
one time the soldiers passed within a mile of the advancing British, but the redcoats, unaware that the continental contingent
was nearby, halted. Howe may have stopped to regroup his men,
or he could have been waiting for reinforcements from Clinton.
But to the Americans, the real reason was Mary Lindley Murray.

Mary, a Quaker and the mother of one of John Jay's colleagues, lived in a dwelling located on what is now lower Park Avenue. It was here that Howe stopped his advance. James Thacher, a surgeon in the continental line, described Mary's activities in his diary. Thacher recorded the war not so much as it actually happened, but how it appeared to the common soldier and the reason for Howe's halt was clear indeed to him:

> Most fortunately, the British generals, seeing no prospect of engaging our troops, halted their own, and repaired to the house of a Robert Murray, a quaker and a friend of our cause; Mrs. Murray treated them with cake and wine, and they were induced to tarry two hours or more, Governor Tryon frequently joking her about her American friends. By this happy incident General Putnam, by continuing his march, escaped a rencounter with a greatly superior force, which must have proved fatal to his whole party. One half hour, it is said, would have been sufficient for the enemy to have secured the road at the turn, and entirely cut off Putnam's retreat. It has since become almost a common saying, among our officers, that Mrs. Murray saved this part of the American army.

Howe's past competence was a general indication that even superb cakes and wine, coupled with an incredibly beautiful Mrs. Murray, would not have been sufficient to delay his advance if the existence of the American forces in the area was known to him. The popularity of the Mrs. Murray story was perhaps an American propaganda attempt aimed at discrediting the abilities of General Howe and raising the morale of the flagging continentals. It was, in effect , a counter-rumor to the British tales concerning the extracurricular activities of Washington.

By mid-September, the British were in complete control of New York City. As the rebels continued their retreat northward, General Nathanael Greene suggested that the city be burned so that Howe could not use the buildings as a permanent headquarters. The plan was supposedly rejected. At this time citizens in the state were largely undecided in supporting the rebellion and had not fully committed their resources in battle. Most men in

*Mrs. Murray's Strategy*, painting by E. P. Moran. Photo courtesy of the Library of Congress.

power believed that the burning of the area's major city would create unnecessary animosities and shore up loyalist power.

But on September 19, fire did break out in New York. Rebels suggested that the British were responsible for the blaze. Loyalists claimed that the job was the work of either the Continental Army or civilian saboteurs. From the Hessian camp at Hell's Gate, Major Carl Leopold Baurmeister was shaken by the event:

> At half past twelve in the night of the 19th–20th a terrible fire started in the northern part of the city of New York. Picked incendiaries, who are still hidden in the city, and a colonel with forty more rogues, who had come from Powles Hook by boat with a favorable west wind, set fire at the same time to many parts of this beautiful city. The weather and the carelessness, not to mention the inadequacy of the watch favored in every way, as it were, this Calamity, which brought about the destruction of 560 houses, including the greater part of the best.

Nine of the miscreants who were caught in the act have been arrested, and others thrown into the flames. One fanatical rebel whose wife and five children could not persuade him to refrain from this murderous arson, mortally injured his wife with a knife when she tried to extinguish the fire with buckets of water. The man was seized by some sailors, stabbed to death, and then hung by his feet in front of his own home. He was left hanging there until the 20th at four o'clock in the afternoon.

Frederick MacKenzie saw another view:

It is almost impossible to conceive a Scene of more horror and distress than the above. The Sick, The Aged, Women, and Children, half naked were seen going they knew not where, and taking refuge in houses which were at a distance from the fire, but from whence they were in several instances driven a second and even a third time by the devouring elements, and at last in a state of despair laying themselves down on the Common. The terror was increased by the horrid noise of the burning and falling houses, the pulling down of such wooden buildings as served to conduct the fire. . . .

More than one-fourth of New York was destroyed in the fire and hundreds were left homeless. Shanties, tents and huts were thrown up as shelter, but soon diseases spread through the squalid "canvas towns." Many left the city entirely. Phoebe Hand, daughter of loyalist Obadiah Hand, was sent to Staten Island while her father fled to Nova Scotia. Her "exile" would prove fortunate, for there she met one Cornelius Vanderbilt. The son of this union would later build a great railroad empire and become the nation's wealthiest citizen.

Washington continued leading his troops northward, followed at a leisurely pace by Howe's men. Sarah Simpson did not find the American retreat particularly pleasant, for she claimed that the fleeing soldiers stole from her 27 sheets, two dozen fine breeches, 60 pounds of tea, 128 gallons of brandy, 110 gallons of rum, 25 barrels of cider and 2,000 pounds of cheese. Evidently Sarah was a storekeep for it was most unusual for an 18th century woman to keep a ton of cheese solely for her family's consumption.

Another victim of the New York campaign was Elizabeth Annesley Lewis, the wife of Francis Lewis, a signer of the Declaration of Independence. When the British ransacked the family home at Whitestone, Long Island, Elizabeth was taken prisoner. Although she would be later exchanged for the wives of a British paymaster general and an attorney general, Elizabeth's health was broken as a result of the treatment she received in captivity. She soon died.

American battle casualties continued to mount. The farmers and tradespeople who had volunteered to fight the American cause were dying far from their homes. Joseph Martin, a sixteen-year-old soldier who was with the army described the burial of another rebel who had fallen on the battlefield. The man was a stranger to Martin's unit, but near a farmhouse the survivors prepared to bury their unknown comrade:

> Just as we had laid him in the grave, in, as decent a posture as existing circumstances would admit, there came from the house, towards the grave, two young ladies, who appeared to be sisters;—as they approached the grave, the soldiers immediately made way for them, with those feelings of respect which beauty and modesty combine seldom fail to produce, more especially when, as in this instance, accompanied by piety. Upon arriving at the head of the grave, they stopped, and, with their arms around each other's neck, stooped forward and looked into it, and with a sweet pensiveness of countenance which might have warmed the heart of a misoganist, asked if we were going to put earth on his naked face; being answered in the affirmative, one of them took a fine white gauze handkerchief from her neck and desired that it might be spread upon his face, tears at the same time flowing down their cheeks. After the grave was filled up they retired to the house in the same manner they came.

Howe halted his pursuit and doubling back attacked Ft. Washington, a rebel stronghold on the east bank of the Hudson. With this fort and a companion installation named Ft. Lee on the western shore, the continentals had hoped to control movement on the river. Both were necessary to prevent British troops from sailing northward and cutting off New England from the remaining colonies in the South.

But at Ft. Washington, the great defeat which had been narrowly averted at Long Island and in Manhattan, finally occurred. In mid-November the fort fell. The Hudson was opened and large amounts of supplies and ammunition fell to the enemy. Nearly 3,500 troops were taken prisoner. One of them was Margaret Cochran Corbin.

Margaret or Molly had followed her soldier husband to Ft. Washington. As a matross, John Corbin was attached to a gunnery team responsible for loading and sponging out the cannon so that it could be fired. When the British attacked the garrison, John was wounded and twenty-five-year-old Molly immediately took a position at the cannon. She too was hit by grapeshot, but not before she had "manned" the gun long enough to be seen by reliable witnesses.

Like many 18th century women, Molly was not a stranger to violence. She had been born on the Pennsylvania frontier in 1751. When she was six, her father Robert Cochran was killed and her mother taken prisoner in an Indian raid.

John Corbin died of his injuries at Ft. Washington. His wounded widow was taken prisoner by the British and sent to New York with the other soldier captives. Molly was eventually released and made her way to Philadelphia. Here she enrolled in the Invalid Regiment, a unit which had been formed as a haven for wounded who were able to assist in the recruiting and training of cadets.

Margaret's injuries did not completely heal. She permanently lost the use of one arm and ultimately became completely disabled. Eventually she made her way to the West Point area and because of various idiosyncrasies, became known as "Dirty Kate." In June of 1779, the State of Pennsylvania voted the heroine of Ft. Washington a grant of $30 and the next month Congress recognized her bravery by approving a resolution of the War Board which read:

Resolved: That Margaret Corbin, who was wounded and disabled in the attack on Fort Washington, whilst she

heroically filled the post of her husband who was killed by
her side serving a piece of artillery, do receive, during her
natural life, or the continuance of said disability, the one-half
of the monthly pay drawn by a soldier in the service of
these states; and that she receive out of the public stores one
complete suit of clothes, or the value thereof in money.

Margaret was also granted authority to draw rations from
army stores. She contended that the privilege included liquor as
well as food, for both were routinely issued to male soldiers. In
1782, Molly submitted a bill for 257 gills of whiskey which she
calculated had accumulated to her account. Major Samuel Shaw,
not knowing if army regulations allowed such liberties, wrote
Washington's aide Tench Tilghman for advice.

Shaw explained that Margaret was far advanced in pregnancy and had an old, decrepit husband. Tilghman replied:
"Granting provision at all to women who are followers of the
army, is altogether a matter of courtesy." He suggested that
Margaret could draw the liquor, but that she should not be given
the entire amount at one time. "Now friend Samuel," inquired
Tilghman, "how comes it, that a woman with an old, decrepit
husband should be far advanced in pregnancy?"

The fall of Fort Washington was followed quickly by the
abandonment of Fort Lee. American forces crossed into New Jersey and began a full scale retreat. However, Howe elected to
turn back toward New York and settle into winter headquarters.
Later military tacticians have accused the general of making a
costly error by not pursuing the fleeing continentals. At this time
desertions in Washington's army were increasing. Many enlistments would soon be up. The total continental force was only a
small fraction of Howe's men.

But several considerations indicate that Howe had good reason not to engage the enemy in battle. Following Washington involved invading alien territory where conceivably rebel Minutemen would equal the size of the English army within hours.
Second, Sir William was not assured that he could even find the
continentals. Rebel soldiers could be released and simply fade
away into the countryside.

The British could be lured far inland, away from supply bases in New York, with their rear flank open to counterattack. The casualties from snipers on the march back from Lexington and Concord had demonstrated the dangers of a retreat through enemy territory. With winter approaching, the prospect of heavy snow became greater. Howe, trapped in the interior of New Jersey or Pennsylvania, could be forced to spend the winter without supplies in an unfriendly territory. Much of his army could be lost before spring. If the general had followed Washington into the interior, the result may not have been a brilliant victory which crushed the American rebellion, but rather a catastrophe similar to that which would befall Napoleon in his disastrous retreat from Moscow.

Washington was thus left free to cross the Delaware into relatively safe territory. The rebellion would continue, but his frustrations at his rapidly disappearing army were evident. It was impossible to halt the desertions. The commander confided to Robert Morris: ". . . you may as well attempt to stop the Winds from blowing." To his brother John Augustine, Washington was more candid: "I think the game is pretty near up."

Depression set in at other quarters. The Congress, notified that British armies were within twenty-five miles of Philadelphia, fled to Baltimore. The names of the signers of the Declaration were still unpublished, and with the failing fortunes of the army, it appeared that they would never be revealed.

Thomas Paine, writing in his pamphlet *The American Crisis*, desperately wished that an American Joan of Arc would rise to lead the forces to victory. "Would that heaven might inspire some Jersey maid to spirit up her countrymen and save her fair fellow sufferers from ravage and ravishment." No such martyr came forward.

The Congress and army were not the only Americans in flight from the British. Fearful whigs leaving their homes in New Jersey and Pennsylvania, packed the roads leading to sanctuary in the secluded upcountry. The family of Annis Boudinot, a gentle poet, was among those most hunted by the invaders. Annis' husband Richard Stockton was a congressional delegate and like her son-in-law Benjamin Rush was a secret signer of the Declaration of Independence. Her brother Elias was also a prominent political figure.

Annis was born in Darby, Pennsylvania in 1736, but after her marriage in 1755, she moved to the Stockton mansion, "Morven," near Princeton. As early as 1758 she had begun publishing poetry, but her verses did not assume political overtones until the coming of the revolution.

Richard, a well-known lawyer, had been elected Chief Justice of New Jersey after being defeated for the post of governor

*Annis Boudinot Stockton,* painting by John Wollaston. Courtesy of the collection of Princeton University.

by William Livingston. He refused the judicial position, perhaps insulted by the political defeat, and chose instead to continue his position in Congress.

In October of 1776, Stockton, with the rank of a colonel, went to inspect the American troops near Albany, but returned home as Annis prepared to move the family beyond the reach of the approaching British. On November 29, the group made their way to Monmouth County. The departure was poorly planned for Annis' young son was left behind and the destination of their flight was actually a well known loyalist stronghold.

Two days after arriving, Richard Stockton and his host were captured and taken to a British prison at Perth Amboy. He was then sent to New York's Provost Jail, placed in irons and kept without food for twenty-four hours. Eventually four additional signers would be captured, but Richard's detention would soon have severe consequences for the American cause and for Annis.

The New York into which Howe settled in 1776 was a gay place, despite the devastating effects of the September fire. The letter "R" had been stamped into the doors of all suspected rebels, but other fine mansions and taverns offered hospitality to the occupying army. Loyalists from surrounding areas such as Long Island and New Jersey actively supported the British forces, whose fortunes seemed so high.

For many years, Manhattan had boasted a cosmopolitan air and a toleration for exuberant living. Unlike staid Boston, the rowdy behavior of the British troops was acceptable in the city. New Yorkers were accustomed to strange activities on the part of crown representatives. Governor William Tryon's wife, Margaret Wake, was extremely eccentric and perhaps bordered on insanity. She rejected most of the social duties expected of a governor's lady and preferred instead to concentrate on her own strange projects. One was the writing and publishing of a treatise dealing with military warfare.

An earlier governor of the province, Lord Viscount Cornbury, was even odder. Convinced that he bore an incredible resemblance to his cousin Queen Anne, the Viscount attempted to make the likeness even more noticeable by wearing women's clothing. Janet Montgomery described him as a large man who "wore a hoope and a headdress, and with a fan in his hand was seen frequently at night upon the ramparts."

Cornbury's wife, who Janet maintained was loved primarily because she had a beautiful ear, was also reduced to eccentricity. When Lady Cornbury's carriage drew up in front of New York's fine houses, some reports suggest that the wary hostesses inside gave immediate orders that all the family's valuables should be hidden.

Lord Cornbury's transvestite habits became so regular that the New York Council demanded his recall. They were successful and Cornbury, returning to England, had his portrait painted while wearing a gown which once belonged to the Queen.

During the winter of 1776–1777, New York found a new society leader in Elizabeth Lloyd, the wife of Joshua Loring. The notorious "Mrs. Loring" would become an integral part of Howe's life in America, but her activities would seriously jeopardize the general's career.

Elizabeth, a native of Massachusetts, probably first met the commander during the occupation of Boston. Accompanied by her husband, she sailed for Halifax with other refugees, but returned to be with the British in Manhattan. Soon the status of both Lorings significantly improved.

Thomas Jones, an ardent loyalist and a judge of the Supreme Court of New York, strongly criticized Howe's relationship with Elizabeth. In his history of New York during the Revolution, Jones wrote:

> Upon the close of the campaign, in 1776, there were not less than 10,000 prisoners, (sailors included) within the British lines at New York. A Commissary of Prisoners was therefore appointed, and one Joshua Loring, a Bostonian, was commissioned to the office, with a guinea a day, and rations of all kinds, for himself and family. In this appointment there was reciprocity. Joshua had a handsome wife. The General, Sir William Howe, was fond of her. Joshua made no objections. He fingered the cash, the General enjoyed the madam.

According to the completely biased judge, Howe spent little time considering the war, but filled his days with dancing, card

playing and bedding with Elizabeth while Joshua misappro-
priated money earmarked for the maintenance of American prisoners. The judge estimated that at least 300 captives starved to
death before February 1777 because Loring siphoned off funds allocated for their subsistence or substituted condemned foodstuffs
for designated rations.

Accusations of fraud would continue to plague Loring
throughout his stay in America. During this first winter in New
York, however, supplies were scarce in the city and difficult to
obtain for even British soldiers. The American prisoners were
probably last in priority when stores were available and undoubtedly would have suffered even if a man of unblemished reputation had been given the supervisory post.

Elizabeth was described as a plump, blue-eyed blonde with a
penchant for gambling. According to some estimates, she had lost
as much as 300 guineas, several thousand dollars, in one night of
card playing. For some years, betting had been a preoccupation
among the public and in the 1760's had become almost a mania in
London. One popular story involved a supposed incident at
White's Coffee House, when a patron burst into the hall and collapsed on the floor. Instead of coming to the man's aid, customers
in the establishment immediately began giving odds on whether
he had died or simply fainted.

Elizabeth's almost mystical control over Howe was the subject of gossip not only in high ranking circles but among the
common folk. A rousing ballad of the day, popular in both armies, commemorated the liaison with the triumphal chorus:

Awake, awake, Sir Billy,
There's forage in the plain.
Ah! Leave your little filly,
And open the campaign.
Heed not a woman's prattle,
Which tickles in the ear,
But give the word for battle,
And grasp the warlike spear.

Although life was cozy in Manhattan, the situation in isolated British outposts in New Jersey was harsher. Rebel raiders,

or farmers protecting their property, were a constant annoyance
to soldiers on detail. Judge Jones noted:

> Nothing could be done without the directions of the
> Commander-in-chief, who was diverting himself in New
> York . . . in the arms of Mrs. Loring. Not a stick of wood, a
> spear of grass, or a kernal of corn, could the troops in New
> Jersey procure without fighting for it unless sent from New
> York. Every foraging party was attacked in some way or an-
> other. The losses upon these occasions were nearly equal,
> they could be called nothing more than mere skirmishes, but
> hundreds of them happened in the course of the winter. The
> British, however, lost men who were not easily replaced.

Officers found problems in another area. Not all American
women proved as anxious to accommodate the British as Elizabeth Loring and the ladies at the "holy ground." From Staten Island, Frances, Lord Rawdon, head of an Irish Regiment and Adjutant to General Clinton, expressed his regret that New York
females were not as yielding as those he had met during the British expedition to Charleston. In a letter to his uncle the Earl of
Huntington, Rawdon discussed the situation:

> The fair nymphs of this isle are in wonderful tribula-
> tion, as the fresh meat our men have got here has made them
> as riotous as satyrs. A girl cannot step into the bushes to
> pluck a rose without running the most imminent risk of
> being ravished, and they are so little accustomed to these
> vigorous methods that they don't bear them with the proper
> resignation, and of consequence we have most entertaining
> courts-martial every day.

> To the southward they behave much better in these
> cases, if I may judge from a woman who having been forced
> by seven of our men, [who came] to make a complaint to
> me "not of their usage," she said; "No, thank God," she de-
> spised that, "but of their having taken an old prayer book
> for which she had a particular affection.

> A girl on this island made a complaint the other day to
> Lord Percy of her being deflowered, as she said, by some
> grenadiers. Lord Percy asked her how she knew them to be

grenadiers as it happened in the dark. "Oh, good God," cried she, "They could be nothing else, and if your lordship will examine I am sure you will find it so."

British troops in the outposts in New Jersey and Pennsylvania were also preying on the neighborhood women. A broadside issued in Bucks County on December 14 decried the experiences of inhabitants who came into contact with the enemy:

> On Wednesday last three women came down to the Jersey shore in great distress, a party of the American Army went and brought them off, when it appeared that they had been all very much abused, and the youngest of them a girl about fifteen, had been ravished that morning by a British Officer.

> A number of young women in *Hopewell*, to the amount of 16, flying from this ravaging and cruel enemy, took refuge on the mountain near Ralph Harts, but information being given of their retreat, they were soon brought down into the *British* Camp, where they have been kept ever since.

The British were not entirely neglectful of military affairs for in mid-December, a raiding party captured General Charles Lee. The seizure was another blow to the Americans despite Lee's constant bickering with many fellow officers. During Washington's retreat from New York, Lee had carried out his own campaign, ignoring the difficulties being experienced by other units. Washington repeatedly ordered Lee to bring his forces into coordination with the main army. Lee had not done so.

Personal conflicts had plagued Lee's earlier career in the British service. Three years after he had first come to America in 1755, he publicly scorned his supreme commander as a "booby-in-chief," and a "beastly poltroon." The same year he assaulted an army surgeon because of a supposed libel and later claimed that the doctor had laid in ambush for him with pistols. In 1760, after attacking Philadelphia constable James Rowan, Les was fined £50 for assault and battery, and required to post a £500 peace bond.

Although he gained the nickname "Mad Lee," Charles was considered a superior officer. He served in Portugal for a time, but because promotion was difficult in the British Army, he became a mercenary in the Polish service. In 1773, he returned to the colonies in retirement as an English officer on half pay. Almost immediately he began touring the provinces, meeting with prominent radicals and speaking out against royal oppression. Backed by powerful Virginians, he purchased a plantation named Hopewell in the Shenandoah Valley and became a neighbor of Horatio Gates, another retired British officer who also became an American general.

Lee was rarely unnoticed and during his travels usually managed to involve himself with leaders who would help to promote his career. During the rebel campaign at Boston, Lee found time to socialize at Mercy Warren's house. She described the meeting in a letter to Adams:

> The Generals Washington, Lee, and Gates, with several other distinguished officers from head-quarters, dined with us (at Watertown) three days since. The first of these I think one of the most amiable and accomplished gentlemen, both in person, mind, and manners, that I have met with. The second, whom I never saw before, I think plain in his person to a degree of ugliness, careless even to impoliteness—his garb ordinary, his voice rough, his manners rather morose; yet sensible, learned, judicious and penetrating: a considerable traveller, agreeable in his narrations, and a zealous, indefatigable friend to the American cause; but much more from a love of freedom, and an impartial sense of the inherent rights of mankind at large, than from any attachment or disgust to particular persons or countries. The last is a brave soldier, a high republican, a sensible companion, an honest man, of unaffected manners and easy deportment.

Mercy would later change her favorable evaluation of Lee and note that he was "without religion or country, principle or attachment; gold was his diety. . . ."

Abigail Adams would also have the opportunity to meet Charles Lee and his constant companion, a dog named Spada. The canine took an evident liking to the future first lady, for on their meeting at a party, it leaped onto a chair and offered a paw to her. According to witnesses, Abigail shook it. Lee was rarely without his hairy companions and at one period had a dozen poodles who followed him about. In addition to Spada, his most controversial pet was a pomeranian which closely resembled a bear.

On December 13, British troops surrounded an inn operated in Basking Ridge, New Jersey, by a Mrs. White. Inside was Charles Lee whose presence had been betrayed by a tory informer. Lee surrendered peacefully when the enemy threatened to burn the tavern. Ironically, the captors were from the same regiment which Lee had commanded during the Seven Years War. Included in the group was Banastre Tarleton who would later gain the nickname "Bloody Tarleton" for his order to kill several hundred wounded Americans at the Battle of Waxhaws. After returning to their own lines, the British celebrated their coup and by some accounts fed liquor to Lee's horse until it was neighingly drunk.

Kidnapping was a favorite ploy of both armies. At various times the British concocted plans to seize both Washington and Thomas Jefferson. The Americans made firm arrangements to abduct General Clinton and King George's son, Prince William. A special target was Benedict Arnold after he had been discovered as a traitor.

The Americans were particularly successful with British Major General Richard Prescott who was taken twice. The most daring capture of Prescott occurred in July of 1777 while he was visiting at the house of John Overing near Newport. The purpose of the visit was social, for Prescott was reportedly apprehended while in bed with a prostitute. The *London Chronicle* parodied the situation in a poem called "On General Prescot being carried off naked, 'unanointed, unanealed'." The poem claimed:

What various Lures there are to ruin man;
  Woman, the first and foremost all bewitches!
A nymph thus spoil'ed a General's mighty plan,
  And gave him to the foe—without his breeches."

Although Margaret Draper had earlier written that it was "quere" that Lee formally submitted his resignation to the British army, this action may have saved his life. Many Englishmen thought that the general should be hanged as a traitor, but others maintained that he had officially resigned from the army and therefore should be treated as a prisoner of war. One Englishman proposed that Lee should be sentenced to be hanged, but pardoned if he would agree to marry Catharine Macaulay. The inference was that it would be a difficult choice for Lee to make.

While the British vaccilated on Lee's future, he was given great freedom in New York, allowed a servant and one of his dogs. In March, Lee surprised the British authorities by presenting a plan by which he claimed they would gain victory in the colonies. Although Lee's critics suggest that this was an attempt to save his own life, he actually may have been attempting to disrupt English plans by passing along erroneous information while appearing to collaborate.

The Americans could not spend a great deal of time mourning Lee's capture, for a new plan of operation was soon to be put into action. Traditionally, when armies entered into winter headquarters fighting ceased until the following spring. Both sides used the period to regroup and relax after a hard summer and fall. It was this custom that Washington considered as he finalized a scheme to reinstate the war in mid-winter.

The target was a large garrison at Trenton manned primarily by Hessian mercenaries. The strategy required that three American columns march separately across Pennsylvania, cross the Delaware and rejoin near Trenton for the attack. On Christmas Day, the rebel units moved out, but almost immediately difficulties were encountered. Heavy snows and ice floes kept two of the wings from crossing the river. Unknown to Washington, these columns returned to camp.

The commander's 2,400 troops who were to ford about nine miles north of the village, were also having problems. John Glover's Marblehead Mariners, who had saved the day at Long Island, were again rowing across difficult waters. The passage at McKonkey's Ferry was partially delayed by heavy snows, but by

3 a.m., most of the men were over and the artillery soon followed.

Emanuel Leutze's painting of Washington Crossing the Delaware, while perhaps inspiring, is inaccurate in many respects. The
vessel drawn by Leutze bears little resemblance to the large flat
bottom durham ore boats actually used in the operation. These
low draft vessels carried thirty to forty men at once, not the cozy
group envisioned by the German painter. The American flag
which is prominent in the painting had not yet been authorized
and if Washington had stood erect in the tightly packed boat as
Leutze suggested, he would have immediately swamped it. Leutze
would have other problems with his giant canvases. Two were
painted, but the original was partially damaged in a fire about
1850. Although it was restored, the painting was completely destroyed in an allied air raid on Germany during World War II.

Washington's march continued toward Trenton. Heavy,
blowing snow made visibility difficult. The army was poorly clad
and many of the men had no shoes. On reaching the outskirts of
the city, Washington found that the two other columns had not
appeared, but elected to continue on with the raid. The soldiers
found that their wet muskets would not fire so the raiders prepared to charge the installation using only bared bayonets.

The Battle of Trenton was brief, bloody and decisive. American units commanded strategic locations within the village before the alarm for defense could be sounded. Many of the
Hessians were drunk after a long day of Christmas celebration.
By 9:30 a.m. the battle was over. About 950 men had been captured along with valuable stores and supplies.

Washington, fearing that escapees would soon bring British
reinforcements from nearby garrisons, evacuated the town almost
immediately. The long march back to the river was begun. Glover's sailors again ferried the troops to safety. The last American
elements arrived in their camp on the evening of December 26,
after nearly thirty-six hours of marching and fighting.

The Battle of Trenton was the last time that many of Glov-
er's men would be called up to perform a major amphibious task.
Privateers were being outfitted in New England to prey upon
English shipping and many of the mariners would leave the army

to join the crews of these vessels. Glover, who had once been a shoemaker, would continue in the army and would be constantly punned as a man "who gave his awl" for his country.

The continentals had not finished their winter offensive and soon moved out again accompanied by 3,000 militia who had joined the force. Margaret Morris, a Quaker living in Burlington, New Jersey, was a witness to the activities of this second maneuver. Born in Maryland in 1737, Margaret was the widow of a Philadelphia merchant. She had moved to Burlington in 1770 to raise her four children near the meeting house of her missionary brother-in-law. Margaret, mistress of Green Bank, the former home of Royal Governor William Franklin, watched the troops come and go from battle. In her diary, the sensitive woman carefully noted their conditions and reactions to the war.

On December 27, elements of the militia set up headquarters in Burlington, and moved into vacant houses or the residences of friendly whigs. The following day Margaret saw them leave for battle: ". . . early this Morning the Troops Marched out of Town in high spirits . . . My Heart sinks when I think of the Numbers unprepared for Death, who will probably be sent, in a few days to appear before the Judge of Heaven. . . ."

The militia were moving out to confront British troops under Lord Charles Cornwallis who was progressing toward Trenton in response to the Christmas raid. Cornwallis had earlier been granted permission to return to England where his wife Jemima was reportedly dying. The leave was cancelled after the British defeat in New Jersey.

On January 2, the American army seemed trapped again, but during the night by leaving their campfires burning the forces managed to slip away and avoid detection. They immediately made a surprise raid on Princeton. Here the rebels were successful, but according to Margaret many may have deserted back to Burlington:

> This Morning between 8 & 9 o'clock we heard very distinctly, a heavy fireing of Cannon, the sound came from towards Trenton, about noon a Number of Soldiers, upwards of a thousand came into town in great Confusion, with Baggage & some Cannon— From these Soldiers we learn there was a smart engagement Yesterday at Trenton, & that they

left them engaged near Trenton Mill, but were not able to say which side was Victorious. They were again quartered on the inhabitants, & we again were exempt from the cumber of having them lodged in our house. . . . About bed time I went in the next house to see if the fires were safe, & my heart was melted with Compassion to see such a number of my fellow Creatures lying like Swine on the floor fast asleep, & many of them without even a Blanket to cover them, it seems strange that such a number should be allowed to come from the Camp at the very time of the engagement, & I shrewdly Suspect they have run away for they can give no account why they came, nor where they are to March next.

The troops stayed five days more and finally marched off to the north. On January 8, Margaret surveyed what they had left behind:

— I went into the house after they left it, & was griev'd to see such loads of provisions wastefully lying on the floor— I sent my Son to desire an Officer in Town to order it away— & he returned his Compliments & desired me "to keep it from spoiling," that was, to make use of it, but as it was not his to give & I had no Stomach "to keep it from spoiling," I sent it to another person who had it taken to the sick Soldiers. . . .

Times grew harder for Margaret. As the daughter of a doctor, she helped to nurse the sick, an important function for women during the war because many male physicians had left to join the army. In 1780 she opened a shop to sell medicine, but was unable to keep it in operation. For a time she lived in Philadelphia, but left when yellow fever struck. She returned to Burlington and in 1816 died at seventy-nine.

Washington followed up his victory at Princeton with other successes at Hackensack and Elizabeth. He then returned to Morristown to await spring. The commander's winter campaign became one of the most important of the war. The American victories had broken the hold of the British in New Jersey, raised the hopes of rebel supporters and saved Philadelphia, at least for a while. The area would remain relatively quiet for nearly six months.

Many whigs who had left New Jersey returned home after the victories. Among them was Annis Boudinot Stockton and her family. Richard's treatment in the British jail had been formally protested by Congress which instructed Washington to threaten reprisals against British prisoners if the signer was not handled more kindly. But during his confinement in New York, Stockton signed an oath swearing to take no further action against the King. As a result, he was soon released and returned to Morven.

Princeton had been ransacked during the foreign occupation. Although Morven had been partially burned, it stood mostly undamaged possibly because Cornwallis had used the structure as his temporary headquarters. But inside, the furniture had been pillaged and several portraits defaced. Two of the three trunks of treasure that Annis had buried in the yard were stolen.

Perhaps even more unsettling was the resentment directed against the Stocktons because of Richard's repudiation of the American cause. Upon his release he resigned from the Congress and indeed took no further part in the struggle. Only gradually did the accusations of his disloyalty fade. Although Stockton's death several years later has traditionally been blamed on his mistreatment in the Provost Jail, it was attributed at the time to a complication of a "cracked lip," perhaps a form of cancer. Although Stockton was removed as a participant in the revolution, Annis continued to support the war effort with her poetry.

In Baltimore, the Congress was elated with Washington's victories. The successes emboldened the members so thoroughly that they agreed at last to make known the names of the signers of the Declaration of Independence. In January, the group formally resolved the copies of the document including the names of the signers, should be printed and forwarded to the various states for public distribution. Mary Katherine Goddard was chosen for the task of printing the full Declaration for the first time.

Mary, editor and publisher of the *Maryland Journal and Baltimore Advertiser* had long been connected with the printing industry. Her mother, Sarah Updike Goddard, was publisher of the *Providence Gazette*. Mary's brother William had earlier been a partner in a scheme to publish the *Pennsylvania Chronicle*, but the paper folded and he moved to Baltimore to set up the publication which Mary would later edit.

Goddard turned the *Advertiser* over to his sister in 1774 and devoted his full attention to establishing a postal service which delivered mail between Massachusetts and Virginia. Congress later incorporated the organization as the nucleus of the American postal service, but Goddard was passed over as head of the program in favor of Richard Bache, Benjamin Franklin's son-in-law. Instead, the originator was named to the subordinate post of Surveyor of the Post Roads and Mary was made Postmistress in Baltimore.

Although numerous newspapers in the colonies were folding during the revolution, Mary continued to expand her paper. She took in outside jobs such as printing the Declaration and by November 1779, reported that her circulation was the largest in the colonies. Like Anne Greene in Annapolis, Mary also had her detractors. In 1776, one George Somerville "abused her with threats and indecent language." Somerville was soundly condemned by the local committee of safety for his attack on the staunch whig publisher.

With the American situation seemingly in hand, a diplomatic offensive was begun in Europe. Benjamin Franklin arrived in Paris as head of a mission aimed at obtaining aid for the colonies. The plan was to play on the animosities which had existed for centuries between Gaulist rulers and Britain. As Catharine Macaulay had warned, France was anxious to take advantage of the opportunity to weaken her rival across the channel.

Franklin became the immediate rage in Paris, particularly among the ladies whom he charmed with Poor Richard's witty sayings and homespun philosophies. Although Franklin rivaled Voltaire as the most famous personality in the world, he chose to assume the guise of a simple provincial, dressing in unpretentious homespun, wearing a coonskin cap and often carrying an apple-tree staff through the royal palaces.

The American minister was as delighted with France as the French were with him. To his step-niece, Elizabeth Hubbard Partridge, Franklin explained:

This is the civilest Nation upon Earth. Your first acquaintances endeavour to find out what you like, and they tell others. If 'tis understood that you like Mutton, dine where you will you find Mutton. Somebody, it seems, gave it out that I lov'd Ladies; and then every body presented me their Ladies (or the Ladies presented themselves) to be *embrac'd*, that is to have their Necks kiss'd. For as to kissing of Lips or Cheeks, it is not the Mode here: the first is reckon'd rude, and the other may rub off the Paint. The French Ladies have however 1000 other ways of rendering themselves agreeable; by their various Attentions and Civilities, and their sensible Conversation. 'Tis a delightful People to live with.

One of Franklin's favorites was Madame Brillon de Jouy, his neighbor at Passy, with whom he reportedly played chess while she lounged in a bathtub. Their relationship became something of a fashionable scandal partially because of her habit of sitting upon his lap in public. But the affair was entirely platonic.

Franklin's closest attachment was to the widowed Anne-Catherine Helvétius. Mme. Helvétius was famous throughout French political circles for the salon she maintained in her residence at Auteuil. Here the whig emissary was a constant visitor, meeting with important statesmen, writers and politicians who could assist in his campaign for recognition and financial aid to America.

Lively Franklin became deeply committed to Mme. Helvétius and not so subtly suggested a tryst was due him: "If that Lady likes to pass her Days with him; he in turn would like to pass his Nights with her; and as he has already given her many of his days, though he has so few left to give, she appears ungrateful never to have given him a single one of her nights, which steadily pass as a pure loss. . . ."

Franklin later proposed to the Frenchwoman, but was rejected because of a vow she had earlier made to remain single in memory of her dead husband. But Abigail Adams was not so taken with the liberated woman's conduct. At a dinner party the Adams attended with Dr. Franklin, Abigail disapproved of Mme. Helvétius' activities:

When we went into the room to dine, she was placed between the Doctor and Mr. Adams. She carried on the chief of the conversation at dinner, frequently locking her hand into the Doctor's, and sometimes spreading her arm upon the backs of both gentlemen's chairs, then throwing her arm carelessly upon the Doctor's neck.

I should have been greatly astonished at this conduct, if the good Doctor had not told me that in this lady I should see a genuine Frenchwoman, wholly free from affectation of stiffness of behavior, and one of the best women in the world. For this I must take the Doctor's word; but I should have set down for a very bad one, although sixty years of age, and a widow.

One Frenchwoman, although intrigued with Franklin, was strongly opposed to an American-French alliance. She was Marie Antoinette, Queen of France and the daughter of Maria Theresa, empress of the Hapsburg Empire.

Despite Marie's objections to the rebels, Louis XVI had enthusiastically supported the American efforts in a variety of non-military methods. French ports were opened to American ships. Supplies and money flowed into the colonies, but the King held back from any formal alliance which would commit French troops to American soil.

The nation's treasury was dangerously low, due in part to Marie's enormous expenses, and a full scale war with England would further deplete the royal coffers. Perhaps more important, a tide of revolution was beginning to rise in France, and although it was largely ignored by the aristocracy, the liberal ideas of the colonies were no more welcomed in official Paris than in London.

Louis, one of Europe's most autocratic monarchs, felt a personal distaste for Franklin's teachings of egalitarianism. Reportedly the King ordered the Sèvres factory to produce a custom made chamber pot decorated at the bottom with Franklin's portrait and the slogan *"Eripuit caelo fulmen sceptrumque tyrannis,"* or, "He snatched the lightning from the sky and the scepter from tyrants." The bowl, a parody of a fast selling medallion bearing the same plaque was sent as a gift to Mme. Diane de Polignac, a friend of the Queen and a supporter of the war.

Across the channel, another admirer of Dr. Franklin's was at work promoting the rebel interests. She was Patience Lovell Wright.

Patience Wright had come to London from the colonies about 1771. Within months she became a well-known sculptress in the most aristocratic circles. Her specialty was the modeling of wax busts and life-sized statues of prominent figures, but she used other talents to secretly gather military information for Franklin.

The *Morning Herald* announced:

> She found herself the avenues to get information of almost every design which was agitated or intended to be executed in America, and was the object of the most active confidence of Dr. Franklin and others with whom she corresponded and gave information during the whole war. As soon as a general was appointed to go out and mount the tragi-comical stage in America, she instantly found access to a part of the family and discovered the number of troops to be employed and their proposed destination.

Patience's background was unusual for a pet of the English upper crust and an active spy. She was born in Bordentown, New Jersey, in 1725 where she lived quietly until her husband died in 1769. In an attempt to support her three children, Patience moved to New York City and began making portraits in wax. Although her earlier modeling had been limited to entertaining her children with models made from dough, her new works were successful. Additional profit came when her studio was converted into a small museum where the public paid to view likenesses of famous people.

Because the American market could become saturated, Patience moved her headquarters to London. Here with the help of Benjamin West, a historical painter to the court, Patience's studio became a popular meeting place for notable clients. She was dubbed the "Promethean Modeler," and her shop was organized similar to the New York venture with the price of admission set at two shillings.

King George and Queen Charlotte were reported to have

often visited Patience to watch her work. The custom was not unusual for the Queen was known to periodically attend the shop of her official potter, Josiah Wedgwood.

A temporary setback came when Patience's New York museum was burned, but some of the figures were saved and the operation was reopened on a smaller scale. *London Magazine* called her work a new style of "picturing" and was enthusiastic about Patience's statute of Catharine Macaulay. In reviewing the sculptress' "museum" the magazine reported:

> Amongst the group of her characters, there are some large as life in conversation, and so natural, that people frequently speak to the dumb figures; the most familiar, of these, is Mr[s.] Macaulay, who may live by the figures of Mrs. Wright as long as in her republican history, wherein she has given us a picture of her mind; but Mrs. Wright has preserved to us the person of this celebrated and patriot female.

When Abigail Adams visited the studio she was likewise astonished at the lifelike quality of Patience's figures. On entering, Abigail was surprised to see two elderly people lounging together in the hall. On closer inspection, she discovered that they were actually wax figures who the sculptress explained were likenesses of her mother and father. Later Abigail observed an elderly clergyman reading a newspaper in the middle of the salon. After several minutes she concluded that he too was made of wax.

Patience's most famous work of this period was a large statue of William Pitt, the Earl of Chatham and an opponent of the King's colonial policy. The work was installed in Westminster Abbey and stood as the only sculpture by an American woman until World War II. During a blitz raid, Lord Chatham's statue was knocked from its pedestal. Although the figure remained undamaged, the head was completely severed from the body and curators felt that to attempt to rejoin the pieces could cause major damage or splitting. Several years later it was placed back on display in two separate pieces.

Patience became an outspoken opponent of the British entry into the war at the beginning of the difficulties. That such an open advocate of the enemy would be allowed to remain in a position where she was privy to high military secrets of her clients was unusual, even by the casual 18th century standards. But the government may have considered her merely a harmless eccentric. Another explanation is that her spying activities were well known and English officials were actually passing false information to her which they hoped would confuse rebel operations.

The artist's business dwindled during the war and in 1779 she wrote to Franklin, inquiring if she should come to France. He replied that the journey was not safe and added that the market for her work would not be as profitable as in London. Characteristically, Patience disregarded the advice and moved to Paris, taking lodging at the same rooming house as that used by Elkanah Watson. Watson, a financial agent for the colonies, soon grew to know the scuptress quite well:

> The wild flights of her powerful mind stamped originality on all her acts and language. She was a tall and athletic figure;—and walked with a firm, bold step, as erect as an Indian. Her complexion was somewhat shallow; her cheekbones high; her face, furrowed; and her olive eyes keen, piercing and expressive. Her sharp glance was appaling; it had almost the wildness of a maniac's. The vigor and originality of her conversation, corresponded with her manners & appearance. She would utter language, in her incessant volubility, as if unconscience to whom directed, that would put her hearers to the blush.

Watson declared that as Patience moulded, she constantly poured forth strange thoughts. He was thoroughly familiar with her work as Franklin's agent and explained:

> The peculiarity of her character, and the excellence of her wax figures, made her rooms in Pall Mall a fashionable lounging-place for the nobility and distinguished men of England. Here her deep penetration and sagacity, cloaked by her apparent simplicity of purpose, enabled her to gather many facts and secrets important to "dear America"—her uniform expression in referring to her native land, which she dearly loved."

She was a genuine Republican and ardent Whig. The King and Queen often visited her rooms; they would induce her to work upon her heads, regardless of their presence. She would often, as if forgetting herself, address them as George and Charlotte.

According to Watson, Patience's strangeness often made her life difficult. One incident occurred late at night when she had wrapped a newly modeled bust of Franklin in a cloth, intending to take it for a comparison with the original. On the way she was stopped at a police checkpoint, which had been set up to apprehend travellers carrying contraband. The officers, unwrapping her parcel and discovering the head, immediately took her into custody. She had already aroused their suspicions because of her loud protests against being stopped and searched. The policemen later said that they had assumed her to be a homicidal maniac who had decapitated some unfortunate and was on her way to dispose of the head.

With the help of women such as Patience Wright, Franklin's mission in Paris gained new successes each month. But just as Franklin had sailed east to seek help in the American cause, thousands of Europeans were making the opposite voyage in the interests of Britain. These were Hessians and other mercenaries from the German states. Unlike the good doctor, their attempts would prove unsuccessful.

# CHAPTER FIVE

# *Armies on the March*

I left Wolfenbüttel on the 14th of May, 1776 at five o'clock in the morning, and in spite of my ardent longing to see my husband again I could only have a heavy heart from the full realization of the magnitude of my undertaking, especially as I had been told repeatedly about the dangers connected with such a voyage. . . . It took all of my courage and tenderness, therefore, not to renounce my only wish, my resolution to follow him. I was told not only of the dangers of the sea, but that we might be eaten by the savages; that people in America ate horsemeat and cats; but all of this was less frightening than the thought of going into a strange country where I did not understand the language. However, in the meantime I was prepared for everything, and the thought of following my husband and fulfilling my duty sustained me throughout the entire journey.

THUS BEGAN THE JOURNAL of the Baroness Frederika Charlotte Louise von Riedesel, who at twenty-nine, was the wife of the commanding general of the Brunswick troops in America. The Baroness, the most patrician campfollower of the American revolution, was leaving home to join her mercenary husband in Canada.

Military life was not new to Frederika, for her father was a Prussian general and had served as Commissary to Frederick the Great. Her own 1762 marriage to Friedrich Adolphus von Riedesel, the future Baron of Eisenbach and a promising young officer, had perpetuated the family's military tradition.

The American campaign presented a great opportunity for German officers such as Riedesel who were partially dependent upon activities in foreign wars as a means for advancement. Thus the Baron had left Brunswick, seeking to improve both his finances and military career by aiding the British.

The Baroness would take thirteen months to complete her journey to Canada. During the trip she was swindled by an 18th century confidence man, befriended by King George, left almost destitute because of the romantic aspirations of a companion and mistaken for a French prostitute by a mob of sailors.

Other women followed the German troops, but none produced diaries of the campaign which feature the elegance and insight of the learned Baroness. Her journals and letters, which cover more than six years, minutely describe the war as seen by an observant foreign woman who was witness to numerous important events.

Early in the rebellion, English officials had realized that their standing forces would be inadequate for subduing the colonies. The conflict was unpopular at home and new enlistments were not expected to provide enough manpower to fight in America and staff British garrisons throughout the empire.

Originally the government appealed to Catherine II of Russia for 20,000 mercenaries. The wily Empress rejected the plea, wishing to remain totally neutral in the action and thus able to play both sides to her own advantage.

The most promising alternative was an appeal to the princes of the German states. There were some 300 of these semi-independent monarchs in central Europe, held together by loose alliances. Many had been joined to the British through marriages of German princesses to English royalty such as George III's own union with Charlotte of Meckenlenburg-Strelitz. The King himself, only the third British monarch in the German Hanoverian line, was still closely tied to the continent.

Clinton opposed the hiring of these mercenaries, claiming that their rate of desertions was high and their loyalty was undependable. Other opponents of the plan feared that desertions

Frederika, Baroness von Riedesel, engraving by J. C. Buttre after a painting by Tischbein. Courtesy of the Manuscripts and Archives Division, The New York Public Library, Astor, Lenox and Tilden Foundations.

would be even greater during the American campaign, for more than 150,000 citizens in the colonies were of German descent.

Several of the princes contacted by England were anxious to provide troops. Not only was money a great incentive, but many German leaders were wary over increasing French power. The new alliance with England would provide a valuable ally in case the French increased their imperialistic ventures.

At least six rulers agreed to supply men, but the terms of the contracts varied widely. The most controversial was a pact with the Duke of Brunswick which contained what would soon be known as the "blood clause." Under this proviso, George III agreed to pay the Duke 30 thalers or about $185 for each of his men that was killed in America. For each wounded soldier, the figure was ten thalers. Although the Duke was required to outfit his army, he would show a large profit in their deaths. Nearly 60 percent of the Brunswick leader's troops failed to return from the war.

Other leaders like the Landgrave of Hesse-Cassel, whose contract did not contain the blood clause, could also profit from the deaths of their men. Instead of reporting casualties, the names of the deceased were continued on payrolls and their salaries poured into the rulers' coffers for years.

Not all European leaders were enthusiastic with the operation. Frederick the Great was disgusted and wrote to Voltaire:

> If the Landgrave had come out of my school, he would not have sold his subjects to the English as one sells cattle to be taken to the slaughter house. . . . Such conduct is motivated only by selfish greed. I pity the poor Hessians who will end their lives unhappily and uselessly in America.

Many Hessians did indeed die on the foreign soil. One out of every four able bodied men in Hesse was shipped out to the colonies. Their numbers were so great that gradually the names of other principalities which had sent troops were ignored and all German troops in America became known as "Hessians."

Occasionally the hired soldiers and their families shared Frederick's displeasure. Stephan Popp recorded in his diary the despair that filled the friends and relatives of the troops when it was known that their destination was the new world:

> It was reported to all companies and made known in the Regiment that we must take to the road within three weeks. Col von Voit would assume command. At the same time, young lads from all walks of life were brought in as recruits. Then there occurred a lamentation. Fathers, mothers, and relatives came daily and visited their sons, brothers and friends. . . . Some for sorrow and dislike could hardly be consoled over the fact that they should be torn away from their parents. Wherever you looked you heard nothing but moaning and groaning.

Whig propagandists attempted to capitalize on the unhappiness of the mercenaries and the seeming exploitation of the blood clause by naming the English-German agreements "the sale of the Hessians." In August of 1776, Congress called upon the hired troops to desert the: ". . . foreign princes who are in the habit of selling the blood of their people for money." Throughout the war, such efforts proved successful and the German desertions would be several times as great as those for the British regulars.

An elaborate system of rewards was offered for those who joined the American side. Most popular were land grants, usually on their frontier, which ranged up to 1,000 acres. One plan would have completely outfitted a deserter for farming, granting to a captain who brought in 40 men, for example, 800 acres of land, four oxen, one bull, three cows and four hogs. Other means were tried. One technique involved lavishly entertaining prisoners who were then sent back to their own forces to spread glowing tales of their treatment at the hands of the friendly rebels.

The spectre of mass desertions did not affect General John Burgoyne in the spring of 1777. Burgoyne was one of the most popular of the British generals in America. Nicknamed "Gentleman Johnny," Burgoyne had seemed destined for a brilliant career at the highest levels of the military when he was a young man. But his fortunes suffered as a result of his elopement with Lady Charlotte Stanley.

Lady Charlotte's father, the powerful Earl of Derby,

strongly resented the marriage, in effect disinherited his daughter and forced Burgoyne to resign his army commission. For several years the pair lived in virtual exile, but at the beginning of the Seven Years War, Derby and his daughter reconciled, Burgoyne returned to the army as a Lieutenant Colonel in good standing and once again began his climb upward. By the outbreak of the revolution, he had somewhat recouped his station, but was still far back in the line of command.

In an effort to recapture the status he had lost as a result of his marriage, Burgoyne returned to England during the winter of 1776–1777 to lobby for a new battle plan which held the promise of quick promotion. The scheme was accepted by the war office and soon the general was back in Canada. Burgoyne's maneuverings continued and soon Governor Guy Carleton, who formerly commanded the military in Canada, was relieved of his non-civilian duties. Burgoyne in the early summer of 1777 stood in control of the entire British army in the far north.

However, things were not proceeding as well for the Baroness. One of her problems was Harriet Van Horne Foy, the American wife of Capt. Edward Foy, a commissary who would become Adjutant General in Canada. General Riedesel had insisted that his wife travel to the colonies only if accompanied by a companion. Harriet Foy was chosen for the job, but the lady was hesitant to leave England and the gay life she was enjoying there. In late 1776, a firm sailing date had been set, but at the last moment, the reluctant Harriet succumbed to warnings of the hazardous voyage told to her by several dashing young officers. She refused to proceed.

Soon the north Atlantic was iced in and a crossing was impossible until spring. The Baroness, whose funds were rapidly being eroded by English inflation, rented a small house for the winter. One bright spot was her presentation at court where she was enthusiastically received by the German-born Queen and kissed soundly by the King. She returned to the palace several times, and finally in mid-April, sailed for Canada with her three daughters and several maids.

Also in the company was the errant Harriet Foy who spent most of the voyage socializing with the ship's captain. The Baroness was annoyed not only with her companion, but with Harriet's maid who led a "dissolute" life and stole wine from the public stores.

On June 11 the Baroness finally arrived off Québec, but here she met with a new disappointment. The Baron and his men had already gone south with Burgoyne to begin the grand plan for the conquest of America.

Basically the strategy was to crush resistance in the northern colonies by separating the British troops into three powerful striking units which would march through New York and meet at Albany. Howe would move a large force out of New York City and progress up the Hudson Valley. Lt. Col. Barry St. Leger, with a contingent including tories and Indians, would leave Montreal and go west, down the St. Lawrence and then overland east through the Mohawk Valley. Burgoyne, heading the major units of the British and German troops, would go almost due south from Montreal, down Lake Champlain and capture Fort Ticonderoga on the way to Albany.

In addition to splitting the colonies, the campaign had two other objectives. One was the capture of known patriot leaders in New York. The other was the rallying of loyalists who were known to be numerous in the area, but were hesitant to take part in the struggle without a major show of British strength.

Burgoyne moved out from St. Johns near Montreal on June 17 with approximately 9,000 Canadian, tory, British and German troops, accompanied by 500 Indian allies and a mass of camp followers. Only 300 women were listed on the official roles, but as many as 2,000 may have informally attached themselves to the party. One of the most prominent followers was Burgoyne's own mistress, the wife of a commissary. Lady Charlotte, whom Burgoyne described to Clinton as: "the truest friend, amiable companion, tenderest, best of women," had died while Gentleman Johnny was intriguing in Canada.

The general's mourning was short lived and he soon turned his attention to the desirable army wife. The Baroness disliked Burgoyne's festive life style on the march and criticized the affair severely: "In fact, Burgoyne liked having a jolly time and spending half the night singing and drinking and amusing himself in the company of the wife of a commissary who was his mistress and, like him, loved champagne."

The advancing British force initially met little resistance, but did have some trouble moving their heavy siege guns through the virgin forests of Canada. As the army approached Fort Ticonderoga, Major General Arthur St. Clair, commander of the American troops inside, gave the order to abandon the fort.

St. Clair would later be court martialed for pulling back without a struggle, but his action was an intelligent one. The British had fortified Sugar Hill, a steep rise overlooking the installation, an overlook previously considered unscalable. St. Clair's position at Fort Tie was thus made indefensible and his retreat actually saved 3,300 men, the last ragged units of the American army in the area.

When the English reached Ft. Tie, a garrison which had traditionally been viewed as the keystone in the defense of the colonies, the installation was deserted.

Farther along at Hubbardton, forward units of the British army managed to catch the rear guard of St. Clair's retreating forces. The invaders were victorious and Burgoyne's vast regiments rolled on virtually unopposed. Just two weeks after embarking, the British reached Skeensborough, a small town 150 miles from their Canadian camp, and the entrance to the Hudson Valley.

Gentleman Johnny was constantly dispatching glowing reports of his rapid progress. Lady Sarah Lennox was not impressed, but like many was fearful of the effects that his Indian allies would have on the situation. She raged to a friend:

> Was there ever such a brute as General Burgoyne, who could find time to compose his bombast nonsense, and his trumbrel, and all his nonsense, and neglect sending a return of the killed and wounded. Only think too of the horrors of employing the Indians, and allowing them to fight their own way. I am not much pleased with my friend Sr. Wm Howe neither, for tho' a most humane man himself he has not contrived to see strict discipline in his army, and I hear of horrible cruelty among them, from too good authority to doubt it.

Philip Schuyler, commander of the northern American troops, attempted to impede the invaders' progress by ordering his soldiers to obstruct the road south. Trees were felled across the path. Boulders rolled into the line of march. Bridges were destroyed. Schuyler further ordered that all fields be set afire and cattle driven away so that the British would be unable to live off of the land.

An English work force of about 200 men was sent to clear the obstructed road south so that the main body of Burgoyne's troops could advance. But near Fort Anne, the party was surprised by a force of about 500 American militia.

One of those present at the attack was Jane Cromer, the wife of a British soldier. As the battle grew fiercer, Jane and Sgt. Roger Lamb set up a temporary hospital for the wounded in a hut near the fighting. After about three hours, the rebels, who had gained the initiative, pulled back, erroneously believing that British reinforcements were progressing down the newly cleared road. The British also retreated, leaving Jane and the wounded soldiers behind.

Burgoyne changed directions as a result of the skirmish and instead of marching down the Fort Anne road, went east through Castleton. Jane and her twenty-three wounded charges waited seven days in enemy territory for relief which did not come. Finally they set out to make their own way back to Skeensborough.

By July 24, Burgoyne had entered Fort Anne, which had been burned by the retreating militia. Lt. William Digby of the Shropshire Regiment found that camping near the ruins was almost unbearable. Still on the ground were the remains of soldiers killed at the battle two weeks earlier. "We saw many of their dead unburied, since the action of the 8th, which caused a violent stench," he wrote. "One officer of the 9th regiment, Lieut. Westrop, was then unburied, and from the smell we could only cover him with leaves."

The Baroness at last caught up to her husband, but she found the free-wheeling British camp not to her liking. Secrecy was non-existent and she feared possible consequences from the open discussion of battle plans. Despite minor difficulties, the way seemed clear for the army all the way to Albany. Hundreds of American sympathizers were leaving the area. Their fears were not primarily of the excesses which could be committed by the British or Germans, but of the looting, burning and murder which they believed the Indians would cause if unleashed.

One of those who left her home was Anne Eliza Bleecker, a poet who lived eighteen miles from Albany at Tomhanick. In great haste, twenty-five-year-old Anne headed south with her four-year-old daughter and her young baby Abella. Anne would die at thirty-one, the last years of her life saddened by the tragic events of the British invasion. Her writings became mournful and although most were not concerned directly with the revolution, their pensiveness stemmed from the death of baby Abella on the 1777 forced flight.

Anne's poem: "Written on the Retreat from Burgoyne," stands as a poignant description of the trials encountered by many on the journey down the Hudson Valley. In the opening lines, the author describes her progress through the thick forests, sometimes carrying her daughters, but always filled with apprehensions of the Indians accompanying Gentleman Johnny. The loss of her home, which had earlier seemed important, paled when she suddenly realized that her youngest daughter was dying:

> Was it for this, with thee, a pleasing load,
> I sadly wandered through the hostile wood—
> When I thought Fortune's spite could do no more,
> To see thee perish on a foreign shore?
> Oh my loved babe! my treasures left behind
> Ne'er sunk a cloud of grief upon my mind;
> Rich in my children, on my arms I bore
> My living treasures from the scalper's power:
> When I sat down to rest beneath some shade,
> On the soft grass how innocent she played,
> While her sweet sister from the fragrant wild
> Collects the flowers to please my precious child,
> Unconscious of her danger, laughing roves,
> Nor dreads the painted savages in the groves!
>
> What thought my houses, lands, and goods are gone,
> By babes remain—these I can call my own!

But soon my loved Abella hung her head—
From her soft cheek the bright carnation fled;
Her smooth transparent skin too plainly showed
How fierce through every vein the fever glowed.

Desperation such as Anne Bleecker's mounted in the area and the morale of the American army continued to drop as the British war machine ground forward. Local volunteers were few and the leaders of the continental troops found it almost impossible to mount any type of counter-offensive. On July 27, however, the death of a tory woman inflamed both whigs and loyalists. The tide rapidly turned away from Burgoyne.

The woman was Jane McCrea, daughter of a New Jersey minister and the fiancee of David Jones, a loyalist officer with the invading troops. For several years, Jane had lived with her brother near Saratoga, but on June 11, she received a message from Jones, asking her to go to Fort Edward to await the army's arrival.

Jane complied and moved north to live temporarily with Sarah Fraser McNeil, a distant relative of General Simon Fraser who led the British advance guard.

On July 27, Mrs. McNeil, her daughter and Jane were surprised and taken prisoner by Indians attached to the British troops. The scouts, not realizing that their prisoners were friends to Burgoyne's cause, intended to take the women back to camp for a reward. On the way an argument broke out among the Indians concerning exactly who would receive the prize for the capture. Reportedly, in order to settle the disagreement, a Wyandot Indian named Panther tomahawked Jane and took her scalp as evidence for his claim. According to Albert Baker, who claimed to be a witness, the war party then stripped the girl's remains, taking her clothes as loot, and rolled her body into a hidden ravine.

Within hours of the incident, news of the murder was spreading throughout New York. Local rage increased when Panther was pardoned by the British commander. Whigs, fearing that enemy victories on the battlefield would expose their own families to similar dangers, rushed to volunteer for duty with the American troops.

Many tories felt that if the loyalist fiancee of a British officer was not safe from slaughter, then their own people in outlying communities were obviously helpless, for frontier raiders seldom inquired about the political beliefs of their victims. The incident undoubtedly lost to the British hundreds of tories who might have joined the King's cause.

Realizing the potential propaganda effect of the murder, General Horatio Gates, who had replaced Schuyler, quickly moved in to make Jane into a martyr. In his protest to Burgoyne, "Granny" Gates described the murdered girl as: ". . . a young lady lovely to the sight, of virtuous character and amiable disposition. . . ." Gates further pursued the matter in emotional terms calculated to increase the anger of local citizens:

> That the savages of America should in their warfare mangle and scalp the unhappy prisoners who fall into their hands, is neither new nor extraordinary; but that the famous Lieutenant General Burgoyne . . . should hire the savages of America to scalp Europeans and the descendants of Europpeans, nay more, that he should pay a price for each scalp so barbarously taken, is more than will be believed in Europe, untill authenticated facts shall, in every Gazette, convince mankind of the horrid fate.

Ironically, the name of Jane McCrea, the tory girl friend of a British soldier, became the war cry of the growing militia units. In later skirmishes, Bourgoyne's men would be met by Americans yelling her name as they charged into battle. The British general, however, remained fearful of losing Indian support if he punished Panther, and refused to retaliate even in the face of mounting criticism from loyalists.

He did gently censor his red allies and prohibited them from taking scalps in similar situations. Even this slight rebuke backfired, for many of the braves from western tribes returned home while others deserted to make their own private war on New York's settlers. One factor complicating Burgoyne's control of the Indians was that many of his volunteers were from tribes such as the Fox, Sioux, Winnebago and Sauk, residents from territory beyond the British "frontier" who did not acknowledge past al-

*Death of Jane McCrea*, painting by John Vanderlyn. Courtesy
of the Wadsworth Atheneum, Hartford.

legiances such as those developed by Sir William Johnson with
the Iroquois.

Burgoyne did attempt to answer Gates' charge, but his reply
was vague, for he suggested that he had been "convinced by circumstances and observation," that it would be "more efficacious"
to take no action against Panther. Burgoyne possibly feared that
retribution against the slayer would cause such strong resentments among the Indians, that they would take massive retaliation
against the outlying communities of the area, both rebel and loyalist alike. He had earlier sought to protect the helpless by announcing at a great parlay held on the Bouquet River on June
23: "Aged men, women, children and prisoners must be held sa-

cred from the knife or hatchet, even in the time of actual conflict." He continued: "You shall receive compensation for the prisoners you take, but you shall be called to account for scalps."

Sgt. Lamb, who had returned to the army after his nursing stint with Jane Cromer, agreed with Burgoyne's decision. In his journal, Lamb insisted:

> Had the execution [of Panther] taken place, there is every probability that the Indians would have retired from the army, massacring every body and destroying every thing before them; thus it would have caused the destruction of hundreds of innocent inhabitants of the frontiers of Canada, if the assassin had been then put to death.

The personal implications of Jane's murder were lost in the larger political ramifications, but according to one report, Jones and his brother deserted Burgoyne's army, and after retrieving Jane's scalp, the pair went north to settle in the Canadian wilderness.

Burgoyne's fortunes continued to deteriorate. On August 3rd, he finally received a communication from Howe and the news was bad. Instead of confirming that he had begun to march toward Albany, Howe wrote that he was sailing for Philadelphia. Only a small protective force under Clinton was being left in Manhattan and no plans had been made to send troops northward. To Burgoyne, the news meant that Washington's army, as well as the growing forces under Gates, would be stationed between the two major British forces. In case of emergency, little help could be expected from the south.

A second blow came two weeks later when the general sent a large force into the new republic of Vermont. Their objective was to seize vitally needed supplies, but near Bennington, John Stark and 2,000 volunteers and rebel militia routed the foraging contingent.

Not only were the food and supplies expected to be gathered by the expedition lost, but more than 200 men had been killed and 700 taken prisoner by the Americans. Burgoyne's army had now dwindled to about 6,000, but hope was still high that the troops could reach Albany and find reinforcements from St. Leger.

The days following the Battle of Bennington were happy ones for the Baroness, if not for Burgoyne who was feverishly seeking ways to resupply his train. General Riedesel spent much of his time with his family, and although food was scarce, the Baroness was satisfied:

> We were very happy during these three weeks! The country there was lovely, and we were in the midst of the camps of the English and the German troops. The place where we lived was called the Red House. I had only one room for my husband, myself, and my children, in which all of us slept, and a tiny study. My maids slept in a sort of hall. When the weather was good we had our meals out under the trees, otherwise we had them in the barn, laying boards across barrels for tables. It was here that I ate bear meat for the first time, and it tasted very good to me. Sometimes we had nothing at all; but in spite of everything, I was very happy and satisfied, for I was with my children and was beloved by all about me.

On September 3rd, the final blow came. Word arrived that St. Leger had turned back. The report was a complete surprise, for no difficulties had been reported during the early part of the march. St. Leger with his 875 soldiers and 1,000 Indians under Joseph Brant had quickly progressed to Ft. Stanwix, and the installation was put under siege.

But problems developed when 800 Americans and 60 Oneida scouts approached under the command of Nicholas Herkimer. A party of St. Leger's legion ambushed the oncoming Americans at Oriskany, but the battle was not a clear victory for either side. As it raged, American troops stole out of Ft. Stanwix and raided the British camp, stealing most of the maps and supplies.

The siege was continued under less favorable circumstances until a loyalist informant brought news that Benedict Arnold was approaching with a gigantic force. Actually, Arnold's troops numbered only about 500, but the tory, a double agent for the Americans, had grossly overestimated the figure. Running short on supplies and deserted by his Indian allies, St. Leger could not continue. He began to retreat back to Canada.

Many British and German officers were growing vehement in denouncing Indians as effective elements in battle. Although the braves were helpful in small frontier raids, army regulars considered most to be cowardly in open warfare. Mary Jemison, the "White Woman of the Genessee," saw a different picture.

Mary had been captured in 1755 by a Shawnee raiding party on the Pennsylvania frontier. At the time she was about thirteen years old. Soon after, she was taken to a Seneca village about eighty miles from Pittsburgh and ultimately was adopted into an Indian family, taking the place of a brave who had been killed in battle.

Adoption was a common alternative to torture or death. At one time, two-thirds of the Oneida tribe were actually Indians or whites who had been captured and adopted. The companions of a red man killed in battle usually tried to bring back prisoners as compensation for his grieving relatives. In most tribes, the surviving family decided the fate of those who were captured. Some were set free. Some tortured. If the hostage had been responsible for the Indian's death, he was usually killed.

But if the family chose adoption, the captive was treated as an equal member of the family. No discrimination was lodged against the newcomer who took the place of the dead Indian.

Mary would live most of her life as an Indian, recounting her experiences years later when contact between settlers and Indians became less violent. Her accounts of the revolution are unique, for they show the conflict as it appeared to a woman who knew intimately both the whig and Indian cultures.

According to Mary, when the war erupted British representatives were sent into her village seeking allies. They boasted that the King's run was as plentiful as the waters of Lake Ontario and his men as numerous as the sands on the shores. If the tribe helped to destroy the whigs, the crown recruiter promised, never again would the red people want for food, land or any other thing.

Many braves agreed to join and the representative outfitted each of the new recruits with a suit of clothing, a brass kettle, a

gun, powder and lead, a tomahawk, a scalping knife and a piece
of gold. Some were evidently undecided or reluctant to actually
take to the field when their help was requested, so the British
again used guile. Mary described the events which led the men of
her village to follow the British to Ft. Stanwix:

> Previous to the Battle of Ft. Stanwix, the British sent for
> the Indians to come and see them whip the rebels; and at the
> same time stated that they did not wish to have them fight,
> but wanted to have them just sit down, smoke their pipes
> and look on. Our Indians went, to a man; but contrary to
> their expectations, instead of smoking and looking on, they
> were obliged to fight for their lives, and in the end of the
> battle were completely beaten, with a great loss in killed and
> wounded. Our Indians alone had thirty six killed, and a
> great number wounded, Our town exhibited a scene of real
> sorrow and distress, when our warriors returned, recounted
> their misfortunes, and stated the real loss they had sustained
> in the engagement. The mourning was excessive, and was
> expressed by the most doleful yells, shrieks, and howlings,
> and by inimitable gesticulations.

Despite the fiasco at Ft. Stanwix, Burgoyne continued to
press ahead. Unknown to him, Clinton had been reinforced with
fresh troops from Europe and already was moving northward
from Manhattan. His plan was to follow the original British blue-
print, by progressing up the Hudson until he met with Burgoyne
at Albany.

Gentleman Johnny, his army reduced by nearly one-third,
moved out of camp intending to forage along the route. He made
slow progress southward. By mid-September, he reached the
country home of Philip Schuyler near Saratoga. Catherine Rensselaer Schuyler, the general's wife, tried to burn her fields so that
the British could not reap the corn and grain ready to be harvested. She succeeded in destroying only about one-fourth of the
crop before the English arrived and saved the remainder for their
own use.

The Americans were not idle. Volunteers continued to pour
into camp following the victory at Bennington and the defeat of
St. Leger. In addition, the murder of Jane McCrea was still

prompting enlistments. For the first time in the campaign, American troops outnumbered the British. The continentals elected to make a firm stand and began digging in north of Albany at Bemis Heights.

As part of their defense, Daniel Morgan's raiders were sent into the countryside to harrass scouting parties of the enemy. His men were not alone, for also roving about the area were Indians who had deserted Burgoyne. These braves were attacking not only country settlers, but British deserters or wounded who had left the main force.

On September 19, elements of the two armies met at Freeman's farm in an all day battle. The Americans finally retreated, but it was not a Burgoyne victory. Of the 1,300 British forces which took part in the action, about 600 became casualties or prisoners.

Burgoyne at last received word that Clinton was coming to the rescue. The relief force was moving slowly northward, burning and looting the homes of whigs along the way.

One victim of the column was Margaret Beekman Livingston, the matriarch of a powerful clan whose family headquarters was Clermont, a mansion on the Hudson. Margaret had privately inherited 240,000 acres from her own family and when her husband died during the first year of the war, she assumed his place as ruler of the dynasty with even greater financial holdings.

The Livingstons had exerted enormous influence on the revolution. Margaret's son Robert was a Congressional delegate, five members of the family had served on the attack at Québec and at least seven were gathering for the battle at Saratoga. Three of Margaret's daughters married military generals; the most famous was a liaison between daughter Janet and General Richard Montgomery, the hero of Montreal. Gertrude Livingston married Morgan Lewis, the future governor of New York and the son of a signer of the Declaration of Independence. Young Lewis was nearby as Clinton approached Clermont, for he was serving as General Gates' chief of staff at Saratoga. Generations later, another Livingston descendant, Eleanor Roosevelt, would become prominent by marrying a president.

Margaret Beekman, known as "the old lady" strongly

*Lady Ackland's Visit to the Camp of General Gates,* engraving after a painting by Alonzo Chappel. Photo courtesy of the Library of Congress.

supported the American war and paid a high price for her allegiance. The great house Clermont was burned by Clinton's men, but Margaret refused to leave the ruins. Instead, she continued on the estate, living in a hastily built cottage until the conflict could be settled and another manor house constructed.

Both Burgoyne and Gates remained quiet until October 7, when they met at the Battle of Saratoga. The Baroness had planned a dinner party for that evening, with Generals Burgoyne and Fraser as her special guests. Instead, Fraser was carried into her house that afternoon, a wounded victim of the battle. Doctors used the Riedesel cabin as a hospital in a desperate attempt to save the soldier, but the efforts were unsuccessful. His physician explained that because the general had eaten a large breakfast, the penetrating rifle ball passed directly through the expanded intestines. If Fraser has abstained at the table, it perhaps would have gone between them, causing less damage. Fraser died of his wounds and was buried the following day on the Saratoga battlefield. According to some reports, the Americans, not knowing that a funeral was in progress, shelled the attending group throughout the service.

The battle was also devastating to Lady Christian Harriot Acland, a friend of Lady Sarah Lennox and the wife of Major John Dyke Acland, a member of Parliament. Lady Harriot had left Montreal after the skirmish at Hubbardton to nurse her husband who was wounded in the foray. After his recovery she remained with the army, often travelling with the Baroness.

The journey had not been simple for the high-bred daughter of the Earl of Ilchester. At one point, the Acland tent caught fire in the middle of the night and she reached safety only after crawling under the edge of the canvas. On October 7th, Harriot received more troublesome news. The Baroness was there:

> Lady Acland had a tent not far from our house; she slept there at night and spent the day in camp. Suddenly a messenger came to tell her that her husband had been mortally wounded and taken prisoner. She was deeply saddened. We tried to comfort her by telling her that the wound was only a light one, and urged her to go to him, as she would surely be permitted to do, in order that he be better nursed. She loved him dearly, although he was a rough fellow who was drunk almost every day, but nevertheless, a brave officer.

Lady Harriot took the Baroness' advice and requested permission from Burgoyne to leave the army camp and head for the American lines. Burgoyne was not enthusiastic about her chances of completing the trip and noted that he had little help to give her:

> After so long an agitation of the spirits, exhausted not only for want of rest, but, absolutely want of food, drenched in rain, for twelve hours together, that a woman should be capable of delivering herself to the enemy, probably in the

night and uncertain into what hands she might fall, appeared an effort above human nature. The assistance I was enabled to give, was small indeed; I had not even a cup of wine to offer her, but I was told, she had found from some kind and fortunate hand a little rum and dirty water. All I could furnish to her, was an open boat and a few lines written on dirty and wet paper to General Gates, recommending her to his protection. . . .

Harriot set out under a flag of truce for the enemy lines, accompanied by her maid and her husband's valet. She was received unharmed by Gates and taken to her husband. John Acland recovered from his battle wounds, but soon died from other causes. Some said he met his death in a duel, others insisted that he fell and hit his head on a pebble.

After the British defeat at Saratoga, Burgoyne ordered a retreat. The wounded were to be left behind with a note requesting that Gates see to their care. Frederika von Riedesel, growing increasingly dissatisfied with the British leadership, was beset with new difficulties as the army secretly slipped away:

> We had been warned to keep extremely quiet, fires were left burning everywhere, and many tents were left standing, so that the enemy would think the camp was still there. Thus we drove on all through the night. Little Frederika, was very much frightened, often starting to cry, and I had to hold my handkerchief over her mouth to prevent our being discovered.
>
> We spent the whole of the 9th in a terrible rainstorm, ready to march on a moment's notice. The savages had lost courage, and everywhere they were seen retreating. The slightest setback makes cowards of them, expecially if they see no chance of plundering. My maid did nothing but bemoan her plight and tear her hair. I begged her to quiet herself, as otherwise she would be taken for a savage.

Conditions became harsher, food was rationed. Loyalists like Mary Swords, who owned a farm in the valley, donated food to the army, but the supply was inadequate. On October 10, the troops again halted near the Schuyler house with Gates in pursuit. Burgoyne ordered the mansion burned, presumably because it interfered with his artillery's line of fire.

That night, the battle broke out again. The Baroness along with other camp followers and the wounded, huddled in the cellar of a farmhouse. As the highest ranking army wife, she took charge as conditions became more crowded and unsanitary. Frederika ordered the basement disinfected with vinegar and when water ran low, arranged for a camp woman to brave the enemy fire to bring more. While the ladies crowded together below, the upstairs of the house was used as a hospital. The Americans did not spare this shelter of sick and wounded, according to the Baroness' narrative:

> Eleven cannon balls flew through the house, and we could distinctly hear them rolling about over our heads. One of the poor soldiers who lay on a table, and was about to have his leg amputated, had the other leg shot off by one of these balls. His comrades had run away from him, and when they returned they found him scarcely breathing, lying in a corner of the room, where he had rolled himself in agony.

The battle continued to rage but soon the British army was almost completely surrounded. Their position was hopeless and Gates demanded their surrender. Burgoyne attempted to delay negotiations, hoping that Clinton would arrive in time to launch a rescue attempt, but unknown to both commanders at Saratoga, Clinton had halted his forward march and turned back toward Manhattan. Finally Gates' patience ended and on October 17, Burgoyne capitulated in a strange agreement called a "Convention," not a surrender.

Under the agreement, the 5,725 men of the defeated forces were not considered prisoners of war. Officers were allowed to keep their side arms and Gates agreed that the entire group would not be interned until the end of the war, but would be sent home as soon as possible. The only restraining stipulation was that the men would pledge to take no further part in the revolutionary fighting.

On "Convention Day," the camp follower who, at the Baroness' instigation had passed through the American fire to bring water to the farmhouse hospital, received her reward. As she stood with her apron held out, about twenty guineas were tossed into it by appreciative soldiers and camp women.

Burgoyne, who days before had ordered the Schuylers' country house destroyed, was taken to be quartered in the family's town house. The stay was short, for soon the entire force, together with a token guard under the command of John Glover, was on its way to Boston.

Unlike Glover's efficient amphibious operations at Long Island and Trenton, the march to Boston was completely unorganized. The general spent much of his time socializing with the captured British officers, and the German troops were left to fend for themselves in the strange country. Often the men went for days without adequate food and were forced to sleep in open fields covered with snow. There were few blankets and tents, and local residents stole many of the captives' horses.

For the Baroness, the going was easier, but was still not pleasant. All along the way, citizens turned out to heckle the wife of the German general. She was quartered in shacks or farmhouses where few niceties were available and her hostesses often vented their hatred of the war upon her. When the army at last neared Boston, the situation was not greatly improved. She wrote:

> We were put up at a farmer's house, where we were given only one room in the attic. My maids slept on the floor and the men in the hall. Some straw on which I had spread our bedding was all we had for a long while on which to sleep, since I had nothing other than my field bed. Our host allowed us to eat downstairs in his room, where the whole family ate and slept together. The man was good, but his wife in revenge for the bother we caused her, deliberately chose to vex us during our mealtime by combing her children's hair, which was full of vermin, often making us lose every bit of appetite, and when we asked her to do her combing outside, or at some other time, she replied, "It is my room; I see fit to stay and to comb my children now." We had to hold our silence, for otherwise she might have turned us out of the house.

Hannah Winthrop saw the main body of Convention troops march into Cambridge and was astounded at their unkempt appearance. In a letter to Mercy Warren, Hannah described the scene when the once impeccable British and German soldiers marched through with their women:

> To be sure the sight was truely astonishing. I never had the least Idea that the Creation produced such a sordid set of creatures in human Figure—poor, dirty, emaciated men, great numbers of women, who seemed to be the beasts of burden, having a bushel basket on their back, by which they were bent double, the contents seemed to be Pots and Kettles, various sorts of Furniture, children peeping thro' gridirons and other utensils, some very young Infants who were born on the road, the women bear feet, cloathed in dirty rags, such effuvia filld the air while they were passing, had they not been smoking all the time, I should have been apprehensive of being contaminated by them.

But farther to the south, Sir William Howe, whose failure to link up with Burgoyne had helped to doom the northern expedition, was in far better circumstances. Howe had sailed from New York for the Chesapeake in an attempt to engage Washington in a major battle and score an important coup by occupying the rebel capital.

After a success at Brandywine where 700 Americans were killed or taken prisoner, Howe continued on toward Philadelphia. When Wilmington fell, alarmed residents in the Pennsylvania metropolis began to panic. The Congress, which had returned from Baltimore, fled again. Philadelphians with strong whig leanings began pouring out of the city.

Little confidence was placed in the ability of the tattered continentals to hold back the British. The rebel supply position was disastrous. As many as 1,000 of Washington's men had no shoes. Many lacked blankets, a situation which probably stemmed from Brandywine where rebel soldiers left their packs on the field. Replacements were unavailable from the public stores, so Washington sent Alexander Hamilton into Philadelphia to beg donations from the residents.

Elizabeth Drinker, a well-educated Quaker living in Philadelphia, noted the increasing bustle in the streets on September
23. The British were just two days from the city at the time she
observed:

> Those men that collected Blankets, &c., in our ward,
> were this afternoon at each of our neighbors, but did not
> call upon us. It is reported, and gains credit, that ye English
> have actually crossed the Schuylkill, and are on their way
> towards us.
>
> Many have had their Horses taken from them this after-
> noon; some going one way, and some another. It is likely
> from ye present prospect of things that we shall have a noisy
> night, tho' at this time, (9 o'clock), I hear nothing like it, but
> we, living back and retired, escape many hurries that others
> are exposed to. All ye Bells in ye city are Certainly taken
> away, and there is talk of Pump handles and Fire-Buckets
> being taken also—but that may be only Conjecture. Things
> seem to be, upon ye whole, drawing towards great confu-
> sion.

Fifteen miles away, Sally Wister also saw the panic and
began to keep a diary of events as they occurred around her.
Sally, the sixteen-year-old daughter of a Philadelphia merchant,
had moved from the city, but planned to return if the British were
defeated. The opportunity did not come, for the American army
continued to retreat. Sally described the scene:

> Yesterday, which was the 24th of September, two Vir-
> ginia officers call'd at our house, and informed us that the
> British Army had cross'd the Schuylkill. Presently after, an-
> other person stopp'd, and confirmed what they had said . . .
> thee may be sure we were sufficiently scared; however, the
> road was very still till evening.
>
> About seven o'clock we heard a great noise. To the
> door we all went. A large number of waggons, with about
> three hundred of the Philadelphia Militia. They begged for
> drink, and several push'd into the house. One of those that
> entered was a little tipsy, and had a mind to be saucy.

I then thought it time for me to retreat; so I figured me (mightly scar'd as not having presence of mind enough to face so many of the military), running in at one door, and out another, all in a shake with fear; but after a while, seeing the officers appear gentlemanly, and the soldiers civil, I call'd reason to my aid. My fears were in some measure dispell'd, tho' my teeth rattled and my hand shook like an aspen leaf.

Some elements of the British army entered Philadelphia that day, but others halted at nearby Germantown. On October 4, the Americans turned back to attack the village. The plan was dependent upon an attack by General Sullivan on the right and by Greene on the left, but fog disrupted the scheme. Greene lost his way and was delayed. When he at last reached the battlefield, American forces began firing upon one another in confusion and the day was lost.

Again Howe declined to follow the retreating army into the countryside and instead retired to Philadelphia to await supplies being brought by his brother's vessels. Admiral Lord Howe's fleet was having difficulties in breaking through rebel installations guarding the Delaware River. Forts along the banks were holding strong and blocking any advancement into the city by water.

But on the land, the continentals continued moving about in haste. Sally noted the action near her house as the rebels took up new positions:

As I was lying in bed . . . Liddy came running into the room, and said there was the greatest drumming, fifing, and rattling of waggons that she had heard. What to make of this we were at a loss. We dress'd and down stairs in a hurry. Our wonder ceas'd.

. . . Sister Betsy and myself, and G.E., went about half a mile from home, where we cou'd see the army pass. Thee will stare at my going, but no impropriety in my opine, or I wou'd not have gone. We made no great stay, but return'd with excellent appetites for our breakfast.

Several officers call'd to get some refreshment, but none of consequence till the afternoon. Cousin Prissa and myself were sitting at the door; I in a green skirt, dark short gown,

&c., Two genteel men of the military order rode up to the door: "Your servant, Ladies" &c., ask'd if they could have quarters for Gen'l Smallwood. Aunt Foulke thought she could accommodate them as well as most of her neighbors—said they could. One of the officers dismounted, and wrote SMALLWOODS QUARTERS over the door, which secured us from straggling soldiers. . . . In the evening his Generalship came with six attendants, which compos'd his family, a large guard of soldiers, a number of horses and baggage-waggons. The yard and house were in confusion, and glitter'd with military equipment. . . .

How new is our situation! I feel in good spirits, though surrounded by an army, the house full of officers, the yard alive with soldiers—very peaceable sort of men, tho!. They eat like other folks, talk like them, and behave themselves with elegance; so I will not be afraid of them, that I won't.

Rather than fear, Sally developed an attachment for the soldiers. She had a brief flirtaion with a Major William Stoddert and formed a set of opinions on many of the men. "Finley is wretched ugly," she commented. "Furnival is most agreeable; but he chats every opportunity; but luckily has a wife!" Like many teenagers, real romance was her ultimate objective: "When will Sally's admirers appear? Ah! That indeed. Why Sally has not charms sufficient to pierce the heart of a soldier. But still I won't dispair. Who knows what mischief I yet may do?"

Unfortunately for her romantic aspirations, Sally had little time in which to work. The troops marched out again on November 1, and the young girl found her neighborhood strangely silent.

Things were not as quiet for Elizabeth Graeme Ferguson, a wealthy heiress living at Graeme Park, her estate near Philadelphia.

In the fall of 1777, Elizabeth had divided loyalties relating to the war. Several years earlier after an unhappy love affair with William Franklin, she secretly married Henry Hugh Ferguson, a penniless Scotsman. When the war broke out, Ferguson became an ardent tory and joined the British. Under Howe he became

*Elizabeth Graeme Ferguson,* artist unknown. Courtesy of The Historical Society of Pennsylvania.

influential and was appointed commissary of prisoners when the army moved into Philadelphia.

Yet Elizabeth had strong ties to the Americans and sympathized with their goals. Before the English occupation of the capital she entertained "Mad" Anthony Wayne, and later wrote to him: "I wish the general cause of America most sincerely well. . . ." Among her closest friends were Annis Stockton and her daughter Julia Rush, both wives of prominent whigs, and many leaders of the revolution.

On October 15, Elizabeth journeyed to the American camp and requested an interview with General Washington. Within days, her name had been permanently discredited and she was considered by some to be guilty of treason. The reason was the widespread publication of a letter written by Washington to Congress which described her visit. The communique revealed:

> I yesterday, thro the hands of Mrs. Ferguson of Graham Park, received a letter of a very curious and extraordinary nature from Mr. Duché, which I have thought proper to transmit to Congress. To this ridiculous—illiberal perfor-

mance I made a short reply, by desiring the bearer of it, if she should hereafter by any accident meet with Mr. Duché, to tell him, I should have returned it unopened If I had had any idea of the contents; observing at the same time, that I highly disapproved the intercourse she seemed to have been carrying on, and expected it would be discontinued.

The note, carried to Washington by Elizabeth, had been written by the Reverent Jacob Duché, a man suspect by both armies. As Rector of Christ Church and St. Peter's in Philadelphia, Duché had been appointed the first Chaplain of Congress. John Hancock had personally notified Duché of the honor, writing that the minister had been selected because of his "piety" and "zealous attachment to the rights of America."

Duché's enthusiasm dulled as the rebels met defeat in the field, and he quickly resigned from the post, claiming ill health and pressing church duties. He requested that the $150 he had earned by his short services to Congress, should be used for the relief of widows and orphans of Pennyslvania soldiers killed in action.

When the British occupied Philadelphia, Duché was arrested, but almost immediately released as a true friend to the King. According to Washington, the letter delivered by Elizabeth, was written in an attempt to even further erode any suspicions which Howe may have held concerning the minister's loyalty.

Duché's famous letter informed Washington that the original leaders of the revolution had been replaced by an uncontrolled rabble and that the Americans had no hope of victory. The former chaplain then requested that the general plead with Congress to surrender, and if the request was refused, then Washington should personally negotiate with the British to end the resistance.

Such letters were not unknown during the war. Even more overt bribery attempts were made to Generals Putnam, Sullivan, Schuyler and Allen. In Paris, similar proposals were put forth to Franklin and Silas Deane. But the Duché letter created a significant stir because it involved the commander-in-chief, a prominent clergyman and a wealthy woman.

As a result of the ensuing controversy, Duché broke all ties to America by sailing for England and leaving Elizabeth to carry on her own defense. Later, when applying for a British pension, he swore that his services to Congress as Chaplain involved no more than reading prayers. In addition, he claimed, he did not believe that the group was actually serious about declaring independence.

Elizabeth, however, soon became involved in a new scheme to end the war, one which would make her even more suspect. The mistress of Graeme Park probably continued her peace ventures not because of any attachment to the British cause, but out of a basic dislike for the violence of war. She may have viewed her approaches to rebel leaders as obligations undertaken solely to end the bloodshed.

For several years, Elizabeth had produced mournful, pensive poetry and by the revolution, had achieved some literary prominence for her translation of Fénélon's "Techemachus." Thus she could have thought that her reputation and wealth would be influential in helping to promote peace.

Elizabeth's new peace plan was developed after the arrival in Philadelphia of George Johnstone, a former governor of Florida who had been sent as a peace commissioner by the British. Despite her earlier experience with Washington, Elizabeth agreed to serve once again as an intermediary between the English and the revolutionaries. This time the mission involved a blatant attempt to bribe her friend, General Joseph Reed.

Elizabeth's relationship with Johnstone probably stemmed from two connections. The commissioner's headquarters was in the home of Elizabeth's kinsman Charles Stedman. In addition, Johnstone's secretary was Adam Ferguson, a relative of her husband.

Even before the furor caused by the Washington mission had quieted, Elizabeth visited Reed, passing along a message that if he used his influence to stop the war, then he would be rewarded with 10,000 guineas and a high post in the government which Britain would establish in the defeated colonies. Reed refused to consider the proposition, but kept Elizabeth's visit secret, evidently in an attempt to protect her already tarnished reputation.

However, Congressman Francis Dana soon publicly announced that Johnstone had made unethical proposals to him, and Robert Morris reported that he too had received a letter from Johnstone which promised that: ". . . honor and emoluments should naturally follow the fortune of those who have steered the vessel in the storm and brought her safely to port."

Although Elizabeth played no overt part in the two additional bribery attempts, she may have had a hand in the composition of Morris' note. One of her earlier poems featured a similar theme concerning a captain and his vessel in times of distress:

> Why mourn the dead? You wrong the grave—
> From storm that safe retreat;
> We are still tossing out at sea—
> Our Admiral in port!

With Morris' announcement, Reed was forced to make public Johnstone's advances via Elizabeth. The angered Congress immediately reacted against the British commissioner by adopting a resolution denouncing the letters and his meetings with an unidentified lady as: ". . . direct attempts to corrupt and bribe the Congress of the United States of America." Most Pennsylvanians knew that the "unidentified lady" was actually Elizabeth Ferguson. Soon they would act against her.

Like Duché, Henry Ferguson left Philadelphia in the midst of the controversy. His prominent activities on behalf of the British had made him a target for rebel wrath. Elizabeth was once again left alone, this time to face the consequences of not only her own ill-advised acts, but also the results of Henry's collaboration with the enemy.

Benjamin Rush offered her moral support, suggesting that a peace with Britain would surely include pardons for loyalists such as Ferguson. Even more important, Rush offered his good offices in case the state chose to take formal retribution against her vast estate: "Can I serve you in diverting the attention of the legislature or Council of Pennsylvania to your property if any-

thing is intended against it?" he wrote. "Most of the gentlemen
of the Council are of my acquaintance."

Rush's help was indeed needed, for the state council issued
confiscation orders against the Ferguson estate. Ironically, almost
all of the attained property had been inherited by Elizabeth from
her wealthy father, but upon her marriage, ownership of the legacy passed to her husband. Thus all property was considered his,
and liable to confiscation because of his unwarranted acts.

In an attempt to save at least a part of her estate, Elizabeth
wrote a defense of her actions. To Reed, she suggested that the
prospect of appearing as a fool was not comforting, but she was
willing to assume the role out of necessity:

> I own I find it hard. . . . knowing the uncorruptness of
> my heart, to be held out to the public as a tool to the com-
> missioners. But the impression is now made, and it is too late
> to recall it. How far, at this critical juncture of time, this af-
> fair may injure my property, is uncertain; that, I assure you,
> is not a secondary thought.

Additional influential friends intervened in the action. Elias
Boudinot, John Dickinson and Robert Morris all spoke in her behalf and through their efforts, a portion of the property was finally exempted from confiscation. The state assembly, convinced
that Elizabeth had been innocently duped into the missions,
passed a resolution noting: "The said Elizabeth appears to have
acted a friendly part to the cause of the United States and to be
in such a peculiar situation as to deserve the protection and in-
dulgence of this commonwealth."

After the war, Elizabeth would live peaceably at Graeme
Park, a semi-invalid, quietly reworking her translations. She
would never again see her loyalist husband.

By December, the Ferguson affair had temporarily calmed.
The armies had remained in their own areas for more than a
month, and it appeared that the winter would be an inactive one.
But Elias Boudinot, chief of Washington's spy ring in the area,
soon knew differently. Boudinot had been reconnoitering the
lines near Philadelphia and had decided to stop for a meal at the

Rising Sun Tavern, a popular meeting place for spies. Here he received some unexpected information:

> . . . After Dinner a little poor looking insignificant Old
> Woman came in & solicited leave to go into the Country to
> buy some flour—While we were asking some Questions,
> she walked up to me and put into my hands a dirty old nee-
> dlebook, with various small pockets in it. Surprised at this, I
> told her to return, she should have an answer—On Open-
> ing the needlebook, I could not find any thing till I got to
> the last Pocket, Where I found a piece of Paper rolled up
> into the form of a Pipe Shank.—On unrolling it I found
> information that Genl Howe was coming out the next morn-
> ing with 5000 men—13 pieces of Cannon-Baggage Wag-
> gons and 11 Boats on Waggon Wheels.

Boudinot had just received a secret message sent by Lydia Darragh of Philadelphia. Lydia was not one of Boudinot's paid informants, but a mortician by trade. The enterprising woman had probably begun her professional career in the city about 1766, when an advertisement under her name appeared in the *Pennsylvania Gazette* announcing:

> The subscriber, living in Second Street, at the corner of
> Taylor's Alley, opposite the Golden Fleece Tavern, takes
> this method of informing the Public that she intends to make
> Grave-Clothes, and lay out the Dead, in the Neatest
> Manner, and as she is informed a Person in this Business is
> much wanted in this City, she hopes, by her Care, to give
> Satisfaction to those who will be pleased to favour her with
> their Orders.

By the time of Howe's occupation, the Darragh family lived in one of the city's best neighborhoods, across the street from the general's headquarters. Although American forces supposedly maintained at least three women spies in the city, Lydia's operation was strictly a family affair.

According to some tales, the mortician had worked out a dramatic, but complicated manner in which to pass along intelligence to the rebels. First she gathered the information. Then her husband William copied it into code on tiny pieces of paper which were then concealed behind buttons on a coat belonging to their fourteen-year-old son John. The boy would then leave the city on some errand, and make his way to the American camp where he would pass the buttons on to his brother Charles, an officer of the rebel line.

Lydia did not have to go far for her intelligence, because part of the Darragh house had been commandeered by the British as a conference hall. Although there was some risk to the English in this loose arrangement, the Darraghs were well-known Quakers who seemingly abided by their sect's policy of strict neutrality, despite their older son's enlistment.

On December 2, the British high command held a late night meeting, long after the Darraghs had retired to their private rooms. Lydia seized the opportunity to eavesdrop on the conference and overheard Howe's plan to leave the city. The unexpected move was planned to surprise Washington's forces, similarly to the American attack a year earlier at Trenton.

Almost immediately the mortician sprang into action, but the complicated code-button arrangement was not to be used in delivering this urgent warning. Instead, the following morning, Lydia requested a pass from the British allowing her to leave the city so that she could fetch flour from a mill about five miles away at Frankford. Here she left her sack and continued on foot to deliver the message.

Lydia probably did not complete the journey all the way to the Rising Sun Tavern, for the description given by Boudinot little resembles the Quaker who was not a "poor looking insignificant Old Woman." Rather, the amateur spy had probably passed her information along to some local female so that she herself could hurry back into the city and arouse no suspicions. If she felt that in the future she could provide other intelligence, Lydia probably would not risk being identified at the Tavern by British sympathizers.

By some accounts, Washington had earlier received information from another woman spy detailing British strength and recommending an immediate attack on the capital. This plan was rejected, but the general acted quickly after receiving Lydia's more valuable message. American troops were moved out to take defensive positions near White Marsh. When the redcoats marched out, expecting to surprise the continentals in camp, they found instead that an almost impregnable defense had beeen set up. For three days, the English maneuvered, attempting to find a weakness in the American lines. Finding none, the attackers returned to Philadelphia, and settled in for the winter. Meanwhile, Washington made his way to Valley Forge.

Lydia was taken for questioning by the British, after the results at White Marsh proved that the rebels had received prior warning of Howe's plans. She was released, however, because of lack of evidence. Lydia and her son Charles were later expelled from the Quaker meeting, he for participating in actions of a "warlike" nature, and she for poor attendance at church meetings. But Lydia's activities would prove more militant than her son's, for her participation in the arena of spying helped to preserve the American troops for six additional years of war.

Philadelphia during the winter of 1777–1778 was a festive sanctuary for the crown's forces. The young ladies of the capital quickly shifted their allegiances to the newly arrived army. As many as one-third of the city's population had fled on Howe's approach, leaving primarily friendly loyalists or neutrals in control.

Howe had not brought Elizabeth Loring with him from New York, but according to a letter by an anonymous loyalist, the general soon found a new love. The charge was widely reprinted in handbills and distributed by the general's opponents in London who sought any means to discredit the soldier. The controversal letter mirrored the growing belief that Howe's lack of military success was due to his own incompetence and suggested that other mistakes made by the general included his lack of an overall battle plan, association with questionable friends who were more interested in gaining wealth from the war than winning it and Howe's "sameful inactivity." The note concluded:

> A great deal has been placed to the account of the General's fondness for, and attachment to, Mrs. L___g; who is beyond compare the Greatest Woman in the World; to

whom all Men must pay their court, if they hope for Prefer-
ment. She is, however, far advanced in her pregnancy, and
was left at *New-York*. But then the General has found another *Desdemona* at *Philadelphia*, even the pretty
Miss, who is now his Excellency's flirt; whilst some known
Adherents to the *American* cause, are become the greatest
and most consequential men at head-quarters. . . . You
think, I dare say, I am descending to tea-table chat and little
scandal. What I tell you, I really believe to be true; and you
will, at some time, hear such evidence of it, as will surprise
you.

Elizabeth Loring, now called "The Sultana," did rejoin her
lover and began to rule Philadelphia with a firm hand. Bawdy
jobs and limericks flew through both the continental and British
armies ridiculing the general's constant attention to her and his
increasing inattention to matters of war. One of the most popular
ditties involved their affair and an ingenious American scheme to
disrupt shipping on the Delaware.

David Bushnell, the inventor of a combination submarine
and torpedo called the *American Turtle*, had perfected a new ar-
mament named an "infernal." Basically, the device was a keg
filled with explosives which would ignite if jostled. In January,
the Americans launched a flotilla of infernals upriver from Philadelphia. The rebels hoped that as the barrels floated toward the
city, many would ram into British ships, explode and create extensive damage to both the vessels and their cargos.

Francis Hopkinson, a New Jersey Congressman, composed a
ballad to commemorate the project and named his song: "The
Battle of the Kegs." Much of the piece is devoted to describing
the reaction of General Howe, who learns of the plan only when
the first kegs began to explode in the city's port:

> Some fire cried, which some denied,
>     But said the earth had quaked;
> And girls and boys, with hideous noise,
>     Ran through the streets half naked.
>
> Sir William he, snug as a flea,
>     Lay all the time a snoring;

Nor dreamed of harm as he lay warm
    In bed with Mrs. L___g.

Now in a fright, he starts upright,
    Awak'd by such a clatter;
He rubs his eyes, and boldly cries,
    "For God's sake, what's the matter?"

At his bedside, he then spied,
    Sir Erskine at command, Sir,
Upon one foot he had one boot,
    And t'other in his hand, sir.

Arise! Arise, Sir Erskine cries,
    The Rebels—more's the pity—
Without a boat, are all afloat,
    And rang'd before the city.


Although the kegs did little lasting damage, they were a morale booster to the inactive troops at Valley Forge. Inside the city, their affect was negligible, for the only significant blemish on the festivities seemed to be a lack of firewood. Elizabeth Drinker observed that the fences were pulled down to stoke the fireplaces and the good times rolled on.

Gambling and drinking clubs were organized at various taverns. A thriving theater was set up to present a series of plays as diversions for the wealthier citizens. According to one report, families sent their servants to the theater early in the afternoon to hold seats for the evening performances.

Private entertaining went on almost constantly. Young Rebecca Franks declared that the pace was quite fatiguing. Rebecca was the daughter of loyalist David Franks, but her name was constantly linked with figures in both armies. After the war, she would marry British Colonel Henry Johnson and return to England with him, but in the winter of 1777, Rebecca was ensconced in the Philadelphia social whirl.

One of her regrets was that her friend, Anne Harrison Paca, could not share the amusement. Anne was the young wife of Maryland's William Paca, a congressional delegate. As a signer of the Declaration of Independence, Paca was high on the list of traitors whose life and fortune were at stake if he should be apprehended. But Rebecca did not see this as an obstacle to his wife enjoying certain gaieties with the British officers in Philadelphia. She wrote Anne:

> You can have no idea of the life of continued amusement I live in. I can scarce have a moment to myself. I have stole this while everybody is retired to dress for dinner. I am just come from under Mr. Black's hands and most elegantly am I dressed for a ball this evening at Smith's where we have one every Thursday. You would not Know the room 'tis so much improved.
>
> I wish to heaven you were going with us this evening to judge for yourself. I spent Tuesday evening at Sir Wm Howes where we had a concert and Dance. I asked his leave to send you a Handkerchief to show the fashions. He very politely gave me permission to send anything you wanted, tho' I told him you were a Delegate's Lady. I want to get a pair of Buckles for your Brother Joe.
>
> No loss for partners, even I am engaged to several different gentlemen for you must know 'tis a fix'd rule never to dance but two dances at a time with the same person. Oh how I wish Mr. P wou'd let you come in for a week or two —tell him I'll answer for your being let to return. I know you are as fond of a gay life as myself—you'd have an opportunity of rakeing as much as you choose either at Plays, Balls, Concerts or Assemblys. I've been now but three evenings alone since we mov'd to town. I begin now to be almost tired. Tell Mrs. Harrison she has got a gentleman in her house, who promises me not to let a single thing in it be hurt and I'm sure he'll keep his word. . . .

"Smith's" was Smith's City Tavern, a wartime hot spot where British soldiers gave weekly parties to return the social invitations from Philadelphia families. Although Rebecca's letter assures that a gentleman quartered in Mrs. Harrison's house had promised to take care of the contents, not all tenants were so thoughtful. When the British vacated the city, some of the best furniture from their commandeered residences went along. Fine books and paintings were carried away by the aristocratic looters who stripped the homes of the absent whigs.

Rebecca remained for additional reveling, but unknown to her, Anne Paca's partying days were numbered. Within three years, the patriot's young wife would be dead.

The festivities were not so cheerful twenty miles away at Valley Forge. Here the Continental Army was almost buried in snow and was surviving on the barest provisions. Meat was rare and often soldiers went for days without bread. Washington reported that one third of his men were unfit for battle because of insufficient clothing. Artillery horses were starving to death and the men were forced to sleep in shifts because of the lack of blankets to keep all warm at once.

Rebel officers did give one significant dinner party. Here no one was admitted that had a whole pair of breeches. Reports of the deprivation reached the outside world, sometimes in the form of rumors. According to one story, the ravenous soldiers were eating the weakest of their comrades. Another tale suggested that mass desertions were imminent. Discipline remained firm. One campfollower was sentenced to a hundred lashes for suggesting desertion was one way out of the situation. An officer received the unusual punishment of having his sword broken over his head for assorted offenses including theft.

But for the generals, the picture brightened considerably with the appearance of their wives and families. Sarah Livingston arrived to visit her husband Major General William Alexander. For several years, Alexander had attempted to establish a claim to a Scottish earldom and although he did not succeed, he insisted in being addressed as Lord Stirling. Alexander's own authentic origins were far from undistinguished. His father had helped to defend John Peter Zenger. His sister had married Peter Van Brugh Livingston, Lady Stirling's brother and President of the New York Provincial Congress.

Revolutionary leaders such as Lord Stirling showed great devotion to their wives throughout the war. Letters between couples of the era indicate that the bonds joining families were often strengthened rather than strained by the long war-time separations.

General Greene, who was constantly foraging for food and supplies at Valley Forge, was passionately in love with his meandering wife Kitty. To her he wrote: "My dear Angel, the contents [of your letter] have wrung drops of blood from my heart. Gracious God, how much I wish to come to you . . . there is not a day or night, nay not an hour, but I wish to fold you to my heart."

Staid George Washington also longed for his wife. He confided to her: ". . . I should enjoy more real happiness in one month with you at home than I have the most distant prospect of finding abroad, if my stay were to be seven times seven years. . . ."

Even John Adams from Puritan New England revealed his affection for Abigail, but not frequently. Adams' letters sometimes seemed cold to his wife, and she suggested that he should include some "sentimental effusions of the heart." In his rare personal notes, Adams did indicate that he missed his wife greatly. He wrote to her: "Alas! How many snowbanks divide thee and me and my warmest wishes to see thee will not melt one of them."

General Henry Knox was particularly devoted to his chubby wife Lucy. "Had I the power to transport myself to you, how eagerly rapid would be my flight," he assured her during one of their first separations.

Lucy was among those women who joined her husband at Valley Forge. Her situation during the war years had proved significantly more difficult than her childhood in Boston as the daughter of Thomas Flucker, the provincial secretary and informant in the case of Dorcas Griffiths. Lucy's marriage to Knox had been opposed by the Fluckers who disapproved of a union with the owner of a bookshop. A popular ditty of the day ridiculed their attempts to prevent the marriage:

> For whoever heard
> Of a case so absurd
> As a marriage deterred
> Or even deferred
> By scolding the boy
> And caging the bird.

Lucy and Henry left Boston after the battles at Lexington and Concord. She would never again see her parents, but their autocratic influence did not fade. Throughout the war and in her later life, Lucy Knox showed complete disdain for the common folk of every area in which she lived. She may have believed that the revolution was a movement which would merely replace the English ruling class with a new level of patrician peers composed of colonial radicals. Many were aware of her feelings. When Knox was sent to Fort Tie to bring back cannon for the bombardment of Boston, there were rumors questioning his loyalty, and some speculation that he planned to betray the continental artillery positions to the British.

During the war, Lucy was constantly on the move, coming to winter quarters whenever possible and then journeying to safety when the campaigns began each spring. She constantly berated Henry for inconveniences caused by the conflict and kept him well aware of the sacrifices she was making on behalf of the cause. From Brookline she wrote continuous complaints of her painful smallpox innoculation and grumbled that she had no "company but Madame Heath, who is so stiff that it is impossible to be sociable with her." From a retreat in Connecticut, she griped that the family who had given her refuge was "as unrefined as yeomanry."

Lucy soon managed to enliven the situation, for after the Battle of Trenton, Knox received a letter from Elisha Hall, Jr., of Wallingford, Connecticut. Hall explained that he had taken pity on Lucy and a Mrs. Pollard, allowing them both to live in his house. After their one month stay, he discovered that all the crockery was broken, the furniture badly damaged and twenty-five gallons of his best West Indian rum had disappeared.

Lucy's extravagant mode of living, her love of finery and penchant for lavish entertaining would become so great that Knox's funds proved completely insufficient to pay their mounting debts. Vast amounts were spent on parties as Lucy attempted to establish herself as a society leader and the family's fortunes earned by various trading ventures and land speculation would be near totally depleted by her excessive purchases.

In 1777, Lucy, who seemed to have inherited her father's propensity for interfering, became involved in a romance between her friend Elizabeth De Blois and Benedict Arnold. Arnold, a persistent suitor even in the face of Elizabeth's coolness, asked "Lady Knox" to intercede on his behalf and sent to her a large chest of fine clothes earmarked for Elizabeth. Along with the treasure, Arnold forwarded a note asking Lucy to provide him with intelligence on his love's true feelings.

Elizabeth refused to accept the trunk and within several months, Lucy was wearing some of the presents herself. Finery was almost impossible to obtain at the time and many of the ladies in her retinue were preparing to divide the remainder of the garments among themselves. Arnold did not choose to accommodate their desires, but instructed his aide to inform them that the trunk and its contents should be preserved intact.

Martha Washington had also come to Valley Forge. The commander's wife traditionally heard the opening and closing guns of every campaign, for no sooner had the last cannon sounded than "Mrs. General" set out for winter camp. Although she travelled in a "plain chariot," Martha did enjoy some flamboyance, for her servants were dressed gaily in scarlet and white. In his war expense account, Washington would later charge the American taxpayers $27,665.30 for her travel costs.

During the early part of the war, rumors circulated that the British planned to kidnap and hold Martha as a hostage. These stories gradually faded and she rode about the countryside with only a small guard, paid for at government expense.

Rather than socialize, Martha seemed to prefer to spend her time organizing camp women into sewing circles to make shirts and socks for the army. A Morristown woman who visited "Her Excellency" at winter camp reported great embarrassment during an audience with the General's lady. While the New Jersey woman, dressed in her finest clothes sat uncomfortably empty handed, Martha, clad in a simple apron, busied herself by knitting stockings for the commander-in-chief.

But retiring Martha Washington was an important figure during the war. Just as her general husband was revered as a great leader of men, Martha was seen as the idol for the war's women. Recognizing this unique station, she attempted to set public examples of ways in which her countrywomen, not as intellectually gifted as Mercy Warren or as personally daring as

Martha Washington, painting by Charles Willson Peale. Courtesy of the Mount Vernon Ladies' Association.

Lydia Darragh, could contribute to the revolution. Although the Virginia housewife served as a pattern for the young nation's "average" females, her own life had been far from commonplace.

Martha Dandridge was seventeen years old when she wed wealthy Daniel Parke Custis in 1749. After eight years of peaceful married life on Custis' tidewater plantation, Martha was suddenly left a widow with two young children and a legacy of more than a million dollars. This "prettiest and richest widow in Virginia" mourned less than two years before marrying Washington, a respectable but decidedly second echelon planter.

By using his wife's financial resources and controlling the inheritances of her children, Washington began building his modest farms on the Potomac into a vast and prosperous estate. Unlike Abigail Adams, Martha gave little attention to everyday business affairs, but contented herself to the domestic areas of child raising and serving as a dutiful wife. The outbreak of the revolution drastically altered this sheltered existence. Martha became a closely watched public figure.

In an effort to conserve foodstuffs, Mrs. Washington retrenched her table at Mt. Vernon, eliminating all but that which was most basic to her family's needs. According to tradition, she also oversaw the development of a particularly frugal form of dressmaking. In the plantation sewing rooms, clothing woven from rough homespun was embellished with strips of silk taken from old stockings. For variety, Martha also pieced damask from discarded chair covers into her dresses.

Mrs. Washington's first major public appearance came in November of 1775 soon after she received an urgent dispatch from her husband, camped with the Continental Army at Cambridge. The general suggested that she leave immediately for Massachusetts in order to pass the winter with him at headquarters. This plea, from normally conservative Washington, was curious in several respects. First, under the best of circumstances the long journey north was a fatiguing experience. In November, the possibility was imminent that heavy snows could make the primitive roads impassable, thus stranding Martha's party in the interior. Attacks from tory sympathizers or British raiding parties were also likely to occur. Finally, the uncertain military situation in Massachusetts made it possible that Washington and his men might move on before Martha could arrive.

Political maneuverings may have lain behind the sudden journey. The couple had been separated for seven months and rumors were increasingly spread that Mrs. Washington, having no confidence in the American efforts, had chosen to live apart from her husband. Throughout the country such doubt and uncertainty as to the prospects of the Continentals were creating a major morale problem. Washington may have hoped that his wife's trip would not only demonstrate her strong rebel allegiances, but would also suggest that the military situation in Boston was well in control.

Martha's winter at Cambridge was the first of her annual pilgrimages to winter headquarters. At snow-bound Valley Forge, her important place in camp had been long established.

The general's lady rarely altered her daily routine. Each morning, except the Sabbath, she attended needlework sessions where camp women knitted or sewed supplies for the troops. In the afternoon, she visited with sick soldiers in their huts. Occasionally she helped in transcribing Washington's orders or correspondence. Ironically, the general would return this stenographic favor many years later when his wife, growing increasingly perturbed at her poor spelling, insisted that he personally copy all of her letters.

Although General Washington developed somewhat of a reputation as a ladies' man, Martha's proper conduct was never questioned. Her married life appeared to be a comfortable one of companionship rather than passion. This apparent lack of romanticism was strengthened after she destroyed all correspondence between the couple, thus leaving no insight for history into their private moments together.

Martha, who constantly referred to her husband as the "old man," had no delusions as to her proper role in life. In describing herself she maintained that she was merely an ". . . old fashioned Virginia house-keeper, steady as a clock, busy as a bee, and cheerful as a cricket." During the harsh days at Valley Forge, these attributes were far more valuable than beauty or wit.

The coming of spring improved the situation at Valley Forge and Greene's foraging began to show results. Adequate food and supplies began flowing into camp to relieve the distress. Another high spot was the appearance of foreign officers such as the Baron von Steuben who set about polishing the military skills of the army's survivors. Von Steuben, whose dossier showed that he held a Lt. General's rank in the Prussian Army, was actually a major who had been unemployed for fourteen years before he met Benjamin Franklin in Paris. Franklin, believing that the Baron's presence in the American army was vital, presumably "doctored" the soldier's record to make his experience seem much more impressive than the actual facts indicated.

Franklin's mission to Paris had finally proved successful, and Louis, despite opposition, at last agreed to enter the war against Great Britain. The mighty fleet of France was detailed to protect the ex-colonies against the sea power of England.

The Frenchmen at camp were unlike their British counter-
parts who seemed to prefer women beautiful but dumb. The
Americans sought homespun qualities in their wives, but the
French delighted in gay, witty and intelligent females. For years
the leaders of French society had made their salons stimulating
retreats for men. Most hostesses studied diligently in order to lead
the learned discussions in the arts, history and politics.

At Valley Forge, Catharine Greene, who had the distinct advantage of speaking French was the epitome of the sparkling
French ideal. Catharine, considered a beauty, became an immediate favorite of the foreign soldiers, particularly Marie Joseph Paul
Yves Roch Gilbert du Motier, the Marquis de Lafayette. Some
jealousy arose because of her relations with the young officers
and General Greene, according to Henry Knox, was not particularly pleased with his wife's outgoing behavior.

Charles Lee was also back in camp after being paroled from
Philadelphia. Before his release, Lee promised not to interfere
with the interests of the crown, but in effect this pledge merely
prohibited him from taking command in a battle situation. He
would almost immediately break the vow.

Lee's arrival at army headquarters was greeted with great
celebration, despite the antagonism between his supporters and
those loyal to Washington. After an elegant dinner on the night
of his return, Lee retired to bed in a back room of Washington's
residence. According to Elias Boudinot, Lee did not appear until
late the following morning. Breakfast was held for him and when
the general finally appeared, Boudinot wrote that he: ". . . looked
as dirty as if he had been in the Street all night." Boudinot soon
pieced together the reason for Lee's erratic behavior: "Soon after I
discovered that he had brought a miserable hussy with him from
Philadelphia (a British Sergeant's wife) and had actually taken her
into his Room by a Back Door and she had slept with him that
night."

Although Lee had obviously adopted at least one of General
Howe's vices, the American officer was not a particular adherent
of the Englishman's style of campaigning. Lee announced:
"Howe shut his eyes, fought his battles, drank his bottle, had his
little whore, advis'd his counsellors, receiv'd his orders from

North and Germain, one more absurd than the other, shut his eyes and fought again."

This ostrich-like behavior finally backfired on Howe. Sir William had submitted a token resignation in November of 1777, perhaps expecting that its rejection would be a vote of confidence for his earlier actions. Instead, notice of its acceptance arrived in Philadelphia in April. Growing criticism of Howe was not the only factor in the decision. London officials were receiving increased opposition for their own handling of the war, the rebellion which many leaders had originally predicted would be quickly and decisively crushed. But already the campaign was three years old and instead of victory, the King's holdings were confined to only a few isolated cities. Most of New England had been completely lost. Deaths and casualties were high. Burgoyne and his men had been captured at Saratoga and France had entered the war against England. Howe was selected to become the scapegoat for the failures of the foreign ministry. Clinton was appointed as the new commander and ordered to move the Philadelphia-based forces back to New York.

The order to evacuate Philadelphia and the change in command were resented by many officers who were loyal to Howe. In a grand gesture, a major celebration was planned to honor the departing commander. This fete, called the meschianza or medley would cost 3,300 guineas or about $86,000, but the price in intangible terms was much greater. Just as Burgoyne's action after the murder of Jane McCrea had alienated British loyalists in New York State, the opulent meschianza would offend and damage relations with tories in the mid-Atlantic area.

The celebration was planned by young John André, a dashing officer who was a particular favorite with the young women in Philadelphia. One of his closest companions was Peggy Shippen, who would marry Benedict Arnold within the year. André would be later captured behind enemy lines and hanged for his involvement with Arnold's treason, but such somber thoughts were not in fashion as the party neared.

Invitations to the fete praised Howe with the slogan "He shines as he sets, but shall rise again more luminous." This elaborate motto was only a sample of things to come. By May 18, the

*Mrs. Benedict Arnold and One of Her Children* (Peggy Shippen), painting by Daniel Gardner. Courtesy of The Historical Society of Pennsylvania.

day of the event, the party had developed into a feast honoring not only Howe, but all the women who had been so hospitable to the occupying troops.

Guests for the celebration gathered at Knight's Wharf, where they were met by a "vast number of boats, barges and galleys" decorated with flags and brightly colored banners. A Philadelphia lady in attendance described the events in a letter to her friend, one Mrs. Bland:

> . . . On a sign from the '*Vigilant*' we all embarked, forming lines, with all the music belonging to the army in the centre. The ladies interspersed in the different boats (the seats of which were covered in green cloth) with the red coats, colors flying, music playing, etc. you may easily sup-

pose formed a very gay and grand appearance; nor were the shore and houses, lined with spectators, any bad object to those in the regatta (the water party so called). We were obliged to row gently on account of the galley sailing slow.

The armed ship—the *'Fanny'* was drawn into the stream and decorated in the most beautiful manner with the colors of every Court or State streaming; amidst the number, the thirteen stripes waved with as much elegance, and as gracefully sported with gentle zephyrs, as any of the number. After passing the above ship we reached the *'Roebuck'* whose men were all fixed on her yards and gave us three cheers as we passed, and as soon as we had got to a distance not to be incommoded by the smoke she fired a salute and was answered by several other vessels in the harbor. At length we reached the place of destination (after lying awile on our oars) opposite the *'Roebuck'* the music playing 'God Save the King.'

The passengers then disembarked and proceeded down ranks of soldiers in dress uniforms to a newly constructed medieval field of honor. Here the guests were greeted by belles of the city clothed in costumes of satins, silks and pearls. Young women singled out for special honors were dressed in opulent Turkish attire. The afternoon's entertainment was a jousting and tilting tournament between officers representing the Knights of the "Burning Mountain" and those of the "Blended Rose."

The group then adjourned for tea in a hall where nearly a hundred mirrors had been set up amid banks of flowers and silver decorations. After tea was dancing. After dancing fireworks. After fireworks was a dinner with 1,200 dishes and more dancing until four the next morning. The only interruption to the gaiety was a bombardment engineered by Alan McLane, who with his band of American raiders, tossed homemade bombs into the British lines.

While participants may have been delighted with the festivities, the event revolted many loyalists. Some had barely managed to survive the harsh winter and others, who had made substantial sacrifices to support the British cause, were facing severe punishments from the returning rebels. Instead of the King's troops moving out to destroy the remainder of the American army at Valley Forge, the tories saw their soldiers feasting and dancing in the protected city.

Even Howe's secretary Ambrose Serle was aghast. He wrote: "Our Enemies will dwell upon the Folly and Extravagance. . . ." Elizabeth Drinker noted: "How insensible do these people appear, while our land is so greatly desolated, and death and sore destruction has overtaken and impends over so many."

The event further undermined Howe's influence in England. Career soldiers often viewed the performance as a blot on the reputation of the army and its unfavorable effects would not be quickly forgotten. Five years later, Sir George Eliott leaving his post at Gibraltar, was asked what he desired as a farewell gesture by his troops. He replied: "Anything but a Meschianza!"

Americans also resented the excesses of the celebration. After the British left Philadelphia, some provincial leaders attempted to prohibit those women who had participated in the party from fraternizing with American officers. General Anthony Wayne was more direct. Following the Battle of Monmouth, Wayne notified his friend Richard Peters:

> Tell those Philadelphia ladies who attended Howe's assemblies and levees, that the heavenly, sweet, pretty redcoats—The accomplished gentlemen of the guards and grenadiers, have been humbled on the plains at Monmouth. The Knights of the Blended Roses, and of the Burning Mount—have resigned their laurels to rebel officers who will lay them at the feet of those virtuous daughters of America who cheerfully gave up ease and affluence in a city, for liberty and peace of mind in a cottage.

In June, Howe sailed out, eastward bound for England and an inquiry into his conduct of the war. Behind he left Elizabeth Loring and Sir Henry Clinton. The revolution had claimed another victim.

# CHAPTER SIX

# *Women Take to the Road*

Commanding officers of Regiments will assist Regimental Surgeons in procuring as many Women of the Army as can be prevailed on to serve as Nurses to them who will be paid the usual Price.

*Order of the Day*
*Valley Forge, Pennsylvania*
May 31, 1778

CLINTON WAS ORDERED to return his army to New York by sea, but setbacks in the war made these directives obsolete by June of 1778.

The French navy was expected off the American coast at any moment, and although not as powerful as the British fleet, Louis' squadrons could inflict costly damage. Any troop ship which lagged or floundered could become easy prey, while storms and other calamities of the ocean presented an even greater risk.

The new commander was hesitant to expose his vulnerable army to the hazards of the sea, for the loss of even one boat would provide casualties as high as a major land battle. Unlike Washington, who conceivably could draw reinforcements from the surrounding countryside, a great loss of men by Clinton might place his army in an untenable position. Additional troops could take weeks to arrive from England.

In addition, thousands of tories in Philadelphia were demanding to be taken to Manhattan aboard the transports. After the British evacuation, the property of these loyalists and even their lives would be at the mercy of returning whigs, many of whom were bent on avenging the wrongs committed while Howe controlled the capital.

The husband of Grace Growden Galloway was one of those clamoring to leave. Joseph Galloway had been a major figure in the Pennsylvania Assembly before the war, but had sided with England in the struggle. Like Elizabeth Ferguson, Grace had inherited considerable property from her father, and her husband had placed the estate in jeopardy by collaborating with the enemy.

Grace remained at the family home, Trevose, in Bucks County to prevent its possible confiscation, while Joseph left Pennsylvania with their only child to join the British. When Howe entered Philadelphia, Galloway returned and was appointed superintendent of police. Grace joined him in the city, but their stay together was brief. Galloway and his daughter planned to leave once again with the British, and later sail on to England.

Because there was not room on the departing transports for both soldiers and loyalists, Clinton elected to send the civilians and their huge piles of baggage by boat. He and his men would progress overland. In one aspect, the General was going home, for his father, Admiral George Clinton, had served as Royal Governor of New York for almost eight years and young Henry had spent much of his childhood in Manhattan.

Clinton marched out on June 17, with a baggage train of 1,500 vehicles that stretched for 12 miles. Almost every item of food and drink needed for the march was to be carried from Philadelphia, for according to Clinton the route northward was a "devoured country." The year's crops had just been planted and whig partisans along the road had removed all livestock and provisions, leaving nothing as potential forage for the foreign army. Even the well ropes and water buckets had been taken so that the soldier's thirst could not be quenched without a major effort.

Although the commander attempted to minimize plundering and other retribution by the discomforted troops, his efforts were ineffectual. The devastation left along the early route of march may have further inflamed those whigs further north to renew their efforts to make the British trip as uncomfortable as possible.

Bad roads, heavy rains and burned bridges complicated the movement, but perhaps the worst obstacle was the extreme heat. Both British and German troops were dressed in heavy winter woolens and by some estimates, the temperature soared as high as a hundred degrees. The rate of advance dropped to five miles a day.

This slow pace enabled the continental troops to cut eastward across Pennsylvania and New Jersey from their camp at Valley Forge, confronting the King's men at Monmouth Courthouse. The opponents were almost equal in numbers, but the British, fatigued by their march and without their heavy cannon, were in a decidedly inferior position.

Charles Lee originally opposed an American attack on the train, but jealously demanded command of the advance units after he learned that Lafayette was slated to lead the rebels.

Most allied officers, confident of a victory, charged into the foray. But instead of success, troops under Lee's direction were soon seen fleeing the field in panic, although they were not pursued by the enemy. Washington rode to the front and found the command in complete confusion. Lee's inept direction was creating panic all along the line. Washington immediately relieved the general and attempted to rally the disorganized troops. Lee would later be court martialled for his actions on the field at Monmouth. His army career in effect ended that day on the New Jersey plain.

One person on the battlefield who did not panic was Molly Ludwig Hays, a camp follower who had been nicknamed Molly Pitcher because of the water containers she carried to the fighting men. Molly's background was modest. As the daughter of a German immigrant dairyman in New Jersey, she had earlier hired out as a servant to a doctor in Carlisle, Pennsylvania. In 1769, at age fifteen, she married John Casper Hays, a settler who later became a gunner with the Pennsylvania artillery.

Molly, though well advanced in pregnancy, was engaged in carrying water to the soldiers at Monmouth when her husband collapsed, possibly from a battle wound but more probably from heat exhaustion. Molly, like Margaret Corbin, decided to take a hand in the fighting. Private Joseph Martin saw her exertions and later noted in his diary:

> One little incident happened, during the heat of the cannonade, which I was eye-witness to and which I think would be unpardonable not to mention. A woman whose husband belonged to the artillery, and who was then attached to a piece in the engagement, attended with her husband at the piece the whole time. While in the act of reaching for a cartridge and having one of her feet as far before the other as she could step, a cannon shot from the enemy passed directly between her legs without doing any other damage than carrying away all the lower part of her petticoat. Looking at it with apparent unconcern, she observed that it was lucky it did not pass a little higher, for in that case it might have carried away something else, and continued her occupation.

Others claimed to have seen Molly at work. Some said she singlehandedly sponged, loaded, aimed and fired the cannon in addition to nursing her husband. Others report that she was also a heroine after the fight when she searched the corpses on the field for wounded who might have survived. Supposedly she found one, a Private Dilwyn whom she carried to safety.

Molly, a tobacco-chewing, hard-swearing woman, returned to Pennsylvania with her husband following the war, but John Hays soon died. Then Molly formed an unhappy union with one George McCauley, whom she reportedly deserted. The State of Pennsylvania recognized her growing financial difficulties and awarded her a pension of $40 for "services rendered in the revolutionary war." For many years she lived on the fringe of the army, washing, cooking and sometimes serving as a nurse.

After Washington had relieved Lee, American units began to rally at Monmouth. At the end of the day, the battle was considered at least a draw, though both sides claimed it as a great victory. The intense heat was cited as a major factor in the outcome, for neither side was able to launch any major offensive drives. As many as one-half of the British casualties were attributed to sunstroke and some reports suggest that Washington's own horse died from exhaustion.

Late that night, after several hours of rest, Clinton's troops moved out and headed for Manhattan. By July 7, most of the party had been ferried into New York. Great numbers were missing, however, for during the march an estimated 600 soldiers, mostly Hessians, had deserted back into Philadelphia where they had been treated so finely the winter before.

The French fleet under the Count d'Estaing arrived off Sandy Hook too late to challenge the British, but at last, the new republic was able to confront their enemy on the sea.

Newport, which had been occupied by the British since it fell to Clinton in December of 1776, was chosen as the target of the first Franco-American expedition. In accordance with the overall plan for recapture, Greene and Lafayette sailed with d'Estaing for Rhode Island, while John Sullivan marched overland through New England with a force of continentals and militia. Among those involved in the expedition were John Hancock, Paul Revere and John Glover.

Although the coordinated attack on the port city was scheduled for August 10, d'Estaing chose a hazardous engagement with Admiral Lord Howe at sea. The maneuvering was cut short by a hurricane which caused extensive damage to both navies and the French, instead of supporting the American land troops, chose to put into Boston for repairs. Sullivan, who had already committed his land forces, barely managed to pull back with the help of Glover's mariners, thus narrowly avoiding defeat.

Stephan Popp was one of those inside the Newport installation. According to his journal, the British position was far from a comfortable one as winter arrived:

> . . . We moved into old, empty, unhabited buildings. Our quarters were the worst of all, but the provisions were a good deal worse. For seven days each man received 2½ pounds of bread and that was mostly baked of rice and Indian cornmeal. This you could hardly eat for bitterness. Instead of meat we received stinking codfish and that so little that it was just according to the proverb: "For dying too much; for strengthening too little."

On holy Christmas Eve it began to snow and lasted until the 27th. The snow lay upon the ground three or four feet deep. The cold was unbearable. In that cold spell nine men of the Brown regiment froze to death and 23 men had their hands and feet frozen.

A woman was found in a hut froze to death with her suckling children in her arms. For the great hunger and cold were alike unbearable.

The Convention Army was also on the move during the fall of 1778. After the initial hardships, the captured forces of Burgoyne found their quarters in Cambridge and Rutland rather satisfactory. In the casual atmosphere of semi-detention, desertions among German troops increased greatly. General Riedesel issued special orders aimed at suppressing the widespread exodus, but his wife grew accustomed to the situation.

The Riedesels moved into one of the best houses in Cambridge and entertained freely. Other captives were delighted to share in the Baroness' lighthearted festivities which helped to relieve the boredom of confinement. One of her parties, given on June 3 to celebrate the birthdays of the Baron and the King, was a riotous affair which created some ill will as it closed with a vigorous singing of "God Save the King." On departing, her guests found that the house had been surrounded by armed whigs, who feared that the well-wined prisoners were preparing to foment a riot.

Although captured officers were forbidden to enter neighboring Boston, the Baroness gained permission to visit the city to see friends. One new acquaintance was a tory Captain named Fenton whose wife and fifteen-year-old daughter had been tarred, feathered and paraded through the town in retaliation for his own loyalist leanings.

The Baroness was not impressed with New England hospitality, particularly in Boston, and noted: "It is quite a pretty city, but inhabited by enthusiastic patriots and full of wicked people. The women, particularly were horrid, casting ugly looks at me and some of them even spitting when I passed by them."

Lt. Du Roi, also a member of the Convention Army, shared her astonishment at the women of the northeast. He recorded:

The girls mature very early; I have seen quite a number of them hardly 17 years old and as big and developed as they would ever be. . . . However they get old very early and a woman of 30 often looks like one 50 years old. The people are very fond of luxury, especially the women, which fondness shows itself in their dress and in their houses. However, the way of living in regard to food is very poor. No German stomach can put up with it.

The men are very industrious, especially in business, but they are selfish and not sociable. The women are exceedingly proud, negligent and very lazy. The men have to do all the outside work, as milking cows, etc. The woman in New England is the laziest creature I know, and not much good for anything.

The citizens of the area were even less enchanted with their unwilling guests. Prices of food had risen greatly as thousands of new mouths competed for groceries. The cost of wood rose to $27.50 a cord.

Lodging was also a problem. Many whigs were incensed by the prospect of being turned out of their houses so that the aristocratic internees could be more comfortably quartered. Hannah Winthrop was infuriated when Harvard College was closed to students and then taken over as a barracks for the prisoners:

Some polite ones say we ought not to look on them as prisoners—that they are persons of distinguished rank. Perhaps, too, we must not view them in the light of enemies. I fear this distinction will be soon lost, Surprising that our general, or any of our colonels, should insist on the first university in America being disbanded for their more genteel accommodation; and we, poor oppressed people, see an asylum in the woods against a piercing winter.

Hannah's feeling were not soothed as time passed. Three months later she was still bothered by the privileges being granted to the prisoners and wrote to Mercy Warren: "Methinks I hear Mrs. Warren wondering how they do at head-quarters in Cambridge. Perhaps her wonder may increase when I tell her the

British officers live in the most luxurious manner possible, rioting
on the fat of the land and talking at large with the self-impor-
tance of lords of the soil."

Congress listened as others voiced complaints similar to those
expressed by Hannah Winthrop. Although the terms of the Saratoga Convention had specified that the surrendered troops would
be returned to England as soon as possible, pressure was mounting to disregard the agreement. Gradually the view prevailed that
although the particular men involved in the Convention would
probably not fight again in the war, their return to England
would simply free others stationed abroad, for revolutionary service.

An attempt by Lord Howe to rescue the troops, coupled
with the skyrocketing expense of maintaining the prisoners in the
Boston area, ultimately made a change of location compulsory.
The Congress at last decided to break the Convention, and isolate
the prisoners by moving them further inland to Charlottesville,
Virginia.

The Baroness set out in November of 1778, riding in a carriage and followed by a supply wagon which frequently lagged
far behind the party. The conditions of her trip to Virginia were
not always ideal. Food was scarce. Often, straw was her only
bedding. Citizens along the way were usually antagonistic.

The Baroness found rebel women most difficult and even
anxious to insult the wife of a mercenary. Much of the general
condemnation of German officers troops stemmed from the widespread philosophy that their participation in the war was perhaps
worse than the British. The Hessians, it was believed, had eagerly
entered the American war and chosen to kill rebels not out of
duty, but for money.

Much of the aggression against the Baroness may also have
stemmed from her own behavior, which could have appeared ar-
rogant to the American woman. The Baroness, like Lucy Knox,
scorned citizens of humble origins. Often she treated her roadside
hostesses as peasants who were expected to be respectfully subser-
vient to her high station.

One incident she particularly abhorred occurred in the house
of an American colonel named Howe. Here the soldier's four-

teen-year-old daughter, seated before the fire, wished aloud that King George III could be with then so that she could ". . . tear out his heart, fry it over these coals, and eat it."

Frederika's contacts with men were usually more agreeable. One bigamously-minded farmer near the Hudson proposed that she become his second wife. In Hartford, she entertained Lafayette and attempted to convert the young Frenchman to the British side. However, her main preoccupation throughout the journey was not with the population, but that of securing food for her family.

Just before reaching New York, the Baroness was confronted with a farm woman who refused to provide any nourishment, even for the hungry Riedesel daughters. Using guile and a cup of tea as a bribe, the Baroness made peace with the woman, but was soon faced with a different dilemma:

> . . . She invited me into her kitchen, where her husband sat chewing on a pig's tail, and, much to my joy, she brought up from the cellar a basket of potatoes for me. When she came back her husband offered her his delicacy. She gnawed on it a bit, then gave it back to him, and he continued feasting on it. I beheld this strange reciprocal entertainment with amazement and disgust. But the man seemed to think that my own hunger made me envious, and he offered me the tail, now thoroughly gnawed. What was I to do? If I refused it, I thought, he would be insulted, and I would not get the precious basket of potatoes. So I took it and pretended to gnaw on it. Then I slipped it into the fire. Thus we were finally at peace with one another. They gave me the potatoes, and I made a good repast of them with butter. Moreover, they gave us three pretty rooms with good beds.

The captive army passed on through New York, Pennsylvania and Maryland, then, after two months and about 650 miles, the marchers finally reached their destination. While the main body of the troops were quartered in makeshift barracks near Charlottesville, the Baroness and her family found more luxurious accommodations at Colle Plantation. The estate was owned by Italian immigrant Philip Mazzei who conducted agricultural experiments there, but had temporarily left America for Europe.

Thomas Jefferson, the Baroness' neighbor at nearby Monti-
cello, claimed that the Riedesel horses, in one week, destroyed agricultural projects which had taken Mazzei three or four years to
develop.

Life at Colle was comfortable for the Riedesels. The family
had at least five servants and money was no problem. Jefferson
sold the Baron a pianoforte and the Baroness became close friends
with Martha Skelton, the future President's wife.

Gardens were planted and with the coming of fair weather,
food was no longer a problem. But the general's health was one
blemish on the situation. Riedesel, worried by inactivity, desertions by his troops and mounting criticism of Germans as effective fighting units, suffered periods of intense depression. His
condition was further complicated by a sunstroke.

The general and his wife received permission to take a cure
at Frederick Springs, now Berkeley Springs, West Virginia. The
citizens of these western lands were as strange to the Baroness as
those of New England had been:

> The Virginians are mostly indolent, which is ascribed
> to their hot climate, but with the slightest inducement they
> are ready in an instant to dance; and if a reel (an English
> or Scottish folk-dance) is played, the men immediately catch
> hold of the women, who then spring up as though possessed.
> But as soon as they are led back to their chairs, they sit
> there like blockheads again. What we had heard about the
> morals of the people in this part of the country does not
> make a favorable picture. For instance we were told that
> two girls had been made pregnant by their own father, and
> that while this created a lot of gossip, it had remained un-
> punished. Another man, who found his daughter-in-law
> more attractive than his own wife, made his son an offer to
> exchange wives, to which the son agreed on the condition
> that, in addition to getting his own mother for his wife, he
> also be given two cows and two horses, which was done,
> and nothing further was said about the affair.

The sojourn in Virginia ended in the summer of 1779 with
the announcement that the Baron was to be exchanged in New

York. In August, the Baroness left Charlottesville and headed
north to freedom.

Although women like the Baroness, Martha Washington and
Lucy Knox were technically camp followers, their lives were as
foreign to the existence of the typical army woman as a general's
position was from that of a lowly private.

As many as 20,000 women may have followed their lovers
and husbands during the American revolution. For all but a
handful, the situation was a fatiguing and dangerous experience.
Unlike the Baroness and Martha who rode in carriages, most
women marched on foot, weighed down with heavy iron pots,
small children and baggage. Instead of comfortable quarters in
manor houses, great numbers of followers slept with the troops in
fields or huts.

When the armies clashed, these women were not automatically removed from the scene to safety, but many roamed the
battlefields serving as water or ammunition carriers, cooks or
nurses. After the action, they looted and stripped the dead for
useful articles. Many foraged not only for their own food, but for
supplies needed by their men. All were confronted with an imminent chance of rape by soldiers who had no companions.

Both the British and German armies, professional organizations unlike the voluntary continentals, had long acknowledged
the need for camp followers. Many women were placed on official rosters, given rations and other privileges. In addition to performing certain intangible duties such as alleviating homesickness
and minimizing desertions, the camp women were responsible for
more specific service duties which freed men for fighting.

Their backgrounds were diverse. Women following the foreign troops were often brought from Europe, as many as 5,000
may have been shipped from England and Ireland alone. Thousands of others, picked up in America by the King's forces, were
not listed on muster roles in many cases. These females were
sometimes Canadian, but were most often loyalists or non-parti-
san spinsters or widows who had no other means of support.

Some had not sought the common law relationship established with near strangers. But a wife who followed her husband
to a distant colony for battle, had little choice of action if he

were killed, other than to attach herself to another trooper. The way back home was often long and arduous. Without funds or friends, it was a difficult journey. Frequently, there was no home to which she could return. Still another contingent of followers was composed of prostitutes who were attracted to the foreign troops by their greater financial resources.

The activities of these trailing females did not always assist the army and in some areas hampered its operation. One of the most damaging practices was the trading of liquor, a common means by which women could secure badly needed supplies. Commanders frequently issued orders prohibiting women from selling whiskey, particularly to the Indians. Burgoyne found the situation so disruptive that he threatened to turn out of camp any woman caught bartering spirits.

Another problem area was looting by camp followers. Although there were times when officers encouraged or permitted the practice, there were other occasions when commanders wished a neighborhood to remain inviolate. In such cases, control over the women of the army proved almost impossible. After the Battle of Bunker Hill, the *British Orderly Book* in Boston noted that action had been taken on one such infraction:

> Winifred McCowan, retainer to the camp tryed by General Court Martial for having stolen the town bull and causing him to be killed, and is found guilty of the same and sentenced to be tyed to a cart's tail, and thereto to receive 100 lashes on her bare back in different portions of the most public parts of the town and camp, and to be imprison'd three months.

One of the most perplexing problems to military leaders, including English, German and American, was the chaos created on marches by women seeking to be near to their men. Often as an army progressed through the countryside, women flocked into the midst of the marching men, wandering along with their children and pots, generally disrupting the advance and drastically slowing the procession.

On August 4, 1777, Washington sought to speed up the

movement of his men by limiting the women accompanying the forces. He ordered:

> In the present marching state of the army, every incumbrance proves greatly prejudicial to the service; the multitide of women in particular, especially those who are pregnant, or have children, are a clog upon every movement. The Commander in Chief therefore earnestly recommends it to the officers commanding brigades and corps, to use every reasonable method in their power to get rid of all such as are not absolutely necessary; and the admission or continuance of any, who shall, or may have come to the Army since its arrival in Pennsylvania, is positively forbidden, to which point the officers will give particular attention.

Washington was constantly seeking to keep the women in the rear of the army with the baggage train. One trying incident was just before the Battle of Brandywine when the commander was particularly concerned with making a favorable impression on the citizens of Philadelphia. Hoping to show that the Continental Army was as disciplined and as powerful as that of Howe, Washington ordered a precision march for the troops in the city's main streets. Camp women were instructed to pass through the outskirts of town with the baggage. The attempt was not successful. One Philadelphian described the scene when the females revolted against the attempt to hide them. The picture was far different from Martha Washington elegantly riding through in her carriage:

> They were spirited off into the quaint, dirty little alleyways and side streets. But they hated it. They army had barely passed through the main thoroughfares before these camp followers poured after their soldiers again, their hair flying, their brows beady with the heat, their belongings slung over one sholder, chattering and yelling in sluttish shrills as they went and spitting in the gutters.

Clinton also paid particular attention to the women of the army. His solution was not to put them in the rear, but to post them under guard. The general ordered: "The women of each regiment will march at the head of it, under the escort of a non-commissioned officer and six men, who will take care that they do not get out of the road on any account."

During the early years of the war, the number of American camp followers was probably far below the figure for the British. This difference was primarily because the rebel forces were usually posted near to their homes, where regular visits satisfied any feelings of loneliness. In addition, much of the American strength was composed of militia who remained at home and were usually called only for emergencies.

Enlistments for continental troops were shorter than for the foreign soldiers, thus making the family separation briefer than that experience by the European men. Finally, many American women were needed at home to care for farms and businesses. If these females had joined their husbands, their whole estates might have been forfeited. But as the war dragged on, the number of rebel camp followers increased. American women, convinced that victory would not be achieved quickly, began leaving their homes in larger numbers.

Life was particularly difficult for camp followers without men. Nicholas Cresswell, a Britisher on his way home to England, observed the tribulations of one such woman in New York. On the evening of June 17, 1777, Cresswell and a friend named Furneval had gone into town, spent the evening at Hull Tavern and were returning to their quarters aboard the ship *Bell and Mary*, when they were interrupted. New York in 1777 had not recovered from the effects of the great fire. Among the gutted houses, they heard a strange sound:

> In our return to the Boat, coming by some houses that were burnt down we heard the cries of a Woman. We searched about and soon, to our great surprise, found a poor Woman in labour, and all alone. She told us she was a soldier's widow and begged we would help her to some assistance. We immediately carried her to the house of a Sadler in the Broadway, whom we raised from his pillow and told him the poor woman's situation. But he absolutely refused to let her stay in his house, declaring that he would not keep

a lying-in Hospital for our W——s. However with threats, promises, and the poor Woman declaring that it was impossible for her to be removed, he at length consented that she might lay in a back shop he had. We immediately removed her thither and made her a very poor bed out of a Bearskin, A Packsheet, and an old Blanket.

The situation quickly became critical and while Furneval went off to seek a midwife, Cresswell stayed with the camp follower, fearing that the saddler or his wife would attempt to turn her out. Neither offered to help and Cresswell began to suspect that he would be forced to make the delivery himself:

> . . . but in the critical minute Furneval arrived with an old drunken woman he had picked up somewhere or other and she refused to perform the office without we would give her two Dollars. Furneval gave her one and I another. She immediately fell to work, I am sure the pains of labour must be violent for the poor woman roared out most horridly. I think, I hear the sound yet in my ears. However, in about ten minutes she produced a girl which was wrapped in the Mother's apron . . . for she had not one single rag prepared for the occasion.

Cresswell bought $2 worth of wine, rum and nutmeg bread as a postpartum feast for the new mother. Within half an hour she was able to sit up. All the while, the saddler's wife remained in bed, loudly cursing the camp follower for the disturbance. About midnight, the men departed, Cresswell giving the army woman about $1.25, the last of his worldly estate. Back at the ship he noted:

> The poor woman is heartily welcome to it and I am happy that I had it in my power to relieve such real distress. Furneval gave her two Dollars and swears he will stand Godfather to the child. I have no intention of doing myself that honour, am in hopes it will be dead before morning. We promised to go and see her in the morning and make her case known to some of the Officers. I hope the drunken jade of a midwife don't rob her before morning. I don't like her looks.

Although the great majority of camp followers were white, it was probably not unusual to find black women accompanying the troops in certain areas. Many free black men volunteered as soldiers during the early days of the war in New England, and in Rhode Island, one entire regiment was composed of freedmen. The number of Negro women with such army units may have been even higher than for white companies, for black females were greatly limited in their job opportunities. Most were servants or completely dependent upon the income that their men earned from low-paying jobs. Many black men who joined the army could not afford to maintain their families in separate households, even if the wives were employed.

After the blockade of Boston, the number of Negro troops decreased for a time, partially because of the resentment created when southern soldiers joined the army and found blacks in ranks higher than their own. For nearly two years, enlistments by freedmen were rejected, but in late 1777 when the manpower shortages in the army became critical, they were once again recruited.

In the south, black women with the American army were usually slaves, serving as nurses or cooks so that the men could apply themselves totally to military matters. General William Smallwood, once the guest of Sally Wister, wrote the President of the Maryland Council: "I should be glad that the Sale of the two Negroe women . . . might be suspended. Their services will not only be valuable to me, but will promote the good of the Service as they will supply the Place of Soldiers—who other ways must be necessarily employed in my Kitchen."

Although the American army theoretically disapproved of employing slaves as soldiers, some southern families did enlist their servants as substitutes under the guise that the black men had been freed. Actually most were returned to slavery when their period as a surrogate soldier was completed.

The women of these black soldiers were probably not free to follow the army. In the south, a formal system of control carefully restricted the movements of slaves. Both men and women were required to have passes from their owners in order to leave their plantations and penalties were severe for those apprehended without proper credentials. By holding hostage the wives and lovers of black soldiers away at war, the southern slave owner helped to assure that his male servants would not be so prone to desert.

In addition to serving as soldiers, black men in the south were often hired out by their owners to the army in order to perform manual labor on projects such as construction work. Ann Lauce, a South Carolina slave owner, received £55 for the services of her servants to continental artillery units. Some black women may also have been loaned to the army for such temporary service.

The British army may also have had black camp women as part of their entourage. But in the South, escaped female slaves were confronted with return to bondage if they were apprehended by whigs. As a result, their presence in the camps was probably not extensive, particularly when the British were moving through enemy territory. Many escaped men in the south were appointed as pilots, scouts and foragers. The activities of these quick moving units were not conducive to including women who might have slowed the progress of the raiding forces.

New York City was the center of activity for British camp followers. Although Lord Rawdon had complained about the lack of cooperative women during the early days of the English occupation, the situation was soon remedied. Prostitutes from the area surrounding Manhattan made the city a lucrative headquarters for their trade. Another source of professionals were German women who had been widowed or deserted since coming to the colonies. Unable to speak English, an obstruction to forming a permanent relationship with British soldiers, many of the Hessian wives became prostitutes in order to survive.

England may have been the most important source of prostitutes if the saga of the "Jackson" women is indeed true. According to this report, as the number of British troops increased in Manhattan, rapes committed upon local women increased so drastically that a major conflict developed between the population and occupying troops. In an effort to calm the situation, officials in the London war office reportedly entered into an agreement with a trader named Jackson. Under the contract, Jackson agreed to procure 3,500 young women at approximately $2 a head and transport them to the army in New York.

According to the legend, trader Jackson virtually kidnapped many of the females from the streets of London, Liverpool and Southhampton, but during the voyage to America, one of the vessels carrying the women was lost at sea. Jackson supposedly substituted fifty black women from the West Indies to fill his quota. Thus the basis for the description of the prostitutes as the "Jackson Whites," and the "Jackson Blacks."

During the six years that the prostitutes were reportedly kept in New York, their surroundings were less than ideal. Confined to a stockade at Lispenard Meadows, now a section of Greenwich Village, the women's sole duties were to satisfy the sexual desires of the soldiers.

According to the tale, their homes were shanties with no sanitary facilities and little protection from the biting cold was provided. Eventually a great number of children were born to women in the group, but the worst trials were still to come.

The situation of one woman in Manhattan was far different from that of the Jackson women. Just as Clinton had replaced Howe as commanding general, Mary Baddeley had supplanted Elizabeth Loring as favorite to the army's highest officer.

In 1767, Sir Henry Clinton had married one Harriet Carter, a gentlewoman who died five years later after bearing five children. After her death, Clinton's public as well as private life degenerated. He neglected his duties in Parliament, ignored his family and in general, lost enthusiasm for all his work. In Mary Baddeley, Clinton found a new love which would last throughout the war and until his death many years later. Like Howe and Elizabeth Loring, Clinton and Mary made no effort to conceal their involvement.

As the daughter of an Irish Member of Parliament, Mary O'Callaghan created a stir when she married Thomas Baddeley, a carpenter who was slated to join the British army and ship out for Boston as a Sergeant-Major. Mary, who may have been still a teenager at the time, was attractive to many men, and in particular one of her husband's superior officers. After their arrival in the rebelling colonies, Baddeley was demoted to private, presumably because of either his or his wife's objections to the advances of the superior.

Clinton entered the situation when he hired Mary as his housekeeper and the pair soon became involved in an intimate, but platonic relationship. In 1776, Clinton intended to take Mary with him on the British invasion of South Carolina, but this plan was thwarted when she became pregnant with Baddeley's child. Instead, the general offered her money for her keep in his absence: ". . . She modestly refused all but what she considered as her wages," Clinton noted, "And although I own honestly I could have been tempted even at that time to a connection with her, her conduct was so uniformly discreet that I never dared hint it."

Mary was a "wretched being" when Sir Henry returned. She had suffered through a severe winter complicated by childbirth, a shipwreck, poverty and illness, but had arrived safely in New York. The general set about to make her life easier, and in the process grew passionately attracted to her. Mary stood firm in her faithfulness to her husband, but while serving Clinton as housekeeper she did provide great economic satisfaction. The general estimated that from her economies alone, he was able to save $10,000 during his American tour. Finally their personal relationship changed. Clinton was able to turn an indiscretion by Baddeley to his own advantage. He later described the event:

> Many months passed; and, though she admitted me to certain liberties, I never could prevail on her to grant the last—until resentment did what opportunity and importunity and a warm attachment could not affect. She dectected her h [usband] in an intrigue with a common strumpet. She came to me directly, told him she would, and surrendered. Whether it was the sincerity and warmth of my attachment to her or the want of both in him I don't know; but she certainly avoided him as much as she in decency could, and attached herself to me. And I will be free to own I did all I could to fix her in that disposition, by representing the danger of her connection with a man capable of such depraved conduct.

Thomas Baddeley encouraged the affair between his wife and the commanding officer, and perhaps in return, Clinton heaped advancements on the soldier. Baddeley was unwaveringly grateful to the general, but later in the war, Clinton's actions toward the husband would put a permanent stain on the commander's reputation and result in Baddeley's death.

Although all was quiet in New York, bloody raids continued on the frontier. By 1778, the neutrality of the great Iroquois League had been abandoned by each of the Six Nations. With it the confederation itself was destroyed. Brant and his siter Molly had used their influence to bring the Onondaga, Cayuga, Seneca and Mohawk into the war on the side of the British. The Oneida and minor fragments of the Tuscarora joined the American cause.

Indian desertions during the battles at Fort Stanwix and Saratoga had not diminished the British use of their red comrades on the frontier. In July of 1778, a force of about 1,000 loyalists rangers and Indians swept down on the Wyoming Valley in Pennsylvania. In addition to burning and looting the countryside, the force defeated a group of rebel settlers near what is now Wilkes-Barre. Joining the rebel elements were Delaware who had long warred with the Iroquois over territorial rights in the valley.

The battle and subsequent events became known as the "Wyoming Massacre." Tales of atrocities committed on whigs flew throughout the country. More than 225 scalps were rumored to have been taken in a single battle. Great numbers of women were reported raped and disemboweled. It was claimed that babies were thrown against log cabins or their brains bashed out with tomahawks. Prisoners were allegedly tortured and then burned at the stake in great numbers. Even the livestock did not escape notice, for the Indians were credited with cutting out the tongues of cattle so that the animals slowly starved to death.

Although Brant received most of the condemnation for Wyoming, he was probably not present, for most of the Indians were not Mohawk, but Seneca and Cayuga. While there was undoubtedly some scalping, looting and murder during the raid, the large-scale massacre which was believed to have taken place probably did not occur. The whigs profited from the growing tales of barbarism, but British authorities, attempting to quell growing discontentment in England against the use of Indians, maintained in vain that the massacre did not happen.

Tories and Indians did little to help the British public relations program, for one month later, another force fell on the Cherry Valley in New York. The "Cherry Valley Massacre" further fed the whig rumor mill, but unlike Wyoming, major atrocities were committed by the invaders. One grisly account reveals: "The wife of the Reverend Mr. Dunlap, a Presbyterian clergyman, was found dead, scalped, and an arm of her body hanging on the limb of an apple tree."

Scalping stories had been favorites since the beginning of the war. In 1776, the British *General Advertiser* had reported that Clinton's men were "scalping, slaying, roasting and eating alive," their captives. But the most popular scalp tale in Europe was one spread by Benjamin Franklin in an effort to obtain sympathy for the American cause.

According to Franklin's elaborate fabrication, the Seneca tribe had sent eight bales of scalps to Governor Carleton to be forwarded as a present to King George. A detailed inventory listing the contents of each bale was published by the Pennsylvania doctor. Bale one contained the scalps of 43 American soldiers and 62 farmers. Bale four was a mixed bag including the scalps of 102 farmers, 18 of which were burned alive after being scalped, one clergyman, and 67 relics of greybeards, old men. The total number of scalps in all was set at about 750.

One result of the numerous atrocity rumors was the growing hatred of the whigs toward Indian women. Escaping prisoners returned from captivity with gory tales of the horrible treatment meted out by tribal squaws. Queen Esther was singled out for particular condemnation and her name soon became synonymous with savagery.

"Crazy" Esther's most notorious feat was the supposed massacre of more than a dozen survivors of a battle at Wintermoot's Fort in the Wyoming Valley. As the whig prisoners sat bound in the camp, Esther reportedly performed a weird death chant while wildly dancing around the group. As a grand finale, the chieftress lopped off the heads of the unfortunate prisoners with a tomahawk.

Esther was a mixed-blood *femme du pays*, or "daughter of the country." Her mother, Margaret Montour, was a French woman who had served as an interpreter for the Iroquois. Margaret held a special position among the Indians of the north, not only because she had served the tribe in peace negotiations, but because of her marriage to two braves, the last a powerful Oneida chief named Carundowana.

The facts of Esther's life are even less well known. The least credible report is that she was actually the illegitimate daughter of a Canadian governor. This would have made Esther a full-blooded European and most contemporary accounts describe her as being at least part Indian. Other rumors suggest that Esther's sister Catharine Montour, was the chieftress of the most prosperous village in the Six Nations. A settlement named Catharinestown was indeed a prominent community, but some maintain that Catharine and Esther were actually the same person.

Benson Lossing who chronicled events of the revolution by interviewing survivors of the conflict years later, learned a different story. Lossing maintained that Esther was a Canadian who in her youth was kidnapped during an early war between the Huron, French and Six Nations. She supposedly married a young chief who died about 1730. Esther is also credited with being the wife of Echogohund, a King of the Munsey Tribe which she ruled as a widow.

Like the Cherokee, some of the northern tribes were matriarchal and women shared the powers of decision making. During the rocky years of the 17th and 18th centuries, men were often absent in war and hunting, so by the time of the revolution, women held significant authority in tribal life and home council. Women may have had direct power to appoint and remove male chiefs and in many tribes females could become leaders themselves.

Reports of tortures practiced by women of northern areas do not suggest that females were assigned the tasks because of any particular pleasure which they derived from the cruelty. Nor does the extensive participation in torture by women suggest that they were more adept at the operation. Instead, the practice is a reflection of the social structure of the tribes, where many women in effect "owned" all members of their clan and were responsible for their charge's welfare both before and after death.

Many tribes believed that the soul of a woman or man who had been killed violently would not rest until the murder was avenged. Torture, rather than direct killing, was the preferred method of this retribution. Torture involved an extended period of suffering during which many relatives and friends of the murdered one could take their own personal vindication. A swift killing, however, provided little lasting satisfaction and was gratifying only to the one person who actually performed the final act.

If live prisoners were not available to be returned to the camp as candidates for the ceremony, slain corpses could be scalped and these trophies returned for symbolic torture, death or adoption. Women could also mutilate the bodies of their slain enemies if no live captives were taken. This post mortem disfigurement may have been an additional method of "torture" needed to set at rest the soul of a relation who had been killed.

In most areas, the rules for torture required that the prisoner be exceedingly brave, if possible. Little emotion was a splendid sign and some tribes ate the flesh of outstanding captives in the hopes that the person's heroism would be passed into the Indian's body.

After the massacres at Wyoming and Cherry Valley, whites increased their actions against the Indians. Timothy Murphy of Schoharie County, New York, claimed to have killed scores of red people and personally scalped at least forty in his life. Murphy's credibility may have been somewhat low, for he also bragged that he had shot General Simon Fraser at Saratoga and then neatly picked off Burgoyne's top aide Sir Francis Clarke.

Frontier women also began to defend themselves against maurauding Indians and tories. All along the mountains, women left alone by their soldier husbands were charged with the protection of their homes. Experience Bozarth of Westmoreland County, Pennsylvania, found herself in the midst of the fighting which broke out after Wyoming. According to one chronicler, Experience distinguished herself during an Indian raid on her cabin by seizing an axe and knocking one attacker in the head, cutting out his brains. With these preliminaries completed, she increased the scope of her defense. A letter by a fellow resident dated April 26, 1779, described her next activities:

> Mrs. Bozarth turned to this second Indian, and with her axe gave him several large cuts, some of which let his entrails appear. He bawled out: "Murder, Murder." On this, sundry other Indians (who had hitherto been fully employed, hailing some children out of doors) came rushing in his relief; one of whose heads Mrs. Bozarth clove in two with her axe, as he stuck it in at the door, which laid him flat upon the soil.

Nancy Quackinbush Van Alstine, a settler in the Mohawk Valley and the mother of fifteen children, was another frontier woman credited with bravery. Although raiders had looted her house, they had not burned it because of her friendship with Sir John Johnson. Nancy, irate over the plunder, supposedly slipped into the Indian camp and stole back her possessions.

The Slocum family was not so fortunate. Francis Slocum was five years old when she was kidnapped by Delaware from her home near Wilkesbarre Fort on November 2, 1778. One month later her father was shot and scalped, but her mother survived the second raid to care for nine other children. Francis' treatment by the Indians was probably similar to that of hundreds of other girls and women who were captured on the frontier during the revolution. One major difference was that Francis was "found" by her original family forty-nine years later.

When Francis revealed her life's history in 1837, captivity stories were extremely popular. Almost immediately she became a celebrity, because of the strange story she related.

Following the raid, Francis maintained that she was taken in by the Indians, treated most kindly and given the name *Ma-con-a-gua*, or Young Bear. She was raised as a typical Indian woman, eventually forgetting her English and severing all connections with whites.

After the revolution, Francis married a young chief and moved into the Ohio territory where her tribe joined forces with the Miami. She had several children, the eldest daughter being called *Kich-ke-ne-che-quah*, or Cut Finger. When the volunteer captive's first husband died, she married a Miami and remained in the area, carefully avoiding any action which would result in her being returned to her white family.

But ultimately Francis was discovered. Although critics originally labeled the lost Francis as a hoax, she supposedly provided her identity by recognizing her long-lost brother Joseph by a deformed finger he had smashed in a blacksmith's shop when he was but two and one-half years old. The war had not treated Francis Slocum badly. She had become an important member of her tribe and lived in a fine log cabin. She owned not only a large tract of land, but also a fine herd of cattle, at least 60 horses and had "savings" of about $1,000.

War on the frontier was not always a battle only between white and Indian. It frequently involved white against white and turned Indian against Indian. Often the distinction was difficult to make. Some tories were convinced that many of the "Indian" raids on their land were actually conducted by their whig neighbors in disguise as red man. Rebels suspected the same subterfuge was being made by loyalists.

Like the Europeans, eastern Indians had long warred amongst themselves over territory, hunting rights and personal vendettas. British soldier Roger Lamb, tells in his revolutionary diary the story of an Algonquian woman who was taken prisoner by the Iroquois. In the village where she was taken, her clothes were removed and she was tied hand and foot for ten days. On the eleventh, she escaped by killing an inattentive guard with a hatchet and concealing herself in a hollow tree as her pursuers searched among the woods.

Once she was forced again into hiding, this time in a pond where she submerged herself among the reeds. Lamb reports that for forty-five days she lived on roots and wild berries, before finally making her way to safety near Three Rivers where she met friendly Hurons. She was naked the entire seven weeks.

In the summer of 1779, with all quiet on the eastern front, the Americans began planning a massive invasion into the area of the Six Nations. Commanding the 4,000 troops would be General John Sullivan, the leader of the abortive Newport attack, and General James Clinton of New York.

Clinton considered the possibility that his troops would mistreat Indian women they might encounter. Like others, the general believed that rape was virtually unknown in the Indian culture, and he recognized that his men could introduce the practice on a large scale if care was not taken. Most of the whig women who had been sexually assaulted on the frontier had probably been raped by tory raiders painted as Indians. Clinton commented that although the Indians were notorious for cruel warfare, "they never violate the chastity of any woman, their prisoner." The general further suggested that special measures should be taken to prevent such "stain" by the American forces.

The Americans marched out in two units. Clinton moved south from New York while the larger force under Sullivan proceeded north from Pennsylvania. Both forces were under orders to capture as many Indian prisoners as possible to be held as hostages against future actions on the frontier. The two groups met on August 22, and in a brief skirmish at Newtown, routed an enemy force.

Treatment of the defeated braves on the frontier was far worse than that accorded by rebels to the formal British and German soldiers in the east. Lt. William Barton of the First New Jersey Regiment noted that following one encounter, his men skinned two dead Indians from their waists down and made two pairs of boot leggings.

As Sullivan moved onward, all signs of Indian presence in the area disappeared, thus making the goal of taking hostages impossible. A second order, the destruction of all native settlements, now became the prime directive of the expedition.

Clinton and Sullivan proceeded into the frontier territory, burning villages and crops ready for harvest. The idea was to make the tribes homeless and foodless during the coming winter, thus forcing them to concentrate upon pure survival rather than warring against the whigs.

Many soldiers kept diaries during Sullivan's campaign. Although most are similar in recording overall events, the details of their stories often vary from journal to journal. One example concerns an aged squaw who had been left behind near Catharinestown and found by the invaders. The entire population of her

village had fled into the mountains, but she was too infirm to follow. Lt. Col. Adam Hubley described the scene as he saw it on
Thursday, September 2:

> We this morning found an old squaw who, we suppose,
> by reason of her advanced age, could not be carried off, and
> therefore was left to our mercy. On examining her, she in-
> formed us that the Indians, on our approach last evening,
> went off very precipitately; that the women and children
> had gone off in the morning to take shelter in some moun-
> tains, until the army had passed them: that Colonel Butler
> promised he would send back some warriors who should
> conduct them by bye-ways to some place of safety. She fur-
> ther adds, that, previous to the squaws going off, there was
> great contention with them and the warriors about their
> going off; the former had determined on staying and sub-
> mitting to our generosity; the latter opposed it, and in-
> formed them that by such a step, the Americans would be
> able to bring them to any terms they pleased; whereas, did
> they go off, they would have it in their power to come to
> more favourable terms, should a treaty of any kind be
> offered. . . .

> Previous to our leaving this place, the squaw which was
> taken here, was left, and a hut erected, of which she took
> possession. A quantity of wood was also gathered and car-
> ried to the hut for her use; she was also provided with a
> quantity of provisions. All these favors had such an effect on
> her that it drew tears from her savage eyes.

Major Jeremiah Fogg said that the woman was a Tuscarora
named Madam Sacho and described her as an "awful object." Lt.
Beatty maintained that she was 120 years old and added that the
red woman had revealed that the town was named after a French
woman who had fled Sullivan's forces with her two daughters.
The chieftress was probably Queen Esther's sister Catharine
Montour.

Lt. Barton was impressed with the woman's village and explained:

> Catharinestown is the most important Senakee town we
> have met with since entering their nation. It derived its

name from French Catharine, who in her infancy was taken
from Canada by the savages, and became accustomed to
their manners, marrying an Indian chief, who was said to be
half French himself, from which marriage she claimed this
part of the country. Here she raised a great number of
horses for sale. Its situation a rich flat on the side of a creek.
The corn and beans raised here afforded us one day's subsistence. The great quantity of corn, &c., which is raised here
more than usual, was occasioned by the British giving them
a premium to encourage them in raising it, so as to enable
them to come down on our frontiers.

The troops marched on and by September 15, had burned
every town and field which lay in their path. Only one, a fertile
settlement named Jenise remained. James Norris, a captain in the
Third New Hampshire Regiment, estimated that the men burned
20,000 bushels of corn in Jenise, primarily on giant bonfires made
from the remains of the village's destroyed houses. Lt. Col. Hubley picked up the story, with the surprise entrance into camp of a
wandering frontier woman:

> Previous to our leaving Jenise, a woman with a child
> came in to us, who had been taken prisoner last year near
> Wyoming, and fortunately made her escape from the sav-
> ages. She, with her bratling, was almost starved for want of
> food; she informs us that the Indians have been in great
> want all last spring—that they subsisted entirely on green
> corn this summer—that their squaws were fretting prodi-
> giously, and continually teazing their warrior to make
> peace—that by promises by Butler and his minions, they
> are fed up with great things that should be done for them
> —that they seem considerably cast down and frightened;
> and, in short, she says distress and trouble seem painted on
> their countenances.

The refugee woman was probably a Mrs. Lester whose husband had been killed and scalped near Nanticoke, Pennsylvania,
when she was taken prisoner. Some say that Mrs. Lester was not
exactly happy about being rescued by the Americans. She was reportedly pleased with the Indians and had been parted from them
only because she was unable to keep up with their rapid travel

through the forests. When she entered the American camp, she actually thought that it was one of the British army. Her stay with the whigs was not to be a happy one. Three days after her arrival, her son died and was wrapped in an old blanket, then buried.

Mrs. Lester's report of the dissention between Indian women and warriors on the issue of peace, reflected a new trend in society of the northern tribes. While women, traditionally the peacemakers, supported a quiet settlement with the Americans, the Indian men had been strongly influenced by the war-oriented tory Colonel John Butler, a British representative. In the history of the northern tribes, such important decisions as war and peace had been traditionally reached through discussion among all tribal members. In this case, the procedure involved outside influences from a European society where women had little place in decision-making. The breakdown of authority of women would continue long after the revolution was over.

The American troops, unable to locate any signs of local Indians, turned back towards Catharinestown after destroying the fields at Jenise. On September 23, the troops reached the aged squaw who had been found on the earlier visit. She was not alone. Near her was the body of a young Indian woman who had come down from the mountains. Col. Hubley reported the circumstances:

> During our absence from this place, a young squaw came and attended on the old one; but some inhuman villan who passed through killed her. What made this crime still more heinous was, because a manifesto was left with the old squaw positively forbidding any violence or injury should be committed on the women or children of savages, by virtue of which it appears this young squaw came to this place, which absolutely comes under the virtue of a breach of faith, and the offender ought to be severely punished.

Most whigs, including John Sullivan, considered the expedition a great success. In the official report, Sullivan proudly claimed that he had not left one settlement or field of corn standing in the entire Indian territory. In addition, he announced that the Indians had been driven west and that whigs could move with ease throughout the entire area.

The project was indeed effective from an American viewpoint. Before the revolution, the Iroquois nation was housed in thirty major villages from the Mohawk River to Lake Erie. Only two of these remained undamaged by 1780. Later that year, when Brant returned to Canajoharie, formerly his home and the most important Mohawk town, he found that rebel settlers had moved in, taking the town, houses and fields as their own. As retribution, Brant burned more than a hundred buildings, took sixty prisoners and killed fourteen of the encroachers.

Mary Jemison could also testify to the success of Sullivan's campaign. All throughout the war, Mary had provided help to Butler and Brant. ". . . Many and many a night I have pounded samp for them from sun-up to sun-rise and furnished them with the necessary provisions, and clean clothing for their journey," she boasted. But in the fall of 1779, Mary reaped a bitter harvest for her assistance:

> . . . Sullivan and his army . . . destroyed every article of the food kind that they could lay their hands on. A part of our corn they burnt, and threw the remainder into the river. They burnt our houses, killed what few cattle and horses they could find, destroyed our fruit trees, and left nothing but the bare soil and timber.

When the Indians returned home, they found that there was not enough left "to keep a child one day from perishing with hunger," according to Mary. With winter approaching, Mary determined to set out on her own:

> The weather by this time had become cold and stormy; and as we were destitute of houses and food, too, I immediately resolved to take my children and look after myself without delay. With this intention I took two of my little ones on my back, bade the other three follow and traveled up the river to Gardeau flats where I arrived that night.

Here two runaway slaves took pity on the homeless band. In return for her family's room and board, Mary was given the job of husking 250 bushels of corn. She observed that the men's aid was actually an act of pure charity, for as she worked with the cobs, at least one always stood guard over her, protecting her and her children from possible harm by Indians or unfriendly settlers. Although Mary was relatively safe, the winter was a hard one for the rest of the displaced Indians. She described their situation:

> The snow fell about five feet deep, and remained so for a long time, and the weather was extremely cold, so much so indeed, that almost all the game upon which the Indians depended for subsistence, perished and reduced them almost to a state of starvation through that and three or four succeeding years. When the snows melted in the spring, deer were found dead upon the ground in vast numbers; and other animals of every description perished from the cold also, and were found dead in multitudes. Many of our people barely escaped with their lives, and some actually died of hunger and freezing.

Mary stayed with the runaway black men all the winter, and in the spring they built a cabin for her. Here she remained.

# CHAPTER SEVEN

# *War Leaves the North*

> It is remarkable that, in early youth, she had a great
> abhorrence of the fleshly cohabitation of the sexes; and so
> great was her sense of its impurity, that she often admonished
> her mother against it; which coming to her father's
> ears, he threatened and actually attempted to whip her. . . .
>
> *Testimonies of the Life, Character,*
> *Revelations and Doctrines of our*
> *Ever Blessed Mother Ann Lee*

AFTER MORE THAN FOUR YEARS of combat, victory for the British in the northeast seemed no clearer than before Lexington
and Concord. American successes on the frontier indicated that
the west provided no avenue for conquering the colonies. Thus,
in 1779, England's attention turned toward the south.

Only isolated engagements had occurred in the lower provinces since 1776 when the British had failed to take Charleston.
But in December of 1778, Lt. Col. Archibald Campbell successfully attacked the rebel stronghold at Savannah and by spring,
whig opposition in the Georgia upcountry was being easily subdued.

The great English push was slowed only temporarily at Kettle Creek, where a small band of American farmers managed to
surprise the King's forces. The whig's success was fleeting, for
soon most of the state was firmly in enemy hands.

Rural areas in northern and western Georgia were the scenes
of some of the most violent and vengeful actions of the war. In

*Nancy Hart, a Heroine of the Revolution*, engraving by F. E. Jones after a drawing by Darley. Photo courtesy of the Library of Congress.

many settlements, tory and whig partisans were of almost equal number. Neighbors commonly ambushed neighbors. Violence rather than reason was the most common solution to disputes, for long standing arguments with local Indians had made hit and run raids commonplace. Grudges were pursued into full scale feuds which were not soon forgiven.

About seventy tories captured at Kettle Creek were condemned to be hanged as traitors, an action almost unknown in the north where loyalists captured in battle were treated as prisoners of war. Although the sentences of most were commuted, five men were executed for chosing the wrong side.

One of the most violent Georgians of the revolution was Nancy Morgan Hart, a six-foot, cross-eyed sharp-shooter, who would become the South's most illustrious heroine. While the exploits of many figures in the rebellion were forgotten after the war, stories of Nancy Hart's deeds continued to grow ever greater with the passing years. By the 1860's, she was revered as a super heroine.

Nancy's background is as undocumented as her later activities, but she was probably born about 1735 on either the North Carolina or Pennsylvania frontier. Some propagandists claimed that she was a cousin to Daniel Boone and Daniel Morgan, but there is no indication that her family was indeed particularly distinctive. By the time of the war, Nancy had settled in a small cabin on the Broad River in Georgia with her husband Benjamin and perhaps as many as eight children.

Like other frontier women, Nancy was uneducated and was probably illiterate. Contemporaries describe her as a clumsy, physically repelling woman who was subject to frequent uncontrollable temper tantrums.

Both Nancy and her husband were present for the fighting at Kettle Creek, an area of such great conflict that it was known as the "hornets' nest." But according to local adventure stories, Nancy's real contributions to the war came at home where she waged a private battle with any luckless tory who happened to pass her way. Nancy is credited with capturing loyalists on roads, in cabins, in the woods, or in any other place where she could gain an advantage. Reportedly she once threw a vat of boiling lye into the face of an enemy agent spying upon her from outside her house. Laughing gleefully at her success, she immediately made him her prisoner.

In other stories, the Georgia heroine is credited with subduing three luckless tories whom she singlehandly escorted to captivity after wading across the Broad River. In another instance, she supposedly disguised herself as a man, walked into the British stronghold at Augusta and, by feining insanity, managed to gather data on upcoming battle plans. In two lesser incidents, she reportedly defended a fort against attacking legions and carried secret information into South Carolina by crossing the Savannah River on a raft she had constructed from logs and grape vines.

The most frequently told tale of the Georgia heroine may be based in part on true facts. Although it has become embroidered through generations of tradition, Nancy Hart may indeed have shown extraordinary courage in at least one incident.

According to this report, five tories, newly arrived from murdering a local militia officer, raided the Hart farm in search of other rebel partisans. Nancy and her twelve-year-old daughter Sukey were alone at the time, for Benjamin had gone to work in the fields.

Five to one odds were evidently too great for even reckless Nancy Hart, so she ostensibly acceded to their demands for dinner, while secretly plotting their capture. She began to cook, sending Sukey for water from a nearby stream, but actually to warn Benjamin of the danger, ordering him to rally the neighborhood. He and his friends were to attack the cabin en masse when a signal was given.

Back at home, Nancy with the help of a jug of spirits, had lulled the tories into false security and was busily stealing their guns. She was discovered in the act, but the alarm, the blowing of a conch shell, was given before the intruders could act. By the time Benjamin and his friends arrived, Nancy had scored another coup. She had killed one tory, mortally wounded another and made captives of the remaining three. The wounded man soon died, and at Nancy's insistence, the others were immediately hanged in her front yard.

Although there is no dependable documentation of Nancy's adventures by reliable witnesses during the war, it may be erroneous to completely reject the basic theory that she was indeed involved in numerous exploits on the frontier. Several difficulties are involved in documenting the history of rural and frontier America during the revolution.

First, unlike the sophisticated urban areas such as Boston and Philadelphia, where the deeds of heroines were recorded by scores of diarists, the sparsely settled frontier had few chroniclers. Even those who could write lived a different type of existence than those in a populated urban environment. For Nancy Hart and her neighbors, the days were filled with difficult physical chores which left little time for maintaining extensive journals or for letter writing. Settlements were isolated and news of events travelled slowly by word of mouth. No newspapers were published in the backwoods of Georgia, and in Savannah, a city under British rule, the successful exploits of a whig woman were unlikely to be touted in the press.

Finally, much of the war on the frontier was fought by local adversaries. No major armies, with their scores of amateur historians recording every event, were witness to the day-to-day skirmishes of the long conflict.

But after the war, citizens all along the Georgia frontier were relating tales concerning Nancy Hart and the stories were remarkably similar in detail. Unlike the Betsy Ross legend which did not spring up for nearly a hundred years after the rebellion, stories of the Georgia heroine were circulating during her own lifetime. Although Nancy may not have actually performed the deeds attributed to her, many of her contemporaries firmly believed that she did.

During the 1820's newspapers apparently began printing accounts of her bravery. Congressman George R. Gilmer suggested that one of the niches in the U.S. Capitol should be filled with a painting of Nancy wading across the Broad River with her loyalist captives. Gilmer also maintained that the various legends had been completely accepted by his mother, a friend of Nancy Hart.

The list of honors continued to increase. An area in her home state was named Hart County. A locomotive was named for her and monuments were erected. During the Civil War, a group of defenseless women in La Grange, Georgia, organized themselves into a mutual protection society called the Nancy Harts. Histories began to appear in which her exploits were accepted as fact. Railroad workers reportedly uncovered several skeletons from beneath the site of her cabin, supposedly indisputable proof of her most famous adventures with the enemy.

But the reputation of husband Benjamin suffered as his wife approached the deity status. Ultimately he was considered as an indigent character, dependent upon his wife for life and subsistence.

Reaction at last set in against the increasingly incredible stories. Some skeptics refused to admit that Nancy Hart had ever existed and considered her a figment of the imagination of Victorian society.

But Nancy Hart did live and her husband actually took an active part in the war as a militia officer. Following the conflict, the family owned at least 650 acres of frontier land, not an inconsiderable total in those days. In the later 1790's, the family moved to Brunswick where Benjamin served as a judge of the Inferior Court. About 1802 he died and Nancy went to live with a son, later moving to Kentucky where she died sometime after 1820.

Even her death failed to halt the flow of legends, for one of her descendants would later write that on the day of her burial, the sun suddenly eclipsed.

Despite the heroics of Nancy Hart, the British, in firm control of Georgia, marched north toward Charleston in 1779.

Ann Manigault observed their campaign. After a brief siege of the city, the Americans were able to turn back the attackers and the British withdrew. For several weeks they remained in the area, skirmishing and plundering, but were finally pushed out of the territory. Ann's diary is filled with minutia concerning her daily social life, but her comments on the war are brief and terse:

> May 4, 1779—Great uneasiness on account of the British troops. 9th—Great Confusion as they were very near. 10th—They were in sight of Charlestown. 11th—Much fireing and it was expected the town would be attacked— Benj. Huger killed by our own people by mistake. 12th— Many flags sent into town. They marched off in the night. 13th—Pretty quiet, but they are very troublesome in the country. 15th—We hear nothing of them. 16th—We are still very uneasy, they are ravaging the country. 17th— 21st—The same, and Genl. Lincoln cannot prevent it. 22nd—Some of our people went to Johnson's Fort, were fired upon, and a good many wounded. 23d—Count Pulawsky had a skirmish with them. 28th—They left James Island and went to Johns Island. 10th—Still there. A little skirmish. 13th—Very hot and dry weather. 30th—They were gone from Johns Island.

On October 9th, American forces supported by elements of the French fleet attempted to retake Savannah. The move failed and further convinced English authorities that a large scale invasion of the south would prove successful. More than 15,000 men with heavy artillery and horses were dispatched from Manhattan to the Savannah River.

Clinton personally led the expedition, leaving only a small force in New York to guard against possible attack by the rebels. Commanding these troops was General Wilhelm von Knyphausen, a Hessian who had the distinguishing habit of buttering his bread with his thumb.

Major General Benjamin Lincoln with a rebel force of only about 5,500 chose to remain in Charleston. Unlike St. Clair who had been in a similar situation at Fort Tie, Lincoln refused to retreat into the country. The whigs thus gambled their major force in the south, on the defenses which had earlier proved unbreakable.

The chance was not a good one. On land the invading legions soon surrounded the city and easily turned back militia attempts to break through with reinforcements. One such skirmish was at Monck's Corner where British officers intercepted American battle plans and were able to defeat the rebel force. An aftermath of the battle was a possibly successful rape attack on three women by British dragoons. The act probably would have gone unnoticed, but the event occurred at Fair Lawn, the home of Sir John Colleton, an important tory.

The situation was even more serious in the harbor where Admiral Marriot Arbuthnot's English ships had cut off all foreign commerce and prohibited any vessels with reinforcements from approaching. The British ships laid down an almost constant bombardment, Arbuthnot, who was constantly feuding with his land based allies, had surrounded himself with a rather rowdy selection of advisors who proposed burning the city and suggested that the vessels ". . . send twenty-four pound shot into the stomachs of the women . . . to see how they will deliver them."

By May 12th, further defense of Charleston became impossible and the city fell after a forty-five day siege. More than 5,000 rebels were taken prisoner, including General Lincoln who would later be exchanged for Baron von Riedesel. Other soldiers were not so fortunate, for many were interned aboard prison ships in Charleston harbor, where they lived on mouldy bread and wormy meat.

Some women were also incarcerated. One report claimed that: "Ladies of the first respectability accused of imaginary crimes, were thrust into the dungeons of the provost, and compelled, promiscuously, to mingle with a motley rabble. . . ."

But the fall of the city was welcomed by hundreds of English sympathizers and soldiers who had been incarcerated since the unsuccessful English invasion of 1776. Many of these loyalists and troops had been neglected, but Elizabeth Thompson, a mantua maker, had not forgotten the needs of a significant number.

Elizabeth and her husband had come to Charleston about 1769 where they set up a shop. But as the conflict with England became more severe, her husband was asked to take an oath of support to the new rebel government. He refused and left the country in 1776. Elizabeth remained and although she was threatened and her slaves confiscated, she suffered no physical harm from the revolutionists.

When the city's prisons began being filled with the enemies of the rebel state, Elizabeth turned her attention to assisting them. She supported captive officers in her house and carried messages, primarily personal ones, from captive soldiers to their nearby army. After the war she would claim a British pension, based partially on this assistance to the friends of the King.

James More, also a Charleston storekeep, supported her petition and announced that as a loyalist she had been of great service to British prisoners. He swore that: ". . . When he was a Prisoner himself, has known several Battles of Rum and other things sent to several of the Prisoners in Distress which he understood came from the Claimanet . . ." More further swore that Elizabeth was a good business woman and was "esteem'd to be worth a good deal of Money."

On the rebel side, women were busily smuggling food and supplies to whigs in the city. The contraband runners were imminently successful until British officials noted that the slim ladies leaving Charleston were returning only a short time later with enormous bulges under their clothes. The occupiers reportedly solved the problem by marshalling a force of tory spinsters to search the errant whig women.

Two Charleston members of the Timothy family were also affected by the British victory. For nearly fifty years, Timothys of both sexes had been associated with publishing in South Carolina. After the death of Lewis Timothy who had "refounded" the *South Carolina Gazette*, Elizabeth, his widow, continued the publication. Later, her son Peter assumed control and the paper became one of the first in the colonies to oppose British rule. Publication was discontinued for a time in 1775 and 1776, but issuance began again in 1777 under the new name of the *Gazette of the State of South Carolina*.

One of Peter's competitors during the war was his sister Mary Timothy Crouch who ran the *South Carolina Gazette and Country Journal*. Just before the city fell to the British in 1780, Mary was able to slip away with her presses and move north to Salem where she began publishing the *Salem Gazette and General Advertiser*.

On December 6, 1780, Mary announced that the goal of her new paper was to publish news concerning: ". . . the safety and welfare of the United States, to the Liberties and Independence of which the *Salem Gazette* will be ever sacredly devoted." But Mary's project failed after less than a year of publication. She announced the closing of the paper on September 4, 1781, because of: ". . . the want of sufficient Assistance and the impossibility of procuring House-Room for herself and Family to reside near her Business."

Peter Timothy did not flee the city and was taken prisoner with the fall of the defenses. He, along with two signers of the Declaration of Independence, was shipped to a St. Augustine prison, but Timothy was later exchanged. Peter and his two daughters sailed for the Caribbean in an attempt to find refuge but they did not complete the journey. The ship was lost in a storm off the Capes of Delaware. Timothy's widow Ann revived the *Gazette* during the last years of the war, and gained even further prominence because of her appointment as official printer for the state.

One woman who did not witness the fall of Charleston was

Elizabeth Shubrick Lynch, the young wife of Thomas Lynch, Jr. Lynch was only twenty-seven years old when he signed the Declaration of Independence, actually as a substitute for his father who had fallen ill in Philadelphia during the congressional session. After adoption of the Declaration, the Lynchs began the journey back to South Carolina, but Thomas, Sr., died on the way. Soon his son also fell ill. In 1779, the signer and his wife set sail for the West Indies on the first leg of a journey to France where Lynch hoped to recover his health. The Lynchs and their ship vanished without a trace, evidently lost at sea.

After the capture of the port city, Clinton returned with much of his army to New York to defend against a possible attack by Washington. Cornwallis assumed control of the southern forces and engineered a program for pressing into the interior of South Carolina.

On May 29, a British force under Banastre Tarleton annihilated the remnants of a whig force at Waxhaws. Tarleton, enraged by the refusal of the whig commander to surrender before the battle, ordered his men to show no mercy. After the fight, the King's soldiers executed the directive with great effectiveness by bayoneting prisoners who had surrendered and also those who lay wounded on the field.

That night Tarleton wrote Cornwallis: ". . . I have cut 170 Officers and Men to pieces. . . ." Actually the figure was much higher, for only 53 of the original 380 members of the rebel force survived to be taken to a church in Waxhaws where local Irishwomen attempted to save them.

The dashing dragoon, henceforth known as "Bloody Tarleton," or "The Butcher," became the most hated and hunted Britisher in America. Back in Charleston, he set up headquarters in one of the city's finest dwellings. When his reluctant hostess complained that she was allowed only one room in her own house, he announced:

"Reflection convinces me that enemies should not be allowed any conveniences."

In London, Tarleton's successes and the fall of Charleston were greeted with great fanfare. The news could not have come at a better time, for the city had recently been racked by a series of bloody riots organized by Sir George Gordon, the brother of Lady Sarah Lennox's lover William Gordon. The opposition forces lost new ground with the American defeat. Their situation had already been greatly weakened when Catherine Macaulay, one of the most influential and erudite critics had created a public scandal.

Catharine was still a prominent figure in 1777 when she, Patience Wright and Dr. Wilson became the brunt of a popular war joke. According to the tale, the trio planned to take the notorious statue of Catharine to Saratoga, and erect it as a monument commemorating the American victory.

But one year later, Catharine's reputation was near totally ruined because of her marriage to William Graham, a twenty-one-year-old saddler's son. Her literary career suffered and her newly issued history received little acclaim.

Graham's motives for marrying a wealthy and much older woman were openly questioned. In addition, his own background appeared somewhat shady. For a time he had been a surgeon's mate on an East India man-o-war, but was better known as the brother of Dr. James Graham, the "Prince of Quacks." James Graham had invented and attempted to market an electrified couch named the "Royal Patagonian Bed," which, if used during conception, was guaranteed to produce healthy children.

Catharine's connection with this strange family was ridiculed by critics at all levels. *Town and Country Magazine* considered Graham a fortune hunter and Catharine somewhat of a fool. The magazine parodied the marriage in a satire of the most famous soliloquy from Hamlet:

> To marry or not to marry, that is the question— whether it is nobler in the mind to pass my days with an old dotard, who can afford me no joys but what arise from political animadversion, sarcastic observation, and ministerial invective—or fly to the arms of the dear beloved youth, who burns with rapture to embrace me, give loose to all that exotic bliss of which I before have known on the downy pillow of sacred Hymen's couch!

English feminist Hannah More was both shocked and disgusted by the marriage. She also feared that the reaction against

Catharine's escapade would harm the English women's movement:

> I knew her to be absurd, vain, and affected; but never could I suspect her of the indecent, and I am sorry to say, profligate turn which her late actions and letters have betrayed. The men do so rejoice and exult; yet have they no real cause for triumph for this woman is far from being any criterion by which to judge the whole sex. She was not femine either in her writings or her manners. She was only a clever man.

Dr. Wilson, with whom Catharine had been living for several years, was perhaps the most upset of all. In revenge for her unfaithfulness, Wilson publicly threatened to expose certain incriminating letters written by the historian. Some claimed that he became completely unhinged and spent much of his time ranting against his former companion. One friend believed he was beyond help and noted that he was ". . . half gone and it would not be a sin to bury him."

Two countries away in Spain, another woman was suffering because of the American war. She was Sarah Livingston Jay, the wife of John Jay, America's emissary to the Iberian state. Sally, the daughter of New Jersey Governor William Livingston, had married Jay five years earlier. As a member of the powerful Livingston dynasty, the young woman exerted great pressure on her husband.

One Spanish observer noted this domination and sought to use it for his country's ends. In describing the Jay couple, the Spaniard announced: "This woman, whom he loves blindly, dominates him and nothing is done without her consent, so that her opinion prevails, though her husband at first may disagree; for which I infer that a little management in dealing with her and a few timely gifts will secure the friendship of both. . . ."

Sally Jay probably could not be bought for a "few timely gifts," for she had been raised in an atmosphere of both wealth and political intrigue. Her father had left the Livingston home in New York to become one of the most powerful men in the colonies and a member of the Continental Congress.

*Mrs. John Jay* (Sarah Livingston), engraving after a painting by Alonzo Chappel. Photo courtesy of the Library of Congress.

As the first whig governor of New Jersey, his outspoken opposition to the King resulted in a bounty being offered for his capture. Livingston, seemingly unconcerned that he was a wanted man, simply commented: "They certainly overrate my merit, and I cannot conceive what induces them to bid so extravagant a sum, having now raised my price from 500 to 2,000 guineas. . . ."

Sally's connections with revolutionary leaders were far superior to her husband's. Her uncle Philip was a signer of the Declaration of Independence and her cousin Robert was a member of the elite committee appointed to compose the document. Her uncle Peter was president of the New York Provincial Congress and her aunt Sarah was better known as Lady Stirling, the wife of General William Alexander.

The Jays left America in October of 1779 to cement the shaky alliance which had brought Spain into the war against Britain. Jay's specific job was to assure that Spain held firm in her belligerency, despite the pressures from other European powers to negiotate a peace. If possible, Jay was also to secure loans or grants from the Bourbon court.

Sally was well fortified with advice and high hopes for the voyage. Her father had specifically warned her against the evils of cosmopolitan Europe and advised that she: ". . . suffer not the Gaities and Amusements of the World, and the particular Avocations of what is called *high life*. . . ." George Washington sent her a lock of his hair as a remembrance and his wishes that she would find: ". . . prosperous gales—unruffled Sea—and everything pleasing and desirable. . . ."

Washington's hopes were not to be granted for the trip was to prove most discomforting. Two weeks out, the vessel's main mast fell because of slack rigging created when the ship moved into the warm waters of the Gulf Stream. The fore and mizzen masts also collapsed, the bowsprit broke and the rudder almost fell into the sea. Sea sickness from high waves plagued the passengers as the boat limped into Martinque for repairs. After ten days, the party boarded a French frigate bound for Spain and barely managed to escape a British man-o-war.

The Jays' trials were not over even after landing. Transportation to the capital at Madrid was inferior and expensive. The longest trek was made in a small cart pulled by two mules with bells around their necks. At night, the family was often overcharged and sometimes slept in rooms next to the livestock. In addition to the bed lice and fleas, the night's rest was often disturbed by the ringing of the animals' bells.

Finally in April of 1780, after a journey of six months, the whig representative and his wife at last arrived in Madrid. Jay received a chilly reception at the Spanish court, a sign of the indifference which would plague the entire mission. During his two years of residence in Spain, Jay did not meet King Charles III. The American was constantly misled, usually by royal courtiers who played him against agents of other powers who were also seeking favors from the Spanish.

Soon after their arrival, Jay was forced to leave Sally, who was pregnant, while he journeyed to the countryside where court was being held in summer residence. The Jays' financial situation was near desperate and little help was expected from the rebelling colonies where funds were scarce. At this time, the American emissary lived in one room of a country inn and lacked funds to buy even a carriage or the mules to pull it. Most important, he could not afford to hire private messengers to carry his secret correspondance to Benjamin Franklin in Paris or to the government in Philadelphia. As a result, the official dispatches were sent by public post, where the missives were usually opened and read by unfriendly agents.

Jay was particularly concerned about Richard Cumberland, supposedly a British playwrighh, but actually an enemy agent attempting to heal relations between England and Spain. Cumberland had not come alone, but had brought to Spain his wife and two daughters who romanced with local officials.

But on July 14, Jay was able to write happier news. To William Livingston he announced: "I give you Joy—there is a little Stranger here, who I hope will one Day have the Pleasure of calling you Grandfather. . . . The Mother is in a fair Way and the Child thrives finely." But the gaiety was short lived. On August 28, a depressed Sally Jay notified her mother:

> On Monday the 22nd day after the birth of my little innocent, we perceived that she had a fever, but were not apprehensive of danger until the next day when it was attended with a fit. On Wednesday the convulsions increased, and on Thursday she was the whole day in one continued fit, nor could she close her little eye-lids till Fryday morning the 4th of August at 4 o'clock, when wearied with pain, the little sufferer found rest in—Excuse my tears—you too mamma have wept on similar occasions.

Jay's grief at the death of his daughter was not counterbalanced by success at court. His negotiations continued to progress poorly. In addition, two powerful monarchs with vested interests in settling the dispute in America to the advantage of England, were purposefully hampering the whig's Spanish venture. They were Russia's Catherine II and Maria Theresa, empress of the Hapsburg empire.

Catherine the Great had closely monitored Jay's progress in Madrid and Franklin's success at the French court. Her attention to the colonial war was not, however, rooted in any philosophical comradeship with either the advocates of democracy or those of absolutism. Instead, Catherine's strongest motivation was the self-interest of the vast country which she governed.

Since Russia under Peter the Great had emerged as a distant member of the European family of nations, its rulers had attempted to maintain a balance of power among the stronger monarchies in the west. A European country with an overwhelming force, whether it was France, England or Prussia, would threaten the independence of Russia. Traditionally, Russian rulers had favored England and opposed France who seemed to be building strong ties with principalities bordering on the imperial frontiers.

But in 1776, Catherine refused to aid England by providing mercenaries for the American campaign. She feared that with a quick victory, England would be greatly strengthened and could then turn imperialistic eyes toward the east. After France and Spain entered the war, however, Catherine urged England to make peace, probably in the hope that George III would not continued to involve his country in a long and costly war, thus enabling France to become dominant on the continent. In 1779, the Russian Empress sent word informally that she would negotiate the dispute and one year later, she tendered a formal offer.

Catherine was one of the most learned and flamboyant of the world leaders. She had spent many of the early years of her unhappy marriage to the Grand Duke Peter III reading histories, political writings and treatises on social philosophy. Her private writings show a deep understanding of the basic concepts of democracy, liberty and freedom.

The works of Voltaire and Montesquieu made vivid impressions on her own political ideas and one of Catherine's first manifestoes after seizing the throne was a criticism of despots. In an

Catherine the Great of Russia. Attributed to Dmitrii Grigore-
vich Levitskii. Courtesy of Mrs. Merriweather Post, Hill-
wood, Washington, D.C.

age when the decisions of most rulers were considered beyond
criticism, she recognized that conflict in a nation was not always
the fault of the citizen and claimed that a leader: ". . . if unre-
strained by humane and benevolent qualities in the sovereign
holding absolute power, is an evil which is often the first cause of
many baneful results."

Catherine originally hoped that all her subjects would enjoy

enlightened rule. Among her private notes are statements which
seem to capture the spirit of the American revolution:

> Liberty, the core of everything, without you there
> would be no life! I want the laws to be obeyed, but I want
> no slaves. My general aim is to create happiness, without all
> the whimsicality, eccentricity, and tyranny which destroy it.

> When you have truth and reason on your side, they
> should be exposed to the view of the people, it should be ex-
> plained that such and such a reason leads to such and such a
> decision. If necessity is based on reason, one can be sure that
> the majority will then accept it. It is truth that induces com-
> pliance, not ostentatious language.

Yet Catherine's rule was based on the strength of the nobility and her generalizations against oppressive power of absolute
monarchs were not sufficiently strong for her to free Russia's
serfs or extend any great power to those outside her hand picked
counselors. When she became one of the first world leaders to be
confronted with revolution, she reacted with the same unbridled
force which George III would later apply to his own difficulties.

The revolt which made Catherine an expert in the field of
revolution began in 1773. Her protagonist was cossack Emelyan
Pugachev who aroused thousands of dissatisfied peasants in Russia's east and southeast. For months the rebels rampaged, robbing
mansions, killing nobles and burning fields. By 1774, the force
was strong enough to march on Moscow, but the threat was
averted when Russia's war with Turkey was ended and reinforcements were able to pull back in time to defend the motherland
against internal overthrow. Pugachev's forces were overcome and
he was beheaded after being betrayed by his own top officers.
But Catherine forbade any retribution against his followers. Gossips in European circles claimed that the revolt was the work of
French agents.

As the American conflict began, the Empress predicted that
the British would be unable to keep their provinces and wrote:
"The colonies have told England good-bye forever." Catherine
had little confidence in the Hanoverian monarch in London, and

ordered: "Do not speak to me about Brother George, because his name is never mentioned to me without making my blood boil."

But England held high hopes that Catherine would aid their cause and like the other warring powers, dispatched courtiers to woo the Russian ruler. Ambassador Sir James Harris was constantly at work in behalf of his country, claiming that with Catherine's help, peace could be achieved. The Empress retorted that Britain could create peace much easier by freeing her American colonies than by fighting them with the military help of Russia.

Harris privately considered Catherine's rule greatly lacking in the finesse shown by other monarchs. But her overt plunges into the international field may have been a result of her strange background which was far different than that of most 18th century leaders.

Catherine, once an obscure German princess, was brought to the Russian court when she was fifteen years old, as the prospective bride of the Grand Duke. Under the tutelage of Empress Elizabeth, then ruler of the vast country, Catherine cast off her identity as a European woman and adopted the customs of Russia. She became fluent in the language of her new land, converted to Russian orthodoxy and changed her name from Sophie Charlotte. Life at the court was rather strange under the eccentric Elizabeth, who claimed to own 15,000 dresses and frequently gave parties where men dressed as women and women as men. Catherine attended these events and noted that they were often dangerous. The women guests were in constant peril of being knocked to the floor by the men's wildly swinging crinolines.

The Grand Duke showed no great mental ability and even after marriage spent much of his time playing soldiers with his dwarfs and valets. The royal marriage was probably not consummated for at least seven years, and the male heir born to Catherine in 1754 was possibly the son of Sergei Saltikov, a prominent Russian nobleman and the first in a long line of lovers.

After Elizabeth died, Peter's reign was brief. Within several months he had managed to alienate almost every segment of society and power. In 1762, Catherine supported by the army, took control. Dressed in the uniform of an officer, she personally led her troops in rebellion. Peter was arrested and died mysteriously several months later in confinement. Soon, another pretender was murdered in prison.

Although Catherine promoted the arts, literature and architecture, she is often remembered best for her long series of paramours. Most of her "favorites" had a semi-official status, but went through a vigorous screening program before they were appointed. Candidates chosen from the ranks of eligibles were meticulously examined by a doctor to satisfy Catherine's concern about contracting venereal disease. They were then tested for physical prowess by one of her ladies in waiting and finally, if completely satisfactory, made their way into the Empress' bed.

Various distractions of court life did not deter Catherine from aggressively performing her duties of rule. In 1780, she made perhaps the most outstanding diplomatic venture of her career by moving actively into the Anglo-American war.

For some time, neutral nations in Europe had been concerned with the harrassment of their vessels by American privateers and British warships. Frequently, merchant ships from the non-belligerent countries would be waylaid and searched for contraband or military cargo bound for one of the nations participating in the war. Often entire boats were seized as "prizes" for carrying war materiel to the enemy.

But the definition of what exactly constituted contraband differed from country to country. As a result, many goods were confiscated by Americans or British which were not considered military supplies by the nation owning the vessels. More and more frequently, the ships of neutral powers were being taken for transporting goods they considered to be non-military products.

Catherine, seeking to increase her prestige and protect Russian commerce, moved to halt the practice of confiscation. In 1780 she called for creation of a league of Armed Neutrality composed of nations such as Sweden, Denmark, Norway, Prussia, Austria and Portugal. Under her plan, member nations would provide armed escorts for merchant convoys, thus assuring that non-contraband products would not be seized by the belligerent powers.

The league was a direct threat for England where a profitable industry had been created in the sale of prize cargos. Although American privateers had periodically harrassed neutral ships, most of their activities were concerned with English-owned vessels and the affect of the league would be minimal on their operations. Many in the colonies considered the organization to be an aid to their cause, for the armed escorts would assure that great amounts of supplies and naval stores would safely reach France and Spain.

In anticipation that the league would be successful, England forced the Netherlands into armed conflict and declared war in December of 1780. By becoming a participant in the conflict, the ships of the Netherlands would not be entitled to the protection of the neutral league and would be easy prey for the English prize hunters.

In addition to the creation of the Armed Neutrality, Catherine sought to codify the various descriptions of contraband by drawing up a specific list of goods considered to be seizable. England did not recognize the list as binding, but the Americans quickly accepted the Empress' standards. Actually the whigs hoped to use the list as a tool for gaining official recognition from the Russian ruler.

Francis Dana was detailed to Catherine's court to negotiate a treaty between the two nations which would formally recognize the contraband list, and in turn the existence of the new American nation. But Dana's situation became much like that of John Jay in Spain. For the two years he remained in Russia, Dana was virtually ignored by the Empress and his mission completely failed.

Catherine, like other European leaders, was primarily concerned with the colonial war only as it affected the continent of Europe, not as it influenced the course of independence in America. The colonial situation of the rebels was of little consequence in the large power struggle between England, France, Spain, the Netherlands and various smaller nations east of the Atlantic. The Empress' 1780 offer of mediation made no attempt to include recognition of American interests. The British privately favored Russian intervention, for they believed that Catherine would be inclined to support their claims against those of other European nations, but would be reluctant to interfere in the actual colonial rebellion. But to assure such favoritism, the British secretly offered to Catherine control of the island of Minorca in exchange for her special favors. Catherine refused the offer.

Europe's second powerful Empress, Maria Theresa, ruler of the Hapsburg empire, was also involved diplomatically in the revolution. Unlike Catherine, Maria Theresa had spent much of her life as a devoted wife, bearing sixteen children and adherring to a strict standard of fidelity to her husband Francis Stephen of Lorraine. Soon after Francis' death in 1765, the Empress considered abdicating so that she could retire to a convent. The plan was discarded, but she did appoint her son Joseph II as co-regent so that much of the burden of rule would be relieved from her hands. The move may have been later regretted, for Joseph, unlike his more conservative mother, was expansionist minded.

Throughout her forty-year-reign, the Hapsburg empress had concentrated on merely maintaining the lands of her inheritance, which included Austria-Hungary, sections of Italy, Yugoslavia and nearby lowland duchies. Although her fortunes were tied to France, partially through the marriage of her daughter Marie Antionette to Louis XVI, the Hapsburg ruler at first refused to become embroiled in the colonial war. But gradually concern emerged that Louis would be unable to continue a long war against England. A victory by George III would leave the Hapsburg territory far more vulnerable to possible invasion.

Just days before the French formally committed troops to American soil, Joseph attempted to block the action. The co-regent, who was planning to invade Bavaria, called upon Louis for the loan of 20,000 French soldiers to combat a possible countermove by Frederick the Great. The transfer of such a large number of French troops to central Europe would have made it impossible for Louis to provide military assistance to America. Moreover, war between Prussia and the Hapsburgs posed a far greater threat to France than the colonial conflict thousands of miles away.

Louis escaped the dilemma by joining with Catherine the Great who announced that she would intervene with 30,000 Russian troops to prevent a war in Europe. The prospects of Catherine's legions near their borders was sobering to both Joseph and Frederick. The prospect of war receded and Louis was thus free to send his men to the colonies.

The Americans, perhaps believing that Joseph would be more receptive to aiding their military venture than his more peace minded mother, sent agents to the co-regent's court. However Maria Theresa's power and influence far exceeded that of her son, and she refused to meet with the American representatives. She further instructed her foreign ambassadors to have no contact with whig representatives and even more important, she banned trade between her territories and the rebelling colonies.

In 1779, Maria Theresa formally offered to negotiate England's controversy with Spain. But the Empress' efforts went no farther. In 1780, she died after catching a cold during a pheasant shoot at Schönbrunn.

Although some diplomatic efforts in Europe were meeting with failure, a far greater danger to the American cause was brewing. General Benedict Arnold, hero of Québec and Saratoga, had become involved in a treasonous plot with Sir Henry Clinton. Arnold was not alone in his intrigue, for his wife Peggy Shippen, was a co-conspirator and may have actually instigated the entire operation.

In late summer of 1780, Arnold was appointed commandant of the rebel fortress at West Point. The job, although not a field command, was important, for the impregnable installation was considered vital in controlling commerce on the Hudson. From the West Point heights, Americans were able to halt any northern advance which the British might undertake to link their Manhattan forces with those of the crown in Canada. Burgoyne's defeat at Saratoga had demonstrated that a New York campaign could not be successful if attempted inland where supply lines were undependable and reinforcements were forced to cross through enemy held terrain.

Arnold's plan was to turn over the West Point garrison and its 3,000 troops to the British in exchange for a payment of £ 20,000. If the scheme succeeded, England's armies would be able to cut the American forces in half, thus opening a two front war. The rebels, desperately short of men in the south, and unable to draw additional soldiers from New England, could be forced into surrendering.

Peggy's deep involvement in the plot was unknown to all but a few conspirators. Her social background made it unlikely that she would be suspect.

Peggy Shippen was the youngest daughter of Philadelphia judge Edward Shippen. Although long a prominent family in Pennsylvania politics, the war had lessened Shippen's income by cutting off patronage from royal appointments. The family was superficially neutral, but returned to the capital from the countryside when Howe settled safely inside the city.

During the winter of 1777–1778, Peggy and her sisters Polly and Sally were belles of society. Judge Shippen's complaints that party dresses and entertaining expenses were straining their reduced budget did little good. Peggy became an intimate of John André, the planner of the meschianza and was scheduled to be one of the most honored guests at the party, until her father forbade her attendance.

When the British moved out, the Americans entered and Arnold was placed in command of Philadelphia. The city was not a particularly desirable place at the time. Lucy and Henry Knox visited, but refused to stay because "it stunk so abominably."

One returning Philadelphian announced that although the city had not sustained permanent damage from the British occupation: ". . . the morals of the inhabitants have suffered vastly." Many of the local young women were showing distinct signs of pregnancy, clear evidence, so he claimed, of widespread fraternization with British officers. The observer suggested that the increasing weight of motherhood being carried by the collaborators on their fronts, should be counterbalanced by an additional counterweight on their rears:

> I cannot yet learn whether the *cork rumps* have been introduced here, but some artificial rumps or other are necessary to counterbalance the extraordinary natural weight which some of the ladies carry before them. You will probably be surprised at this, but you may rely on it as a fact: indeed many people do not hesitate in supposing that most of the young ladies who were in the city with the enemy and

wear the present fashionable dresses have purchased them at
the expense of their virtue. It is agreed on all hands that the
British officers played the devil with the girls. The privates,
I suppose, were satisfied with the *common prostitutes.*


Some attempts were made to ostracize the women who had
been receptive to the advances of the British soldiers, but American officers after a hard winter at Valley Forge were desperate
for female companionship. Soon the city's party rooms were filled
again with the young belles. This time, however, they danced
with Americans, not redcoats and performed steps called "Clinton's Retreat," "The Defeat of Burgoyne" and "The Success of
the Campaign."

Rebecca Franks, who had earlier asked Anne Paca to join
the gaiety, was reveling with renewed enthusiasm, but she did
not find admirers in all corners. Rebecca met her match for sarcasm in Charles Lee when she publicly ridiculed the general for
wearing patches on his pants. Lee reacted characteristically by
sending her the trousers and challenging her to a duel. In a
widely published letter to her, Lee maintained that the trousers
were actually fashionable riding breeches which she would discover on examining them:

> I say, I dare you, and your whole junto, to your worst; turn
> them, examine them, inside and outside, and if you find them
> to be green breeches patched with leather, and not actually
> legitimate *sherry vallies,* such as His Majesty of Poland
> wears. . . . I will submit in silence to all the scurrility which,
> I have no doubt, you and your abettors are prepared to pour
> out against me in the public papers, on this important and
> very interesting occasion. But Madam! Madam! Reputation
> (as "Common Sense" very sensibly, though not very uncom-
> monly observes,) is a serious thing. You have already injured
> me in the tenderest part, and I demand satisfaction; and as
> you cannot be ignorant of the laws of dueling, having con-
> versed with so many Irish officers, whose favourite topic it
> is, particularly in the company of the ladies, I insist on the
> privilege of the injured party, which is, to name his hour
> and weapons; and as I intend it to be a very serious affair, I
> will not admit of any seconds; and you may depend upon it,

Miss Franks, that whatever may be your spirit on the occasion, the world shall never accuse General Lee with having turned his back on you. . . .

P.S. I have communicated the affair to only my confidential friend _____, who has mentioned it to no more than seven members of Congress and nineteen women, six of whom are old maids; so that there is no danger of its taking wind on my side; and I hope, you will be equally guarded on your part.

While Lee and Rebecca were publicly sniping at one another, Arnold was courting Peggy Shippen with the same enthusiasm that he had shown to Lucy Knox's friend Elizabeth De Blois. He was also using the same words, for the general had merely taken his earlier love letters to Elizabeth and slightly reworked them before dispatching copies to Peggy.

Although Arnold was a thirty-eight year old widower and Peggy a young eighteen, the courtship was successful. On April 8, 1779, they were married and as a wedding present, the general purchased a large estate named Mount Pleasant. Lavish expenditures such as this had constantly placed Arnold deeply in debt. In Peggy Shippen, he had found a mate who enthusiastically endorsed his concept of deficit financing.

For some time Arnold had been dissatisfied with the American leadership. He frequently complained that the army had not sufficiently recognized his services with promotions and financial rewards. The commandant also developed a slightly shady reputation for questionable business ventures relating to the conflict. On one occasion he was court martialled and reprimanded by Washington for using government wagons to transport private merchandise for sale. But unknown to the military tribunal trying him, Arnold had become involved in a situation which could prove far more harmful than the use of military transports for private gain.

One month after his marriage, Arnold contacted Joseph Stansbury, a Philadelphia merchant with connections to Clinton in New York. According to Stansbury, Arnold volunteered to do anything within his power to assist the British.

The continued use of Stansbury to carry messages between the two camps proved dangerous, so the conspirators concocted a new plan whereby Peggy would write seemingly harmless shipping lists to Clinton's aide John André. Actually the notes were coded messages to the British commander from Arnold.

Clinton originally hoped that Arnold would be placed in command of the southern army, but British successes at Savannah and Charleston had lowered the importance of that post. With the southern wing of the American service almost completely destroyed, West Point was chosen instead as the target.

In August of 1780, the carefully laid plan was threatened. Arnold's past complaints that he had not received a responsible post had been noted and the government chose to reward him belatedly by giving him control of the left wing of the army, one of the most powerful positions in the entire military. For Arnold the news was a disaster. Although he would be more influential in the assignment, he would be forced to work in close conjunction with other generals. Without an independent command, it would be almost impossible for him to turn over any part of the army without being immediately discovered.

Robert Morris was with Peggy when the news of her husband's new appointment arrived. Instead of joy, he reported that she went almost completely out of control and had "hysteric fits." Arnold had already begun to secretly move his funds to London and considered the new honor a great tragedy. A crisis was averted when he insisted that his battle wound, suffered at Saratoga, had not yet healed and that field command was impossible. Instead, he requested and received the West Point post.

Peggy remained in Philadelphia for a time after Arnold had left to organize his new command. She evidently began to renew old flirtations and gossips linked her name with that of Chancellor Robert Livingston, Sally Jay's cousin. The news reached Arnold by way of a letter from his sister Hannah:

As you have neither purling streams nor sighing swains at West Point, 'tis no place for me; nor do I think Mrs. Arnold will be long pleased with it. . . . Though I expect it may be rendered dear to her for a few hours by the presence of a

certain chancellor; who, by the by, is a dangerous companion for a particular lady in the absence of her husband. . . .
I could say more than prudence will permit. I could tell
you of frequent private assignations and of numerous billets
doux, if I had an inclination to make mischief.

Peggy soon joined Arnold at West Point, where the plot
with Clinton was nearing its climax. Correspondence between the
two generals was proving difficult, for a series of rebel guardposts
had been set up to ring Manhattan and the line was almost impossible to penetrate.

It was agreed that John André would go upriver on the ship
*Vulture*, to complete the final transaction when Arnold actually
turned the West Point plans over to the British. The rendevous
between the American commander and one of Clinton's closest
friends and aides was important in illustrating that both sides
were indeed committed to the action.

The secret meeting went well, but after Arnold had delivered the necessary documents, it was too late for young André to
safely return to the British ship. Arnold suggested that the officer
discard his military jacket, partially disguise himself, and make his
way back to Manhattan on foot. Armed with a pass from the
West Point commandant, André thus set out, traveling under the
name of John Anderson.

The plan soon miscarried and the officer was apprehended
by the rebels. But André's captors, not knowing that Arnold was
involved in the scheme, notified the general that one John Anderson had been made a prisoner and certain important documents
had been discovered in his possession. When the news arrived,
Arnold held a brief conference with Peggy, and then rushed
from his house and headed south toward the British vessel *Vulture*, still awaiting André's return. Peggy secluded herself in her
room.

Soon to arrive on the scene was General Washington, still
ignorant of the entire plan. Washington, a friend of both Arnold
and Peggy, had scheduled a routine inspection of the West Point
fortress and was surprised to find the commander absent on his
arrival. The whereabouts of Arnold remained a mystery until

later in the afternoon when the incriminating documents taken from André arrived by messenger. General confusion followed the realization that Arnold had indeed betrayed his command, and in the midst of the chaos, Peggy swung into action.

Still in her room and now only partially clad, Peggy feined delirium. Arnold's sympathetic aide Alexander Hamilton described the scene:

> . . . The General (Washington) went up to see her, and she upbraided him with being in a plot to murder her child. One moment she raved, another she melted into tears. Sometimes she pressed her infant to her bosom, and lamented its fate. . . . in a manner that would have pierced insensibility itself. All the sweetness of beauty, all the tenderness of a wife, and all the fondness of a mother showed themselves in her appearance and conduct. We have every reason to believe she was entirely unacquainted with the plan; and that the first knowledge of it was when Arnold went to tell her he must banish himself from his country and from her forever. She instantly fell into a convulsion and he left her in that situation.

Peggy's innocence was also stressed in a letter which Washington received that evening from Arnold. With the advance warning, the turncoat general had managed to reach the *Vulture* and had then turned his attention to saving his wife. "She is as good and as innocent as an angel", Arnold wrote and the Americans chose to agree. Peggy was allowed to make plans for returning to Philadelphia.

Meanwhile, André was scheduled to be hanged as a spy. Although the British claimed that he was merely obeying the orders of a superior officer when Arnold instructed him to remove his military garb behind enemy lines, there was one hitch to the defense. Arnold and André did not belong to the same army.

Washington offered to exchange André for Arnold, but Clinton was forced to refuse. To return a loyalist who had sought sanctuary would arouse other tories and discredit the word of the crown. Thus while the two Arnolds went free, the young British officer was executed.

At least two citizens had a suspicion that Peggy was not as innocent as she appeared. On her return trip from West Point, Peggy stopped for one evening at The Hermitage, the home of her friend Theodosia Prevost in Paramus, New Jersey. Theodosia, the widow of a British officer killed in the West Indies fighting, was being vigorously courted by Aaron Burr. Burr happened to be visiting that evening, and his later memoirs, describe Peggy's arrival:

> As soon as they were left alone, Mrs. Arnold became tranquilized and assured Mrs. Prevost that she was heartily tired of the theatricals she was exhibiting. . . . that she had corresponded with the British commander, and that she was disgusted with the American cause and those who had the management of public affairs, and that through great persuasion and unceasing perseverance she had ultimately brought the general into an arrangement to surrender West Point.

Although Burr kept Peggy's secret for many years because of their past friendship, other whigs received the traitor's wife with hostility. Arnold's defection was not taken lightly and the situation was further complicated by Peggy's earlier complicity during Howe's occupation of Philadelphia. Elizabeth Drinker recorded one not so cheerful phase of the city's reaction, an effigy parade in "honor" of Arnold:

> On seventh day last, ye 30th ultimo was exhibited and paraded through the street of this City, a ridiculous figure of Genl Arnold, with two faces, and the Devil standing behind him pushing him with a pitchfork. At ye front of ye cart was a very large Lanthorn of green paper, with a number of inscriptions setting forth his crime &c. Several hundred men and boys with candles in their hands—all in ranks; many Officers, ye Infantry, men with Guns and Bayonets, Tag, Rag &c., somewhere near ye Coffee-House, they burnt ye Effigy (instead of ye Body, as was said in ye Papers.)

Despite pleading from Judge Shippen, the Supreme Executive Council of Pennsylvania, on October 27th, ordered Peggy to leave Philadelphia and prohibited her from returning before the end of the war. Peggy joined her husband in New York, and began a life which was to prove far from happy. Rather than improving their financial situation, the Arnolds had entered into an alliance which would cause increasing monetary hardships. Arnold would never be accepted into the society he hoped to dominate. Although he had deserted his own nation to aid England, many of the King's subjects would always consider his conduct in the West Point affair as reprehensible.

The Arnold plot was not the only conspiracy confronting New Yorkers in the fall of 1780. Near Albany, Ann Lee, founder of the nation's Shaking Quakers, had been jailed for counselling men to avoid their military service. Many considered her to be a British agent, sent to hamper the American cause. Others maintained that she was a witch.

"Mother Ann," as the woman was known to her Shaker flock, was far from an enemy saboteur. To the true believers, she was a female messiah, and living proof of the dualism of God. Her followers believed that just as Jesus was the personification of God in male form, Mother Ann Lee was God appearing as a woman.

The founder was born in 1736, the daughter of a blacksmith in Manchester, England. She received little formal education, but worked for a time as a velvet cutter in a textile mill and as a cook in the Manchester Infirmary. Ultimately she joined the fledgling Shaker sect.

In 1762, Ann married Abraham Standerim and mothered four children, all of whom died in their infancy. The trauma of these four deaths would permanently mark Ann's philosophy and her religious leanings increasingly assumed more mystical aspects.

By 1766, Ann had become one of the church's most prominent leaders and was attracting new converts with her magnetic preachings. The established founders gradually fell away from the flock as Ann gained power with her own personal form of theology. The basis of her personal creed, was that cohabitation between the sexes was the source of all evil. Pride, greed, envy and all other sins stemmed directly from sexual competition. Her solution to the problem, and thus the only real path to salvation, was celibacy.

As the cult became increasingly more vocal, reaction began to appear from established churches. Ann was jailed and later claimed that she had been given no food or drink by the authorities during one two week period of incarceration. She survived, she revealed, by divine guidance and the help of a friend who secretly managed to feed her milk and wine through a long stemmed pipe pushed through her cell's keyhole. Recruiting ultimately slacked off in England, and because the sect could not perpetuate itself through progeny, Ann and a small band of her followers left for America in 1774.

The early years of their settlement in the new land were not easy. No wealthy backers were found and the leader was forced to become a washerwoman. Later testimonies report that during this time of trial, she lived in a completely bare room, with no fire and only a cold stone on which to sit. In 1775, Abraham deserted her for another woman.

But by 1776, the cult had become more affluent and was able to purchase land about eight miles from Albany for a utopian colony named Niskeyuna.

The Shakers were largely self-sufficient. Most were artisans or farmers who immediately began building a complete community to house the masses of converts who were expected to appear at any moment. The members were to be disappointed, for during the first three years at Niskeyuna, only one new convert was attracted.

News of the movement was spreading, however. But not all the reports were favorable and the twisting rites performed by the Shakers were often condemned as pagan. Their beliefs of sexual separation were considered superficial by writers such as James Thacher who reported in his diary that news of the group had reached the American army:

> We are just informed of a new order of fanatics who have recently introduced themselves into our country, pretending to be a religious sect; but if reports be true, they are a disgrace to both religion and to human nature. . . . The method which they practice under the name of religious worship is so obviously impious, as to exceed the bounds of credibility; but we have the particulars from eye witnesses,

who have been admitted to their midnight orgies. They spend whole nights in their revels, and exhibit the most unbecoming scenes, violating all rules of propriety and decency. Both sexes, nearly divest of clothing, fall to dancing in extravagant postures, and frequently whirl themselves round on one leg with inconceivable rapidity, till they fall apparently lifeless on the floor. A spectator asserts, that the fantastic contortions of body in which their pretended religious exercises consist, bear the semblance of supernatural impulse.. . . .

At last visitors began coming to Niskeyuna in large numbers, perhaps prompted by curiosity created by reports such as Thacher's. Soon Ann's spell-binding addresses made many return as converts. Hundreds crowded into the settlement to hear the female messiah announce what she claimed to be the words and ideas of God.

The sect could have continued unmolested for many years, but the war prompted Ann to add one dangerous new tenet to her teachings. This was the creed that Shakers could neither take up arms, nor shed blood into the revolution. She also proclaimed that they should not take the oath of allegiance to the new government of rebels, or agree to obey future laws of the republic. The rationale for the refusal was that her followers could not pledge in advance to support legislation which could possibly be oppressive or unjust.

Most opposition to Ann's teachings had formerly come from rival religious groups who were threatened by the rising popularity of the sect. With her new anti-war, anti-government stand, the religious critics were joined by whigs who had tolerated her unorthodox religon, but were enraged by her political dogma.

Ann was accused of witchcraft. Rumors flew that she was a British soldier disguised as a woman so that he/she could set about to foment a counterrevolution.

On July 24, 1780, the commissioners for Detecting and Defeating Conspiracies in New York, issued a warrant for Ann's arrest and the detention of two of her apostles. The justification was that the three ". . . by their conduct and conversation disturb the publick peace and are daily dissuading the friends to the

American cause from taking up arms in defence of their Liberties."

Two days later lawman Jacob Kinney reported that he had apprehended the wanted Shakers and had brought in three additional adherents who were also counselling military evasion. The committee ordered that the group be interrogated as to their exact beliefs. Although the four men prisoners were later released, Ann and a companion named Mary Partherton vehemently renewed their commitment to pacifism. On August 26, the commissioners ordered that the two women should be taken to Poughkeepsie and from there forced to join the British in New York City.

Public reaction to Ann's imprisonment was immediate. Although many citizens did oppose her stand against the war, the colonies were filled with descendants of European immigrants who had been forced to flee their native lands because of religious beliefs. In the midst of a revolution being fought supposedly for personal freedoms, the expelling of a citizen for religious beliefs was repugnant to many. Although some of Ann's believers were staunch tories, there was no firm proof that she was in the pay or control of a foreign power, and her prohibition against violence applied equally to the friends of the King.

On December 4, after she had been imprisoned without trial for nearly five months, the commission yielded to the public clamour. The members may have decided that Ann was more of an eccentric than a threat, but nevertheless required that she be placed under a £200 bond to assure her good behavior:

> Resolved upon the Application of William Lees, that Ann Standerren (who was some time ago sent to Poughkeepsie on Account of her Influence in bringing over Persons to the Persuasion professed by the People called Shaking Quakers the said Persuasion having a Tendency to alienate the minds of the People from their Allegiance to the State by inculcating an Opinion of the Unlawfulness of taking up Arms in defence of the American Cause) and it appearing that many of the Persons of the said Persuasion have been reformed and that no further Evil is to be apprehended from her Influence or Example therefore resolved that the said Ann

Standerren have Permission to return to Nistageune . . . not saying or consenting to any Matters or Things inconsistent with the Peace and safety of this and the United States.

The ban against the preaching of non-violence was not obeyed by Ann who was soon back to the pulpit preaching to ever larger crowds. The imprisonment had made her a martyr and converts flocked to her side. A second colony was set up at New Lebanon, New York, to handle the overflow.

Despite the hardships of the war and her stay in jail, Ann began an evangelical tour of New England. Here the Calvinist doctrine was still strong and the anti-tory feeling much greater than in New York. Unlike the more flexible Anglican Church, great numbers of New England's religious leaders rose up against her tenets. The old accusations that she was either a British agent or a witch surfaced again in the ultra-patriotic sections of the northeast. As a result, both Ann and her fellow travellers were stoned and beaten in many towns in which they appeared.

Sometimes the leader did find a somewhat receptive audience such as in Harvard where she assured the congregation that physical threats were not new to her. In England, she said, she had been bound hand and foot by attackers who attempted to throw her out of a loft window. Accounts of the whippings and beatings which Ann Lee continued to receive became important parts of the Shaker religion. Testimonials by her followers at this time are filled with graphic accounts of various lashings and beatings she was subjected to.

One testimonial described an event which took place about forty miles west of Harvard, during a speaking tour to Petersham. A mob had gathered in front of the house at which Ann was lodging, but the group did not remain out of doors for long:

> . . . they seized fire-brands and searched the house, and at length found her in a bed-room. They immediately seized her by the feet, and inhumanly dragged her, feet foremost, out of the house, and threw her into a sleigh, with as little ceremony as they would the dead carcase of a beast, and drove off, committing at the same time, acts of inhumanity and indecency which even savages would be ashamed of.

In the struggle with these inhuman wretches, she lost her cap and handkerchief and otherwise had her clothing torn in a shameful manner. Their pretence was to find out whether she was a woman or not.

Ann Lee was not the only woman preaching chastity and peace during the war. Jemima Wilkinson, a farmer's daughter, was gathering her own flock in Rhode Island.

In 1776, Jemima, who was eighteen, fell into a deep trance. She arose thirty-six hours later and informed those nearby that she had died, gone to heaven and spoken with God. She reported that her body had been taken over by a spirit named Public Universal Friend, or Friend for short.

Jemima found a wealthy backer in Judge William Potter of South Kingston, who supported her for nearly six years. During the revolution she spent much of her time gaining adherents and healing the ill. Once, for example, she announced that she would walk on water, but when spectators lined the beach, she refused to perform the miracle because of their obvious lack of faith in her power.

Friend also failed in an attempt to raise from the dead, Judge Potter's daughter Susanna. Ultimately, Friend left the state and with a small band of followers settled in a colony near Seneca Lake on the frontier. The clan grew from 25 to 260 in just two years and prospered financially.

Jemima was soon reaping most of the monetary benefits of the colony, but doing little of the work. She did perform some missionary acts among the Indians, but the red peoples did not elect to join her cult. Friend also eliminated her requirement for chastity, reportedly because it interfered with her own private activities. Dissatisfaction spread among her flock and membership decreased. In 1819, the Friend, who had developed a severe case of dropsy, passed away.

# CHAPTER EIGHT

# *Secrecy Behind the Scenes*

> My Dear Tomm,—I have just received you letter with
> the account of my losses, and your almost ruined fortunes by
> the enemy. A severe blow! but I feel not for myself, but for
> you; 'tis for your losses my greatly beloved child that I
> grieve; the loss of fortune could affect me little, but that it
> will deprive my dear children of my assistance when they
> may stand most in need of it. . . . Independence is all I want
> and a little will make us that. . . .
>
> *Eliza Lucas Pinckney* to her son Thomas, May, 1779

AMONG THOSE MOST vitally concerned with Arnold's defection
were the numerous rebel spies working in the Manhattan
area. In October of 1780, most did not know how much information Arnold could betray concerning their operations and identi-
ties.

Soon after arriving at West Point, Arnold had requested a
list of all American contacts in New York. The plea was refused.
Thus Washington's middleman with the New York spy rings,
Major Benjamin Tallmadge, was able to assure most of the opera-
tives that their covers would remain unbroken. But Tallmadge
was unable to allay all those concerned, and for a time, many
agents in the British held city halted their activities.

The Manhattan and Long Island spy organizations had provided valuable information to the commanding general concerning enemy troops' strengths and operations. One of the most

effective units was headed by Robert Townsend, code name Culper, Jr. Townsend's sister Sarah also participated to a minor degree in the organization.

For several weeks following Arnold's arrival in the city, there was no indication that any agent had been betrayed. In late October, however, two valuable workers were arrested and jailed. One was Hercules Mulligan, a tailor who had once served as a contact for Nathan Hale. The other was a woman, identified in American records only as agent 355.

355 was a close companion of Townsend and held his complete confidence. He had earlier written: ". . . by the assistance of a 355 of my acquaintance, [we] shall outwit them all." Their relationship was evidently much closer than friendship for 355 reportedly bore a son to Townsend after she was imprisoned.

The shock of her jailing was so upsetting to the ring's leader that for a time he left the secret service. Tallmadge was informed by a fellow conspirator:

> Several of our dear friends were imprisoned, in particular one that hath been ever serviceable to this correspondence. This step so dejected the spirits of C. Junr. that he resolved to leave New York for a time. I earnestly endeavoured to prevent it but could not. . . .

Hercules Mulligan was soon released. The action was promising for 355, because armies traditionally dealt less harshly with women agents than with men. Most females who were apprehended were confined for a brief period and then released with an admonishment. Agent 355 was not so fortunate. Although no trial was held, she received a dreaded punishment for any prisoner, confinement to the prison ship *Jersey*.

By 1780, the *Jersey* was not so much a ship as a floating death house filled with disease. Thousands died aboard the various seaborne confines anchored off Long Island and the *Jersey* ranked highest in these grim figures.

Once the vessel had been a powerful war ship that carried 400 officers and men. In 1776, it had brought Hessians to the colonies and was later used as a hospital and storage ship. As the war progressed, prisoners increased in number and the British once again converted the vessel. Masts were removed, slits cut in the hull and the *Jersey* was ready to be packed with American captives.

Conditions were intolerable. As many as 1,400 men were stuffed below decks with inadequate facilities or clothing. Food was usually spoiled. Rats and lice transmitted disease from piles of excrement. Medical attention was almost unknown. Diseases such as smallpox, yellow fever, typhus and dysentery ravaged the weakened prisoners.

To captive Thomas Andros, the vessel was contaminated to its very core: "For the whole ship, from keel to taffarel, was equally affected and contained pestilence sufficient to desolate a world: disease and death were wrought into her very timbers."

Although the guards enjoyed certain amusements such as tossing apples into the hold and watching the prisoners fight for a taste, diversion for the captives was mostly absent. The most sought after opportunity for the prisoners was to be placed on burial detail. Each morning several men were allowed to row to the nearby sand flats to throw those who had not survived the night into shallow graves. On returning, the diggers often brought back bits of earth and grass for their fellow prisoners to smell. Often the burials accomplished little, for high tides frequently dislodged the newly covered corpses. Soon the remains would float back to the ship, bobbing about in the water from which the captives drew their drinking supply.

Thomas Dring was not yet twenty-five when he was thrown into the *Jersey*'s hold. Although he does not mention the presence of 355 in his journal, he does describe another woman, one who was able to alleviate some of the misery of those on the ship:

> One indulgence was allowed us by our keepers, if indulgence it may be called. They had given permission for a boat to come alongside the ship, with a supply of a few necessary articles, to be sold to such of the prisoners as possessed the means of paying for them.
>
> This trade was carried on by a very corpulent old woman, known among the prisoners by the name of "Dame

Grant." Her visits, which were made on every other day, were of much benefit to us, and, I presume, a source of profit to herself. . . .

When our guard was not composed of Refugees, we were usually permitted to descend to the foot of the Accommodation ladder, in order to select from the boat such articles as we wished. While standing there, it was distressing to see the faces of hundreds of half-famished wretches looking over the side of the ship into the boat, without the means of purchasing the most trifling article before their sight, not even so much as a morsel of wholesome bread.

Her arrival was always a subject of interest to us; but at length she did not make her appearance for several days, and her approach was awaited in extreme anxiety. but alas! we were no longer to enjoy this little gratification. Her traffic was ended. She had taken the fever from the hulk and died, if not in the flower of her youth, at least in the midst of her usefulness, leaving a void which was never afterwards filled up.

Women were periodically allowed to bring food, clothing and bandages to the ship, but probably forbidden any close contact with the captives. Among the ladies who ministered to the rebel prisoners in the city were Hercules Mulligan's sister Sarah Whaley and a pair of her firends. One lady, the widow of a sea captain named Adam Todd, had originally left Manhattan, but returned when she discovered that one of her maids was masquerading as mistress of the house and taking in boarders. Margaret Whetten, also a sea captain's widow, not only aided rebel prisoners, but reportedly harbored whig spies in her house.

These three women may have spent the greatest part of their fortunes in charity to those who were confined, for a testimonal published after the war sought to raise funds for them. The petition stated: "As their circumstances are doubtless impaired by their attention and charitable donations to the prisoners, we humbly conceive they merit some acknowledgement from their country."

Most of the captives of the prison ships were sailors from the rebel navy or crews of privateers. Some, like 355, were political prisoners, while other detainees did not fit into either category.

Philip Freneau was imprisoned in New York harbor after he was captured while a passenger on an American ship taken off the Capes of Delaware. When Freneau became ill, he was transferred to a hospital ship, probably because of his favored status as a non-military detainee. Here security was less stringent and he managed to escape. Freneau, who in later life would become one of the young nation's greatest poets, almost immediately set about to capture the horrors of his floating jail. The result was a propaganda poem published in 1780 and entitled "The British Prison Ship." He wrote:

> The various horrors of these hulks to tell—
> These Prison Ships where pain and horror dwell,
> Where Death in tenfold vengeance holds his reign,
> And injuried ghosts, yet unavenged, complain,—
> This be my task! Ungenerous Britons, you
> Conspire to murder those you can't subdue!
>
> Remembrance shudders at this scene of fears:
> Still in my view some English brute appears—
> Some base-born Hessian slave walks threat'ning by—
> Some servile Scot, with murder in his eye,
> Still haunts my sight, as vainly they bemoan
> Rebellions managed so unlike their own!
>
> Swift from the guarded decks we rush along,
> And vainly sought repose—so vast our throng.
> Three hundred wretches here, denied all light,
> In crowded mansions pass the infernal night;
> Some for a bed their tattered vestments join,
> And some on chests, and some on floors recline,
> Shut from the blessings of evening air,
> Pensive we lay with mangled corpses there;
> Meagre and wan and scorched with heat, below,
> We loomed like ghosts, ere death had made us so!
>
> And yet so pale! that we were thought by some
> A freight of ghosts from Death's dominion come.

Agent 355 died on board the *Jersey*, and like many others her body was never identified. At the end of the war, the ship was abandoned. Over the years, worms ate through the timbers and the vessel finally settled to the bottom of the sound.

Spying during the revolution was relatively amateur and uncomplicated. Agents would mingle in enemy camps freely, for townspeople often visited troop settlements and unknown faces were not considered unusual. Women were particularly popular as spies and frequently served as messengers or couriers. With the great number of men away from home at war, a lone woman riding through the countryside was not a conspicuous sight.

One professional was Ann Bates, a former Philadelphia schoolteacher who also raised bees and sheep. Ann may have been a double agent, but her final loyalties were probably to the British, for most of her known exploits involve missions which proved ultimately favorable to them.

Ann's husband was Joseph Bates, a British armourer, but the life of an ordinary camp woman evidently held no allure for her. The ex-schoolteacher volunteered to spy on the continentals, and thus began a three year career of successful missions in New York, New Jersey and Pennsylvania. Major Duncan Drummond, Clinton's aide and Ann's contact, reported that she was one of the most dependable spies in their entire operation and stated: ". . . her information as to matter and fact, was far superior to every other intelligence."

The agent's preferred mode of operation was to visit various rebel camps while disguised as a peddler. Once inside, she would move about supposedly selling her wares, but actually counting men, supplies, artillery and generally evaluating the level of morale. Often Ann marched along with the moving rebel armies, dropping back from company to company, counting men and weapons, until she had progressed through the entire train.

Despite her almost constant series of missions, Ann was arrested only once. She was held for two days near White Plains, but released unharmed for lack of evidence. Ann was not particularly concerned with the jailing, but did complain that the matron who had searched her had stolen her silver shoe buckles, a silver thimble, a silk handkerchief and three dollars.

The Americans never again came close to capturing the elusive woman. When Clinton's troops shipped out for South Carolina, Ann accompanied her husband, and in 1781, the pair sailed for England.

Soon they were in desperate need of a £10 pension which had been promised but not delivered to them. Ann was bitter about the treatment which she considered to be a shabby reward for her long and dangerous service to the crown. She suggested that if she had performed the same tasks for the Americans, they would have been much more considerate of her needs.

Things were progressing more cheerfully for the Baroness von Riedesel. After leaving Charlottesville with the belief that her husband would be immediately exchanged in Manhattan, Frederika began a leisurely pace northward. Near Baltimore, she noted in her journal that she saw a snake eat a live frog and was delighted when the snake was slit open and the frog jumped out alive.

For about ten days she rested at the estate of Charles Carroll and his wife Mary Darnall. Carroll was considered to be the wealthiest man in America. Although his personal fortune was valued in millions of dollars, he avidly supported the colonial stand and was the only Catholic signer of the Declaration of Independence.

Carroll was thought to be particularly elegant and cultivated in a period where manners were often lacking in both men and women. Much of his polish probably stemmed from his long European education, but the Baroness found him to be less than gracious and called him "brusque and stingy, and not at all a suitable mate for his wife. . . ."

Mary Carroll, her husband's cousin, had become friendly with the Baroness at Frederick Springs. During their visit with her, the Riedesels planted a friendship garden which Mary later maintained. Although Charles Carroll would live to be ninety-five, the oldest surviving signer of the Declaration, his wife Mary died in 1782, at age thirty-three.

After their stay in Maryland, the Baroness' party journeyed on to Elizabethtown, New Jersey, expecting to be taken into Manhattan. But here news arrived that the exchange had been delayed and the group back-tracked to Bethlehem, Pennsylvania. Here they lodged at an inn for about six weeks and on departing were presented with a bill for $32,000.

Finally, in November, the Riedesels were allowed to cross over to New York, and the Baron was formally exchanged at a later date. Riedesel was soon appointed as a British Lieutenant General and his wife set about to establish her reputation as a lavish hostess. The family lived in the elegant house of William Tryon, the former royal governor, but all was not rosy. Inflation was increasing prices throughout the area. Two days of food provisions cost $800, indicating that the tab in Bethlehem may not have been completely outrageous. Firewood was practically non-existent and for tinder, the soldiers were forced to cut down many of the great trees lining New York's boulevards.

The Baron was given command of the combined installations on Long Island and there, because of her service to the wounded during the Battle of Saratoga, Frederika was given a full dress parade of honor, and allowed to review the troops.

The Baroness' long trek in America was nearing an end, for her husband at last received orders to leave the rebellious colonies and take up a command in Canada. The war had left its mark on the family however. The Riedesel daughters could not speak their native tongue, and the Baroness had difficulty in speaking any language but English. The Baron was still subject to fits of depression.

The war also was affecting German women who had not elected to come to America with their mercenary husbands. One example was the four year struggle by Major Baurmeister to secure relief for his sister at home.

Baurmeister's sister was the wife of Lt. Col. Balthasar Bretthauer, a Hessian officer who had been stationed at Trenton. After Washington's successful raid on the New Jersey installation during December of 1776, most German officers who had been attached to the garrison were considered to be guilty of neglect of duty. Bretthauer, although wounded in the fight and taken prisoner, was one of those considered *persona non grata*. By the summer of 1778, the condition of the officer's family was near poverty. Baurmeister intervened for his sister and on August 24, wrote for help to his patron Baron von Jungkenn:

> May I humbly beg your Lordship to recall my sister Bretthauer's three boys at some propitious moment, for this poor family cannot possibly subsist on a pension of six thalers a month. I know that the unhappy father of these innocent children is in bad repute and that the punishment meted out to him by His Serene Highness is just, but I also know that His Highness will have pity and not permit these boys to be impoverished through his anger. My sister wrote a touching letter to me. I will help her, but in the near future I shall be able to give but little assistance. Will your Lordship please pardon with this humble request.

There is no evidence that Baurmeister suffered for his bold but "humble request." But there is also no evidence that it prompted any aid for his sister. Col. Bretthauer died at Dumphries of his wounds and his widow's six thaler pension, about $4.40, was of little help in raising her family. By September 10, 1780, Baurmeister was ready to broach the subject again to the Baron:

> May I once more beg your Excellency to have pity on my helpless sister in Breuna. I wish I might move your Lordship to lighten her terrible burden of having to raise three small sons. Your Excellency could do a great deed of mercy for these orphaned children, whose suffering, due to having lost their father so early, has made me shed many a bitter tear. I hope that Lieutenant Colonel Bretthauer did not deserve such disgrace and punishment as to cause a widow with small children endless suffering. I pray your Excellency to pardon me for showing what I feel for a suffering sister. I would not do it, had I not the greatest confidence in your Excellency, knowing that you are the only one to find ways and means of helping the destitute.

This time the major's perseverance paid off. More than a year later, His Excellency had granted at least one small favor. Once again Baurmeister wrote:

If I have correctly interpreted my sister's letter, dated Carlshaven, November last year, my humble request has been fulfilled in that she is graciously permitted to live free of charge in the hospital there. With the warmest feeling of gratitude I recognize in this benevolent deed the same gracious kindness which I, enjoying your Excellency's efficacious protection, shall praise as long as I live. . . .

Although the major was ultimately successful in improving the lot of his sister, the effort had taken nearly four years. The case was by no means typical of the plight of most German widows. Sister Bretthauer was the wife of an important officer and her brother was a direct correspondent with one of the most prominent men in the country. The situation of a private's survivor without friends in high places must have been much more difficult.

In the colonies, captured German prisoners were faring little better. Under some local regulations, these men could be bought out of prison, usually for about £30 and by women who used them as forced labor while their own husbands were away at war. More compassionate females were involved in freeing the German troops stationed in Manhattan. Here the rate of desertion climbed steadily higher, aided in part by local women who smuggled dissatisfied Hessians across to rebel-held New Jersey.

In the South, Cornwallis had moved up in command. The capture of Burgoyne, coupled with the removal of Gage and Howe, had depleted the ranks of the British high command. Cornwallis, formerly far back in the line of promotion, now held the position of commander of the British field forces in the south.

In the summer of 1780, Cornwallis planned to subdue the deep south, and then march northward to conquer the middle colonies. The rebel militia in the Palmetto State presented no real obstacle, but word arrived of a more dangerous threat. Continental forces under Horatio Gates were marching through North Carolina in a rescue effort.

The British moved out to meet them, and on August 16, the contestants clashed at the Battle of Camden. General Gates was one of the first and fastest to flee the battlefield as the English gained the advantage. By the following day, Gates had fled seventy miles, while his men retreated behind him on foot or scattered throughout the countryside. Gates would later be relieved of his command, primarily because of his speedy departure.

Much of the fighting in the south involved not major battles such as that at Camden, but minor skirmishes between local tories and whigs. In these encounters, many of the participants were volunteers, without the supplies and matériel carried by formal, standing forces.

The rate of death from wounds was probably much higher, for the injured were often left unnursed for long periods or carried home in wheelbarrows to be tended by the soldiers' womenfolk. Entire families tended to become involved in the local bouts, for in these clashes the families of combatants often lived within sight and sound of the action.

One countrywoman from Pleasant Green, North Carolina, found the waiting too much to bear. After her husband had marched off to confront the tories, she felt strangely compelled to follow. The woman, a Mrs. Slocum, left an account of her impulsiveness and a description of the war as seen by the wife of a whig partisan:

> The cool night seemed after a gallop of a mile or two, to bring reflection with it, and I asked myself where I was going and for what purpose. Again and again I was tempted to turn back; but I was soon ten miles from home, and my mind became stronger every mile I rode that I should find my husband dead or dying. . . . When day broke I was some thirty miles from home, I knew the general route our army expected to take, and had followed them without hesitation. About sunrise I came upon a group of women and children, standing and sitting by the road-side, each one of them showing the same anxiety of mind which I felt.

> Stopping for the few minutes I inquired if the battle had been fought. They knew nothing, but were assembled on the road-side to catch intelligence.

> The sun must have been well up, say eight or nine o'clock, when I heard a sound like thunder, which I knew must be cannon. It was the first time I ever heard a cannon.

I stopped still; when presently the cannon thundered again. The battle was then fighting!!

Mrs. Slocum continued toward the sound of the cannon and soon saw a group of about twenty men, most of whom had been wounded. In the mist of them she recognized her husband who was badly hurt. She dismounted and rushed to help him:

> I remember uncovering his head and seeing a face crusted with gore from a dreadful wound across the temple. I put my hand on the bloody face; 'twas warm; and an un-known voice begged for water. . . . it was not my husband but Frank Cogdell. . . . A puddle of blood was standing on the ground about his feet. I took the knife, and cut away his trousers and stockings and found the blood came from a shot hole through and through the fleshy part of his leg. I looked about and could see nothing that looked as if it would do for dressing wounds, but some heart-leaves. I gathered a handful and bound them tight to the holes; and the bleeding stopped. I then went to others. . . .

She continued to nurse the wounded, both of her own side and those of the enemy. She begged that mercy be shown to the captured tories and was told that only those guilty of "murder and houseburning" would be further harmed. Finally, Mrs. Slocum did find her husband: "bloody as a butcher, and as muddy as a ditcher." But he was alive and unhurt. Then she rode home.

Battle wounds were not the only health hazard for southern based soldiers. Outbreaks of malaria and yellow fever demobilized much of the British army after Camden. Another problem for the King's troops was the South Carolina militia which was be-ginning to cause significant damage in the state's upcountry. The foremost leaders of these dissident elements were Francis Marion, known as the "Swamp Fox," and his rival Thomas Sumter, nick-named the "Gamecock."

Unrest had also broken out along the Appalachian and Blue Ridge Mountains. Without the prospect of aid from the Conti-nental Army, frontiersmen decided to join together to fight against the British. Although the threat of Indian attack was always imminent, many settlers determined that the danger from tories and English forces in the east was more pressing.

On September 25, more than 1,000 frontiersmen gathered at Sycamore Shoals on the Watauga River in what is now east Tennessee. This informal army of mountain men was completely distinctive from the usual force taking the field. Many wore buckskins, rode family workhorses and carried hunting rifles as weapons. Their opponents were also distinctive, for the crown supporters were composed entirely of tory volunteers and included only one Britisher, their leader Major Patrick Ferguson. Any confrontation between the two forces would be almost entirely American in composition.

By October 7, the mountain men, led by William Campbell, the husband of Patrick Henry's sister Elizabeth, had crossed the Blue Ridge. Meanwhile, the loyalists had gathered atop Kings Mountain in preparation for a major battle. Their site was ill-chosen, for although the tory regiment had the advantage of height, they were soon surrounded by Campbell's men who were able to maneuver almost unseen among the trees in the dense forest.

The battle lasted only one hour before the Americans received word of the enemy's surrender. This did not stop the fire of some mountaineers, who continued to gun down the defenseless loyalists. Some would claim that in the thick underbrush, news of the surrender did not reach all of the Minutemen. Many more would admit that the slaughter was deliberate and in retribution for Tarleton's no quarter order at Waxhaws.

Patrick Ferguson, struck by at least eight rifle balls, was one of those killed in battle. The dashing young officer had come to Kings Mountain in typical flamboyant style, accompanied by two mistresses known as Virginia Sal and Virginia Paul. Sal, a red-haired admirer who may have moonlighted as a cook, was also killed during the fighting. After her dead lover had been wrapped in a raw beefhide, they were reportedly placed together in the same grave. In 1945, a physician from Kings Mountain opened the officer's burial place to discover if the somewhat romantic rumor was indeed factual. Inside he found the bodies of two people, a man and a woman.

Not all of the soldiers killed in the battle were interred, and during the coming days, wolves, dogs and hogs feasted upon the remains of those who had been left unburied.

Virginia Paul was reportedly unconcerned about the death of Ferguson. With other prisoners, she was taken to Burke Court House near Morgantown, North Carolina, and later sent to the British lines.

The American success at Kings Mountain stalled Cornwallis' advance into North Carolina for about three months. The commander pulled back from his installation at Charlotte and re-entered South Carolina in an attempt to reorganize tory elements which had largely disappeared after the October slaughter at the hands of the mountain men. This lull enabled the whig high command to replace Gates with Nathanael Greene.

Catharine Littlefield Greene would follow her husband to South Carolina. In the roster of the wives of the top rebel commanders, "Kitty" Greene is unique, for her behavior was far removed from the typical, mild-mannered, obedient army wife.

Catharine was born on Block Island, Rhode Island, in 1753, but most of her early life was spent with relatives in Warwick. Like Sally Jay, Catharine's youth was filled with associations with patriot leaders. One uncle was governor of the colony, another a delegate to the Continental Congress. Famous travellers such as Benjamin Franklin were frequent guests at the Warwick house.

Throughout her life, men found Catharine a brilliant conversationalist. Although she had little formal learning, her wit and intelligence assured that she usually could depend upon at least one protective admirer.

In 1774, Catherine married Greene, the owner of an ironworks who was already embroiled in the struggle against England. Greene was read out of the Quaker meeting for his military activities, but continued to take an active part in the rebellion. Three days after the battles at Lexington and Concord, he was made a Brigadier General by the Rhode Island Assembly. By June of 1775, he was appointed to the same rank in the Continental Army. Of the fourteen senior officers commissioned at this time, only Greene, Gates and Washington would serve until the end of the war.

Catherine's first winter with the army was during the siege of Boston where Elizabeth Gates, the English born wife of the general, scandalized the camp by arriving in a man's riding habit instead of a demure dress such as that worn by the other officers' women. The Rhode Island bride may have been intimidated by older, more sophisticated women in camp, for little was written concerning her activities.

Greene may have added to his wife's insecurity during the early days. Inviting her to winter headquarters at Morristown the following year, Greene not so delicately suggested that she had much to learn. After noting that she should write Lucy Knox if she needed any new dresses, the general announced:

> Remember when you write to Mrs. Knox you write to a good scholar, therefore mind and spell well; you are defective in this matter, my love; a little attention will soon correct it.

> Bad writing is nothing, if the spelling is but good. People are often laughed at for not spelling well, but never for not writing well. It is said it is ungenteel for gentlemen to make observations upon ladies' writing. I hope you won't think it unkind in me. Nothing but the affection and regard I feel for you makes me wish to have you appear an accomplished lady in every point of view.

Catharine soon became too accomplished for her husband's liking, for she developed into a femme fatale of succeeding winter camps and was the life of most of the most high level social events. Greene wrote to his friend Jeremiah Wadsworth that her behavior was displeasing, an ironic note for Wadsworth himself would later become one of Catharine's intimates. She would confide to him that during the Pennsylvania winter at Valley Forge, she had been propositioned by at least one foreign officer, but did not reveal her answer to the invitation. Lucy Knox observed the tension and noted that "all was not well with Greene and his Lady."

The following year, Catharine arrived in camp with her finest party dresses, and even somber George Washington was not immune to her charms. In March of 1779, Greene confided to a friend: "We had a little dance at my headquarters. His Excellency and Mrs. Greene danced upwards of three hours without once sitting down."

Kitty Greene would find fertile new ground for levity in South Carolina, but at least once she would be in grave danger of capture by the enemy.

Soon after Greene assumed command of the southern forces, he ordered that Daniel Morgan advance into South Carolina, harass the enemy along his line of march and make foraging simpler by dividing the American troops into smaller units. Travel was painful and difficult for Morgan who was recovering from malaria and had developed both sciatica and hemorrhoids. His destination was supposedly a close kept secret, but the British were able to detect his goal with the help of a loyalist woman who had penetrated the American camp. On December 30, tory spy David George relayed her information to Cornwallis:

> My wifes sister Last Night came to my house out of strong Rebel Settlement up at Princes fort; by her I have heard the Design and Intention of the Rebels; as far as their Captains have any Knowledge; as she came she Informs me that she got into some of their Camps on the south side of the Pacolate River . . . she understood from Captain Francis Princes and Henry Princes Wives; That they were waiting for Colonel Morgan and Colonel Washington who was on their March; in order to Join them, Morgan with five or six hundred Light horse had Crossed Broad River at Smiths ford a few dayes agoe . . . . they intend to march against Ninety Six and Augusta; they say they will have Three Thousand men; to go against Them places: but I have alwayes observed that they always make the Most of There men.

Cornwallis detailed Tarleton to track Morgan and intercept the force if possible. On January 17, "The Butcher" fell upon the whig force at Cowpens, appropriately named because of the large number of hogs confined in the area. Tarleton was soundly defeated and barely managed to escape capture himself. British losses were 929 men captured, killed or wounded. The American figure was 72.

Morgan turned back into North Carolina and wrote Greene that he was in great pain: ". . . I am violently attacked with the piles, so that I scarcely can sit upon my horse." Virginia Major St. George Tucker, also on his way to meet Greene, was more enthusiastic. To his wife Frances Bland, who was managing the couple's 1,300 acre estate Matoax, Tucker wrote: "The lark is up, the morning gray, and I am seated by a smoky fire to let my dearest Fanny know that her soldier is as blithe as the mockingbird which is at this moment tuning his pipe within a dozen yards of me."

At Guilford Courthouse, Cornwallis engaged the combined rebel forces and won a pyrrhic victory which almost destroyed his own troops. The British officer chose to regroup and turn into Virginia, rather than press his questionable advantage with Greene's survivors. Although the Americans had not suffered heavy casualties at Guilford, the army was considerably weakened because of enlistments which were coming due. Greene himself had gone for six weeks without changing his clothes or sleeping in a bed, and each day his situation became more vulnerable. He determined that to pursue Cornwallis would be foolhardy, and instead chose to head into South Carolina to gather supplies and to attack the chain of forts stretching north and west from Charleston.

Thomas Sumter with his volunteers and militia had been plaguing the enemy in this area all during the spring of 1781. In March, the Gamecock had made a daring raid behind British lines to rescue his wife in the High Hills near Cane Savannah. The move had been mishandled and had alienated much of Sumter's badly needed force.

Mary Cantey Sumter was eleven years older than the Gamecock. After the death of her first husband William Jameson, she had taken control of a 10,000 acre estate near the Santee River and successfully managed the operation. Infantile paralysis in her youth had disfigured the South Carolina woman and left one side of her body partially immobile. But one year after she married

Sumter in 1767, Mary at age forty-four produced a healthy son.

Before their marriage, Sumter was a store operator of modest means, but when he moved to Mary's estate, his position changed significantly. He expanded her holdings and entered into additional commercial ventures. By the time of the war, Sumter was one of the most prominent men in the colony, and as an ex-soldier, was given command of major elements in the state militia.

In May of 1780, Mary and her son moved for safety to the family's summer cottage. Here a British detachment sent to capture Sumter attacked the house, pillaged the contents and burned the building. Reportedly Mary was in extreme ill health and had to be carried from the structure before it was fired. The partial invalid moved once again, this time to the High Hills. By March of the following year, Sumter felt her to be in further danger, for the enemy had accelerated their attempts to capture him. Mary could conceivably be kidnapped and held as a hostage to trap the officer.

With a band of rebel raiders, the Gamecock rode to rescue his wife. According to reports, her health had become so poor that she was strapped to her horse so that she would not fall off and cause a costly delay. The party was attacked near Stirrup Branch, but managed to drive off the opposition and cross safely into whig territory.

Although Mary was saved, the entire foray created deep-seated resentment between Sumter and many of his troops. The volunteers who composed his army were annoyed that their lives had been risked not in direct confrontation with the British, but in an effort to rescue the privileged family of the commander. In order to combat their disenchantment, Sumter devised a scheme aimed at raising great numbers of formal and more disciplined State troops. But payment for the men would be impossible, for there was no existing governmental body to authorize military expenditures. Instead, the Gamecock planned to compensate his men with slaves confiscated from loyalist plantations.

Under this plan, the salary for each ten month period of enlistment ranged from one slave for a private to three and one-half for a colonel. Clothes, horses and supplies would also be provided in the "wages," along with a guaranteed share of any booty which could be looted from the tories.

Francis Marion was appalled at the program. One of his main objections was the potential dissolution of slave families which would be split up under the pay schedule. An additional objection was that Marion considered confiscation of slaves and property to be illegal, the move would not be authorized by any official legal body. Although he refused to participate in the enlistment program, other officers endorsed the concept enthusiastically.

One of the most vital targets along the chain of British frontier garrisons was Ft. Motte. Here the English had converted a mansion strategically located on a high bank, into an armed post. About 165 men were quartered about the manor house, which was the seat of a large plantation owned by Rebecca Brewton Motte.

In early May, American troops surrounded Ft. Motte and Rebecca was allowed to cross through the lines to join them. Rebecca's husband Jacob had left her extensive land holdings when he had died, but unfortunately the legacy also included numerous debts and mortages on most of the property. The widow, with several children to support, took control of the plantation and succeeded in reducing much of the liabilities.

Earlier in the war, the widow had sent slaves to help construct defenses at Charleston, but the action at Ft. Motte would demand a more significant effort on her part.

The unsuccessful besiegers received word on May 11 that Lord Rawdon was approaching with reinforcements for the surrounded garrison. In a desperate attempt to take the fort before their arrival, Rebecca conferred with rebel leaders and decided that her house should be burned. Flaming arrows were shot into the roof, and the British, in greater danger of being roasted alive than being shot, almost immediately surrendered. The event probably would have delighted Benjamin Franklin who had maintained that American troops should be trained in the use of bows and arrows as well as guns.

Rebecca's house was partially saved by a concerted fire-fight-

ing effort and by evening she was able to give a dinner party for
rebel officers and their high-ranking prisoners. According to
Henry Lee, whose son Robert would take part in a great civil
war of the future, Rebecca seemed to harbor no resentments:

> The deportment and demeanor of Mrs. Motte gave a
> zest to the pleasures of the table. She did its honors with the
> unaffected politeness which ever excites esteem mingled with
> affection. Conversing with ease, vivacity, and good sense, she
> obliterated our recollection of the injury she had received;
> and though warmly attached to the defenders of her coun-
> try, the engaging amiability of her manners left it doubtful
> which set of officers constituted these defenders.

The loss of the manor house would not have meant total
ruin for Rebecca Motte, for she also owned a town house in
Charleston and at least two other plantations. But the burning
was only one in a long series of setbacks which would deplete
her holdings. When peace was finally established, she was nearly
bankrupt. However, Rebecca began to rebuild her fortune by
buying sub-standard land on credit. Most of her purchases were
huge tracks of swamp which she converted into fertile rice fields.
Ultimately she was able to pay off her debts and those of her
husband. Once again Rebecca became a wealthy woman.

After the fall of Ft. Motte, American forces moved upland
and laid an unsuccessful siege at the crown garrison at Ninety-
Six. Commander of the target was Col. John Harris Cruger,
whose wife Anne was a member of New York's tory De Lancey
family. By many accounts, Anne was apprehended by Greene
during the siege, but instead of being held hostage as in the case
of Lady Johnson, Anne was placed under a protective guard and
returned to her husband when the attack proved futile.

One of Anne's earlier experiences was reported in detail by
Judge Thomas Jones, the tory historian who had so soundly condemned Howe and Elizabeth Loring. According to Jones, in November of 1777, radicals broke into the De Lancey mansion
Bloomingdale, in New York. Anne's sister Charlotte was struck
with a musket. Jones' niece Elizabeth Floyd, a visitor, was set

afire when a rebel threw a burning drapery over her. Mrs. De
Lancey avoided harm by first hiding in a cupboard beneath the
stairs and then in a dog kennel.

Anne managed to escape in the confusion and tried to hike
overland to warn the King's troops camped about two miles
away. Instead, she became disoriented in the night and walked
about seven miles in the wrong direction. Finally she was taken
in by an innkeeper on the Kingsbridge Road. Anne recovered
from her experience, but two years later was again trapped by
the enemy. While sailing from New York to join her husband
stationed in Savannah, her ship was taken by the Count d'Estaing.
From on board she watched the French bombardment of Savannah, but when the vessels withdrew in defeat, she was sent ashore
and rejoined her husband.

After the unsuccessful ploy at Ninety-Six, Greene, Marion
and Sumter continued moving about in South Carolina during
the remainder of 1781. Although their confrontations with the
enemy usually resulted in their retreat, heavy casualties were ex-
tracted each time from the British. The pendulum of victory had
begun to swing toward the Americans. Gradually the English
and loyalists were forced out of the interior of the state and gathered for a last stand on the Atlantic coast.

Eliza Wilkinson, one of those affected as the British were
pushed back, lived on Yonge's Island, about thirty miles south of
Charleston. During most of the conflict, her house had been left
untouched, but in the closing years of the war, plunder became
common. In an irate letter to a friend, Eliza described her vain
pleadings with one group of looters who had forced their way
into her house and were busily carting away her possessions:

> I ventured to speak to the inhumane monster who had
> my clothes. I represented to him the times were such we
> could not replace what they'd taken from us, and begged
> him to spare me only a suit or two; but I got nothing but a
> curse for my pains; nay, so far as his callous heart from re-
> lenting, that, casting his eyes toward my shoes: "I want them
> buckles," said he, and immediately knelt at my feet to take
> them out, which, while he was busy about, a brother villian,
> whose enormous mouth extended from ear to ear, bawled

out: "Shares there, I say; Shares." So they divided my buckles between them. The other wretches were employed in
the same manner; they took my sister's ear-rings from her
ears; hers, Miss Samuell's buckles; they demanded her ring
from her finger . . . . after bundling up all their booty, they
mounted their horses. But such despicable figures! Each
wretch's bosom stuffed so full, they appeared to be afflicted
with some dropsical disorder. . . .

After these original raiders had left, others descended upon
the house and took what was left:

> Since writing the foregoing epistles, we have been hum-
> bled to the dust, again plundered, worse than ever plun-
> dered! Our very doors and window shutters were taken
> from the house, and carried aboard the vessels which lay in
> the river opposite our habitation; the sashes beaten out; fur-
> niture demolished; goods carried off; beds ripped up; stock
> of every kind driven away; in short, distresses of every na-
> ture attended us.

But Eliza Wilkinson's losses could not match the enormous
damage inflicted on the estates of South Carolinean Eliza Lucas
Pinckney, who may still rank as the most successful businesswoman in American history. Perhaps no other citizen was as in-
strumental in bringing prosperity to the colony as this inventive
Englishwoman.

Eliza was born about 1723, the daughter of British officer
George Lucas and his invalid wife. In 1737, Lucas moved to
South Carolina from his post on Antigua. He assumed that peace
would soon be formalized between England and Spain, and that
he would no longer be needed at his island outpost. But war
broke out again and he was forced to return to the island, leaving
sixteen-year-old Eliza in charge of the large plantation he had settled near Charleston. The separation would be permanent, not
temporary as they both expected, for soon Lucas was appointed
Royal Governor of Antigua and Eliza was established as a prominent planter.

While still a teenager, she was responsible not only for the
primary estate Wappoo, but also for two additional farms. The

job was demanding, but Eliza found time to write a friend in
London:

> I have the business of 3 plantations to transact, which
> requires much writing and more business and fatigue of
> other sorts than you can imagine. . . . By rising very early I
> find I can go through with much business. . . .

The young enterpreneur did have time to read the classics,
but more important, she began to investigate the possibilities of
adapting various foreign crops to the soil and climate of the
southern colonies. With the help of Dr. Alexander Garden, a
botanist for whom the flower gardenia was named, Eliza established large experimental gardens where exotic plants from
throughout the world were planted.

Her idea was to diversify the economy of South Carolina,
which was heavily dependent upon rice production. In July of
1739, she seemed discouraged that her efforts had not yet succeeded in finding a viable alternative and noted:

> I wrote my father a very long letter on his plantation
> affairs . . . on the pains I had taken to bring the Indigo,
> Ginger, Cotton, Lucern, and Cassada to perfection, and had
> greater hopes from the Indigo—if I could have the seed
> earlier the next year from the East Indies,—than any of
> ye rest of ye things I had tryed . . . . also concerning pitch
> and tarr and lime and other plantation affairs.

Some of the experiments continued to fail, but within three
years she had successfully cultivated a healthy indigo crop, proving indisputably that the product could be grown in America.
Other planters adopted the indigo plant, and soon it rivaled rice
as the major crop of the colony. Profits from harvests poured into
Eliza's coffers and her plantations became among the finest in the
south.

Eliza continued her agricultural experiments on projects
such as the introduction of mulberry trees needed for the growing of silkworms. The program was ultimately dropped as im-

practical and her visions of a great silk industry in South Carolina were erased.

The young planter developed independence along with her managerial talents and thus when her father wrote to suggest that she select between two men he had chosen as prospective husbands, Eliza replied that she liked neither and preferred to live a single life. By 1744, her views had changed and she married Col. Charles Pinckney, a man twenty-five years older than she and a widower for only a few months. Pinckney added his estates to Eliza's holdings, but was involved in politics to a greater degree than in planting. He served as speaker of the South Carolina Assembly, was a member of the powerful Royal Provincial Council and was Chief Justice of the colony's Supreme Court.

For several years the family lived in London, where Pinckney was commissioner for the colony. But the pleasant life of the Pinckneys was soon to end. Just months after the family returned to South Carolina in 1758, Pinckney died and again Eliza assumed control of the plantations' operations.

Because much of her financial success was due to British bounties on rice and indigo, Eliza seemed a prime candidate for the loyalist fold. But with her two English educated sons Thomas and Charles Cotesworth, she chose to support the drive for independence.

Although Pinckney had been a royal official, the family also maintained close ties with revolutionary figures. Charles Cotesworth had married Sarah Middleton, the sister of Arthur Middleton, a signer of the Declaration and the daughter of Henry Middleton, president of the Continental Congress. Son Thomas would marry Elizabeth Motte, daughter of the mistress of Ft. Motte.

Soon after the British gained a foothold in the colony, Eliza's property became a target for plunder. In 1779, her largest plantation was almost completely destroyed as Major General Augustine Prevost moved his troops from Savannah to Charleston. Here, most of her valuables had been secreted. The losses continued to mount each month. Eliza Pinckney saw her vast fortune stolen, her houses burned and her years of agricultural experiments destroyed. By 1782, she was unable to pay a bill of £60 owed to an English friend. In a letter asking for an extension on her debt, Eliza carefully outlined the reasons for her inability to pay:

It may seem strange that a single woman, accused of no crime, who had a fortune to live Genteely in any part of the world, that fortune too in different kinds of property, and in four or five different parts of the country, should in so short a time be entirely deprived of it as not to be able to pay a debt of under sixty pounds sterling, but such is my singular case. After the many losses I have met with, for the last three or four desolating years from fire, and plunder, both in Country and Town, I still had something to subsist upon, but alas the hand of power has deprived me of the greatest part of that, and accident the rest.

The labor of the slaves I had working at my son Charles' sequestrated Estate by Mr. Cruden's permission, has not produced one farthing since the fall of Charles Town. Between thirty and forty head of tame cattle which I had on the same plantation, with the same permission, was taken last November by Major Yarborough and his party for the use of the army for which I received nothing.

My house in Ellory Street . . . which I immediately rented at one hundred pre annum sterling, was in a short time after filled with Hessians, to the great detriment of the house and annoyance of the tenant, who would pay me no more for the time he was in it, than twelve guineas. . . .

My Plantation up the path, which I hired to Mr. Simpson for fifty guineas . . . was taken out of his possession and I am told Major Fraiser now has it for the use of the Cavalry, and Mr. Simpson does not seem inclined to pay me for the last half of the year 1781. To my regret and to the great prejudice of the place, the wood has also been all cut down for the use of the Garrison, for which I have not got a penny. The negroes I had in town are sometimes impressed on the public works and make the fear of being so a pretence for doing nothing. . . . I must, though reluctantly, beg your patience till I can raise as much.

Wealthy patriots such as Eliza Pinckney were not the only citizens to feel economic hardships. As the war dragged into its sixth year, the fire of patriotism which had once prompted Minutemen to leave their homes, burned lower, partially extinguished by financial difficulties. Many were tiring of the long struggle which they had expected to be won years before. Soldiers in the army were largely discontented, wages and rations were often delayed for months before they were finally distributed.

The salaries, when they were paid, were totally insufficient to support either the single soldier or those with families. Inflation was constantly shrinking the value of the continental dollar. Thomas Jefferson required $30,000 in travelling expenses for a journey from Virginia to South Carolina. Once there he discovered that 100 yards of fencing for a prison compound cost $500,000. The future president also paid $3,000 for two doctor visits.

In January of 1781, dissatisfaction in the army peaked and a major mutiny broke out in the ranks. More than 1,500 members of the Pennsylvania Line, who had not received pay or rations for ten months, left the main camp at Morristown, technically as deserters. With them went 500 women and children. Despite pleas from the high command, the group refused to return and instead occupied Princeton.

Their departure from headquarters had not been peaceful. Describing the scene to Washington, Anthony Wayne wrote:

> A very considerable number of the field and other officers are much injured by strokes from muskets, bayonets, and stones. Nor have the revolters escaped with impunity. Many of their bodies lay under our horses' feet and others will retain with existence the traces of our swords and espontoons.

In Manhattan, Clinton viewed the incident as an indication that mass mutiny was imminent among the Continental Army at large. In a show of sympathy, he sent a brigade to assist the mutineers if they wished to defect. In a more grandiose scheme, he detailed fifty carpenters to Staten Island to build a bridge into New Jersey in case the Americans requested sanctuary.

Clinton did not benefit from the split, for the disagreement was only temporary. Negotiations between the mutineers and the army proved successful and the rebels returned peacefully to camp.

Joseph Reed feared that the unrest could spread to other units and developed a plan for satisfying the soldiers' grievances by appealing to the vanity of their wives: "A new gown, silk handkerchief, and a pair of shoes, etc., would be of little expense," he suggested, "and I think as a present from the State would have more effect than ten times the same laid out in articles for the men."

Reed added that if the state's Executive Council did not undertake to implement his scheme, he would outfit one woman himself and hopefully others would volunteer to do the same. The finery would be given only to the women of those men remaining in the service and Reed assured the Council that with these rewards, the soldiers would "do their duty better than ever. . . ."

Reed's plan was not adopted and although there would be other mutinies during the war, none would be on the grand scale of the Pennsylvania Line action.

Another effort to improve the soldiers' lot was undertaken by the whig women in Philadelphia. Unlike their more independent sisters in other locations, the actions of the capital's females had been primarily limited to passive assistance. The "at home" support described in a letter from one Philadelphia lady, was typical of the activities of most urbanites during the early war years:

> I will tell you what I have done. My only brother I have sent to camp with my prayers and blessings; I hope he will not disgrace me . . . . had I twenty sons and brothers they should go. I have retrenched every superfluous expense in my table and family; tea I have not drank since last Christmas, nor bought a new cap or gown since your defeat at Lexington, and what I never did before, have learnt to knit, and am now making stockings of American wool for my servants, and this way do I throw in my mite to the public good. I know this, that as free I can died but once, but as a slave I shall not be worthy of life.

But Esther De Berdt, Joseph Reed's English wife, felt that more was needed than mere boycotts or verbiage. Esther began to rally her friends in a campaign to raise money for the relief of the almost destitute rebel troops and before the project was completed, most of the capital's women had joined in the project.

Many of the sums contributed to the Philadelphia campaign fund were made at some sacrifice to the donors. One black maid gave seven shillings, six pence, probably a large share of her monthly earnings. From France came contributions from the Marchioness de Lafayette who pledged 100 guineas and the Countess de Luzerne who sent $6,000. Ultimately more than 1,600 women contributed a total of $300,000 in money and jewels.

Esther Reed did not live to see the end of her successful drive, but died in the fall of 1780 at age 34. Her successor was Sarah Bache, the daughter of Benjamin Franklin.

Sally Bache was knowledgeable in finances and thoroughly familiar with the growing problem of inflation. She had earlier complained that her servants were required to take two baskets to market, one in which to carry the food and the other for the money needed to purchase it.

Franklin's daughter completed the fund raising project and in a corollary campaign organized the Philadelphia women into sewing groups and oversaw the production of 2,200 shirts for the army. Sally had not always adhered to the virtues of thrift and domestic economy which she portrayed during the late years of the war. Earlier she had requested her father in France to secure certain desirables for her, which were unavailable in the war-torn colonies. Franklin was horrified and retorted from Passy:

I was charmed with the account you give me of your industry, the table-cloths of your own spinning, etc. but the latter part of the paragraph that you had sent for linen from France because weaving and flax were grown dear; alas, that dissolved the charm; and your sending for long black pins, and lace, and *feathers!* disgusted me as much as it you had put salt into my strawberries. . . .

The war indeed may in some degree raise the prices of goods, and the high taxes which are necessary to support the war may make our frugality necessary; and as I am always preaching that doctrine, I cannot in conscience or in decency encourage the contrary, by my example, in furnishing my children with foolish modes and luxuries. I therefore send all the articles you desire that are useful and necessary, and omit the rest; for as you say you should *"have great pride in wearing any thing I send, and showing it as your father's taste;"* I must avoid giving you an opportunity of doing that with either lace or feathers. If you wear your cambric ruffles as I do, and take care not to mend the holes, they will come in time to be lace; and feathers, my dear girl, may be had in America from every cock's tail.

Benjamin Rush's wife Julia Stockton was also connected with the money raising project. Rush explained to John Adams that she had developed into one of the staunchest supporters of the revolution and that with the women fully mobilized on the rebel side, the war was assuredly won:

If there is a single philosopher in the cabinet of St. James's, he will advise immediately to make peace with America. "The Romans govern the world," said Cato, "but the women govern the Romans." The women of America have at last become principals in the glorious American controversy. Their opinions alone and their transcendent influence in society and families must lead us on to success and victory. My dear wife, who you know in the beginning of the war had all the timidity of her sex as to the issue of the war and the fate of her husband, was one of the ladies employed to solicit benefactions for the army. She distinguished herself by her zeal and address in this business, and is now so thoroughly enlisted in the cause of her country that she reproaches me with lukewarmness.

The difficulties in recruiting new soldiers to the army were as numerous as retaining those already on duty. But in Massachusetts, one able-bodied young citizen who had attempted to join the service had been rejected. Her name was Deborah Sampson and on her second enlistment attempt she would be successful.

Deborah was born in 1760 in Plymouth County, Massachusetts. Like many other children of extremely poor families, Deborah was indentured at an early age and until she was eighteen, she lived and worked with the family of Jeremiah Thomas, a farmer in Middleboro. After her period of servitude was completed, Deborah remained with the family, learning to read and write and serving for a time as a school mistress. But eventually her peaceful New England life was rejected. Deborah decided to join the army.

For her first try, she borrowed a suit of men's clothing from one Sam Leonard, and promptly enlisted at the local recruiting station under the name of Timothy Thayer. Her masquerade was successful. Unfortunately, Deborah chose to celebrate her victory at a nearby tavern where she behaved so riotously that she was recognized. The town was scandalized. The local Baptist Church lifted her membership. According to some stories, Sam Leonard went into shock and never again wore that particular suit.

But Deborah was not discouraged; instead she concocted a new plan. This time she made her own suit and hiked to Uxbridge where there was less chance that she would be recognized. Here she was welcomed into the army as infantry private Robert Shurtleff, a volunteer in the Fourth Massachusetts Regiment.

Deborah was soon shipped out to West Point and for eighteen months served undetected. Such a masquerade would be probably impossible in modern warfare, but during the 18th century it was difficult to discover. Deborah was about five feet eight inches tall, not an unusual height in an era when most men six feet tall were considered near giants. Army shirts of the day were loose fitting and by binding her breasts, Deborah evidently managed to appear not significantly different from her fellow soldiers. The lack of a beard was not an obstacle, for the desperate continentals were enlisting teenage youth into the ranks. In addition, there was no entrance physical examination for the American army, and bathing was usually confined to washing of the face and hands.

The best chance of detection would occur if Deborah was wounded, a distinct possibility for she was an energetic trooper, often taking part on raids out of West Point. In one hand-to-hand skirmish with tories at Tappan Bay, Deborah was slashed on the head with a saber. At East Chester, she was shot in the thigh with a musket ball, but concealed the wound and nursed herself back to health.

Deborah may also have seen action at Fort Tie, and claimed that she was with the American forces at the battle of Yorktown, but her real downfall came in Philadelphia. Here she fell ill with a "brain" fever and was taken to the infirmary. Dr. Barnabas Binney, attending the soldiers, penetrated her disguise, discovered her real sex, and moved her to his house for convalescence. Some legends report that the doctor kept Deborah's identity a secret until young women began to ogle the handsome "Robert." Reportedly, one girl became so infatuated that she presented the soldieress with six shirts, a gold watch and twenty-five Spanish dollars.

Although Deborah was considered a good soldier who distinguished herself by never getting drunk, she was immediately dismissed from the corps when her sex was made public. She returned to New England and in 1784 married Benjamin Gannett, a farmer from Sharon. Within several years she had given birth to three children.

Later Deborah took to the stage as a public speaker, probably to supplement the growing poverty of the Gannett family. She was perhaps the first woman lecturer in the United States and performed not only in Massachusetts, but in Rhode Island and New York as well. The rousing finale of her act was supposedly a smashing success. For this she dressed in her old army uniform and marched about the stage in a brief drill.

In 1804, Paul Revere took an interest in her welfare and wrote Massachusetts Congressman William Eustis for help. The silversmith explained that Deborah was ". . . a woman of handsome talents, good morals, a dutiful wife and an affectionate parent." Revere had been impressed by both Deborah's desperate financial straits and her character. He confided to Eustis:

> We commonly form our idea of the person whom we hear spoken of, whom we have never seen; according as their actions are described. When I heard her spoken of as a soldier, I formed the idea of a tall, masculine female, who had a small share of understanding, without education, and

one of the meanest of her sex.—When I saw and discoursed with [her] I was aggreeably surprised to find a small, effeminate, and converseable woman, whose education entitled her to a better situation in life.

As a result of Revere's intervention, the heroine received a £34 pension from the Massachusetts legislature and a $4 a month stipend from the Federal government. But financial problems still beset the family and in 1806 she was forced to ask Revere for a loan of £10. In 1820, Congress raised her pension to $8 a month for the rest of her life. The increase may have been due to her claim that her only possessions were her clothes, worth about $20. On April 29, 1827, the retired soldier died, impoverished at age sixty-seven.

Ten years later, Benjamin Gannett applied to Congress for a widower's pension. He claimed that he was a sickly eighty-three years old, completely indigent and with his daughters was forced to live off of charity. In addition, Gannett requested repayment of about $600 which he maintained he had spent during Deborah's last years for doctor fees. The medical bills were probably for the treatment of the wound which she had received at East Chester, for the musket ball had never been removed from her thigh.

The House Committee on Revolutionary Pensions investigated Gannett's petition and found that Deborah's original records had been destroyed when the British burned the capitol during the War of 1812. The Committee decided that there existed no real basis for granting Gannett any relief, but the members were touched by the strangeness of the case:

> ". . . the whole of the American Revolution records no case like this, and "furnishes no other similar example of female heroism, fidelity, and courage." The petitioner does not allege that he served in the war of the Revolution, and it does not appear by any evidence in the case that such was the fact. It is not, however, to be presumed that a female who took up arms in defence of her country, who served as a common soldier for nearly three years, and fought and bled for human liberty; would, immediately after the termi-

nation of the war, connect herself for life with a tory or a
traitor. He, indeed, was honored much by being the husband
of such a wife; and as he has proved himself worthy of her,
as he has sustained her through a long life of sickness and
suffering, and as that sickness and suffering were occasioned
by the wounds she received and the hardships she endured
in defence of the country, and as there cannot be a parallel
case in all times to come, the committee do not hesitate to
grant relief.

Gannett died before he could collect the $80 a year he was
awarded, but Deborah's heirs did receive $466.66 in a settlement.
America would further remember her strangest revolutionary
daughter. On April 10, 1944, a new liberty ship rolled down the
ways from the Bethlehem shipyards in Baltimore. Her proud
name was the *Deborah Gannett.*

# CHAPTER NINE

# *Independence at Last*

In this city, the fair sex, although they are not the prettiest I have seen, form a very agreeable and in general, very well bred society. Perhaps the oppressively hot climate of Virginia has some influence upon the inhabitants; it is probably the reason for their being less gay and much less active than those in the North.

*The journal of Baron Ludwig Von Closen*
Williamsburg, Virginia, November, 1781

AFTER RECUPERATING from the battle of Guilford Courthouse, Cornwallis proceeded north relatively unopposed and entered Virginia with renewed confidence. But William Dickson, a southern planter, was enraged by the conduct of the Britisher's entourage.

According to Dickson, the troops of the enemy were trouble enough, but even worse were the southern loyalists and camp followers who had attached themselves to the English:

The outrages were committed mostly by a train of loyal refugees, as they termed themselves, whose business it was to follow the camps and under the protection of the army enrich themselves on the plunder they took from distressed inhabitants who were not able to defend it.

We were also distressed by another swarm of beings (not better than harpies). These were women who followed the army in the character of officers' and soldiers' wives. They were generally considered by the inhabitants to be more insolent than the soldiers. They were generally mounted on the best horses and side saddles, dressed in the finest and best clothes that could be taken from the inhabitants as the army marched through the country.

Lafayette, who had been sent south with a force to confront Benedict Arnold raiding on the Virginia coast, evacuated Richmond as Cornwallis approached. The British continued on, intending to meet with reinforcements and supply ships near Portsmouth. Only the southern heat seemed a problem. Soldiers were told not to expose themselves to the direct sun's rays or lie on the bare earth. Cannon were kept watered and sunstrokes were common. But soon more severe problems confronted the army camped near Yorktown.

French squadrons, newly arrived from the West Indies, defeated the British fleet and cut off any aid Cornwallis might have received by water. Lafayette moved his men forward to threaten the English from the front. In a final blow, Washington arrived with 7,000 American and French forces.

Cornwallis was completely surrounded on land. Nearly 30,000 allied troops and sailors were matched against his 6,000 men. In the bay were two dozen French ships with heavy cannon which could be used to bombard the vulnerable British camp. After a siege of less than three weeks and isolated skirmishes, Cornwallis surrendered his forces. The defeated troops marched out to captivity to the strains of a British air entitled: "The World Turned Upside Down." Lafayette wrote: "The play, sir, is over."

But although Yorktown would prove to be the last major battle between the armies of America and England, the war was far from over. The capture of the crown forces in Virginia was indeed impressive, but the British still had contingents of men in New York, South Carolina and on the frontier.

In Manhattan, Clinton was having not only professional difficulties as commander of the British forces, but personal troubles as well.

The general did not consider his relationship with Mary Baddeley secure as long as her husband remained in the area. Therefore, Baddeley was detailed to Charleston, supposedly in a safe, noncombat assignment as a barracks master. The elated husband seemed grateful for the advancement and notified Clinton his hopes that: ". . . it may please the Almighty to assist you in all your undertakings and to crown your end with everlasting honor and happiness."

Baddeley's end was much more imminent than Clinton's. The summer after arriving in Charleston, the barracks master died of a fever. New York gossips suggested that the general had intentionally sent the husband of his mistress into an unhealthy area in the hopes that she would soon be a widow. There was some background for this charge, for the port city was a notorious death trap. At least 800 of the 2,100 American prisoners incarcerated after the fall of Charleston were dead within 13 months, most of them from assorted diseases.

Yet Clinton maintained that rather than wishing to harm Baddeley, the transfer had been made to assure that Mary's husband would not be in danger with a battle regiment in the field.

Death from fever was not a particularly unusual event, for medical practices during the war were primitive and hospitals more hazardous than the battlefield. Most soldiers made every attempt to avoid confinement in infirmaries, for during the conflict, an estimated ten times more soldiers died from diseases contracted in hospitals than from combat wounds in the field.

Usually several men shared the same cot and thus one contaminated patient could infect many bedfellows. Hospitals were likely to be rampant with the bacteria of typhus, typhoid, putrid fever, dysentery, malaria and meningitis. Pneumonia was frequent, but smallpox, formerly a greatly feared disease, had come under control by 1781 because of compulsory innoculations for new recruits.

But smallpox had taken its toll during the days when it was still rampant. Martha Dangerfield Bland, the twenty-five-year-old wife of a Virginia colonel, had avoided the sickness by innoculation. Although this prevention had left severe scars, Martha still considered herself more attractive than most women without the disfigurements: "I shall be pitied with them," she wrote of the unsightly marks, "However, every face almost keeps me in countenance. Here are few smooth faces, and no beauties, so that one does very well to pass."

The medical department of the American army passed through various reorganizations during the war in an attempt to promote efficiency, but despite these attempts, the level of services remained grossly inadequate. The most prominent medical writings of the day were of little help to the stricken. Most recommended amputation for all compound fractures, and suggested that saber wounds should be either further enlarged or covered with dry lint. A musket wound was usually treated by removing the ball and covering the sore with flannel dipped in oil, or with a poultice composed of bread and milk.

Because trained doctors were scarce, most of the attention given to the sick soldiers was by para-medical surgeon's mates or by women nurses. A 1777 reorganization of the continental medical staff recommended that one matron and ten nurses should be employed for every hundred wounded. The matron's task was to supervise the general operation of the hospital, oversee the supplies and direct nurses in non-medical matters. For this, she was to receive $0.50 per day and one food ration, a payment equal to about twice that of a sergeant in the service. Nurses were to be paid $0.24 and also to receive a food ration.

A later reorganization ordered that seven matrons and thirty nurses should be employed for every fifteen hospital doctors and surgeons. This relatively high percentage of female help was probably never obtained.

As poor as were the conditions in hospitals, the medical situation in British prisons was far worse. In New York, where Joshua Loring was responsible for the captives' welfare, most sick detainees were left entirely to the care of women who volunteered their services. The abilities of the English professional staff who were available were questionable, particularly to Elias Boudinot, a rebel who investigated the treatment of his comrades in detention.

Boudinot reported that in addition to general neglect, the captives were sometimes helped along to death by at least one

British paid surgeon. Reportedly the instigator was a Frenchman who had been jailed himself while the Americans held Manhattan, but released and appointed as a surgeon when the British took control.

Boudinot claimed that the ex-convict was so successful in increasing the number of deaths among rebel prisoners, that he was given a raise in salary by the enemy. The irate whig had received confirmation for his charges from two escaped prisoners who reported to him:

> . . . That they were sick in the Hospital under the care of the above Frenchman—That he came & examined them, and gave to each of them a dose of Physick to be taken immediately—A Young Woman their Nurse made them some private sign not to take their Physick immediately—After the Doctor was gone, she told them that she suspected the Physick was poison—That she had several times heard this Frenchman say that he would have Ten Rebels dead in such a Room and five dead in such a Room, the next morning, and it was always so happened. They asked her what they should do—she told them their only chance was to get off, sick as they were, that she would help them out, and they must shift for themselves.—They accordingly got off safe & brought the Physick with them. This was given to a Surgeon's Mate who afterwards reported that he gave it to a Dog, and that he died in a very short time.

Rumors, such as the saga of the French doctor, which had been common throughout the conflict, gradually evolved into fully believed legends as the war drew to a close. Some would be passed down through generations and find their way into legitimate textbooks on the period. The subject matter was far reaching for while some tales involve deeds of great infamy, others describe heroic actions of spectacular courage. Many of the legends of the revolution involve the adventures of women; some may be rooted in actual fact, but have probably become distorted by generations of imaginative story tellers.

Several of the most commonly related stories involve females who served as messengers for the armies. The most famous cou-

rier was South Carolina's Emily Geiger who was captured by enemy
scouts while carrying a secret paper to Thomas Sumter. Enterprising Emily promptly ate the dispatch and the British, finding
no incriminating evidence set her free. She successfully continued
her journey and delivered the message verbally.

In the same state, Mary Dillard is credited with carrying a
warning to Thomas Sumter of an impending attack by Tarleton.
The Americans, who were reportedly eating and completely unaware of their danger, were alerted just in time to spring into action and avoid a disastrous suprise raid. Mary Blackstock, who
lived nearby, informed the Gamecock that she would not allow a
battle on her land, but her prohibition was not heeded and the
fight began over her protests.

Jane Thomas, visiting her husband in prison at Ninety-Six,
reportedly overheard a British plan to attack the rebels at Cedar
Springs. Jane dashed sixty miles on horseback to notify her rebel
friends, and is credited with a second adventure when she supposedly rallied her daughters and a son-in-law to repel an enemy
attack on an ammunition supply.

Behethland Moore is a lesser known folk heroine who was
only fifteen when she was employed as an intelligence messenger.
While accompanied only by a friend named Fannie Smith, Behethland is credited with canoeing up the Little River to carry an
important message to Col. Henry Lee.

Grace Waring and Rachel Clay, both married to brothers
named Martin, preferred to work together. After disguising
themselves in men's clothing, the pair set off to capture a British
messenger, something in the spirit of the women of Groton. Supposedly the women apprehended not only a courier with his important documents, but two officers escorting him.

Other women performed similar services for the British.
Dicey Langston of Laurens, South Carolina, was about fourteen
when she gathered information for the crown. Elizabeth Henry
of Ninety-Six was thrown out of her house by her own disap-
proving husband for performing the same service.

Some legendary women performed their notable deeds in
their own homes. Martha Bratton was once slashed with a reaping hook because of her sarcasm to the British and blew up a

powder supply she had been left to guard rather than turn it over to the enemy. Unfortunately she had to destroy her own house in the process. The wife of one Samuel Otterson is also credited with a demolition of gunpowder. In retribution, the opposition allegedly cut off her skirt to the waist.

One Nancy Jackson, living near Fair Forest Creek, kicked a marauding tory down a flight of steps and North Carolina's Sarah Dickinson is credited with singlehandedly capturing five tories who were looting her house. Quaker Hannah Gaunt managed to subdue a similar raider by hitting him over the head with an axe, even though she herself had been wounded.

Another thriller concerns the wife of Thomas Heywood, a Charleston woman who refused to illuminate her house during a mass celebration of the British victory at Guilford Court-house. In retaliation, the English threatened to burn the dwelling and when she later repeated the same defiance, tory women gathered outside to throw bricks and garbage through her windows. The excitement proved too much for her sister Mrs. George Hall who died in an upper room during the females' riot.

Creole Sally St. Clair is credited with masquerading as a man so that she could follow a rebel sergeant on his assignment. Romantic Victorians claim that the soldier was completely ignorant of Sally's deception, until she was killed at the Battle of Savannah.

South Carolina women are not the only ones to be heralded as folk heroines. Anne Frisby of Cecil County, Maryland, organized her servants into a small army and defended her Patuxent River estate against attackers. In Pennsylvania, Rebecca McLane has taken her place in dubious history for making breeches for her husband out of linen tablecloths.

Quick thinking Mrs. Fisher of New Castle, New York, concealed a whig neighbor in an ash heap during a search by the enemy, but in Connecticut, one Mrs. Griswold chose to hide her husband in a meat barrel.

Northern spies on the distaff side do not seem to have been as successful at avoiding detection as their southern sisters. Margaret Moncrieff, daughter of a British engineer, was captured for gathering intelligence, but was released with the help of influential friends. Mrs. John Rapelje of Brooklyn disregarded the rebel tea boycott, and as retribution, whigs fired a cannon ball into her house. She reportedly became so irate that she revealed rebel troop movements to the British.

In New England, Mrs. Nathan Sargent, desperate to contribute metal for bullets, not only melted down her pewter tableware and clockweights, but also donated all the name plaques from her family's tombstones. The local cemetery also came in handy for one Mrs. Horry who used a marble vault top to hide her potato crop.

But the most famous yarn of all concerns Philadelphia seamstress and upholsterer Elizabeth Griscom. Betsy was born on January 1, 1752, the eighth of seventeen children of Samuel Griscom, a builder who reportedly helped to construct Carpenter's Hall.

In 1774, Betsy was read out of the Quaker Meeting for eloping with upholsterer John Ross. The pair set up shop in Philadelphia, but in 1776, John was killed by an explosion while serving with the state militia.

Betsy's poor luck with husbands would continue. Seventeen months later she married Joseph Ashburn, a sailor who was captured at sea and incarcerated in Plymouth's Old Mill Prison. Ashburn died in 1782 and about a year later, Betsy tried a third time; this marriage was to John Claypoole, a family friend.

Revolutionary writers made no mention of any particularly significant contribution which widow Ross performed during the war. But a hundred years after the Boston Massacre, Betsy's grandson William J. Canby began a project which would make the seamstress the most famous woman of the revolution.

In March of 1870, Canby, in an address to the Pennsylvania Historical Society, announced that his modest ancestor had made the first American flag. Although he presented no conclusive documentation, Canby maintained that some thirty-four years before, Betsy while on her deathbed, had revealed the story to him. Canby had been eleven years old at the time. Three affidavits were presented as evidence, but these statements, by Betsy's daughter, grandaughter and niece, did not claim that the witnesses had seen her make the flag, merely that they had heard her claim she did.

The story in a more sophisticated era may have been eyed as merely a romantic legend. More than ninety years had passed since the event and no mention of the deed had been recorded by observers or survivors of the war. However, Canby's story was almost immediately accepted as fact. One reason may have been Philadelphia's gala bi-centennial which was rapidly approaching. The public, imbued with patriotic zeal, may have been accepting claims which would normally have required more extensive proof.

By the time a closer examination was made, numerous textbooks had already incorporated the Betsy Ross legend into print and it was generally accepted as a proven fact. Millions of Americans believed indisputably that the humble seamstress had created history.

However, a core of skeptics sprang up in an attempt to debase each point of the claim. In a hotly contested debate, charges and countercharges were made; lawsuits were threatened. One complication in the historical debate was the creation of the Betsy Ross Memorial Association, a group formed to perpetuate the Philadelphia woman's memory and purchase the home where she reportedly lived. The Association sold more than two million memberships, many to schoolchildren at $0.10 each.

Opponents claimed that only a small fraction of the total funds collected actually were designated for the house purchase while thousands of dollars were given to promoters of the scheme. When the small dwelling on Arch Street was at last bought by the Association, opponents did not quiet their cry. Instead they claimed that the structure was not the actual building in which Betsy had lived.

Like Philadelphia, the frontier also had folk heroines whose exploits came to be accepted as true fact. Elizabeth Zane is one example. Elizabeth, a teenager, had reportedly taken refuge in Ft. Henry when the area was invaded by renegades and Indians. After a six hour battle, powder began to run low and the young girl was selected to fetch additional supply stores outside the protective walls. Her mission was allegedly successful and thus the defenders were able to hold out until reinforcements arrived. A similar tale is told concerning a number of women at Bryan's Station near Lexington, who went out of a besieged fort to bring back water. The attacking Indians were said to be so astonished that the females were able to return unharmed.

These two frontier tales illustrate that sex was no criterion for protection in times of danger. Life was less luxurious for the women of the frontier. Unlike the rebellion on the Atlantic seaboard where war was fought primarily in major battles between formal armies, the revolution in the west entailed constant hit and run raids involving Indians, tories and whigs. There were no "safe" winters or springs when opposing forces were resting in camp. While their husbands roamed the frontier, pioneer wives assumed almost total responsibility for day to day activities such as farming the land or defending the home. Sarah Jolly, wife of a scout, became so irate at one marauder plundering her house that she broke his arm with a stick.

During hazardous attacks on community settlements, women were chosen for the most dangerous tasks, so that the more skilled men could be left available to do the actual fighting. One common tactic in understaffed garrisons was the dressing of women in men's clothes. The male impersonators then paraded about openly to give the impression that great numbers of defenders were in attendance.

However, many pioneer women in revolutionary vignettes did take part in various stages of combat. Angelica Vrooman moulded bullets while Mary Hagidorn defended a New York fort with a pike. Near Herkimer, the wife of John Christian Shell saved the day when her family's cabin was attacked. As the invaders stuck their rifles through the wall boards to fire, Mrs. Shell bent the barrels from inside the house, so that they would misfire.

The wife of John Merrill in Nelson County, Kentucky territory, chose an axe as her defense. After her husband had been wounded and she had personally dispatched four Indians, the situation became critical. The remaining attackers climbed to the roof, intending to enter by way of the chimney. Mrs. Merrill quickly tossed a mattress onto the fire. When two Indians became overcome with smoke and fell onto the hearth, the pioneer woman efficiently killed them with her axe.

Anne Bailey was undoubtedly an authentic figure on the frontier and one who became so adept at moving secretly through the forest that she was tagged the "White Squaw of the Kanawha."

Anne was born in Liverpool in 1742, but came to the colonies as a child. Here she married Richard Trotter, a frontiersman who was killed in a battle with the Indians in the Great Kanawha Valley where the two had settled. Almost immediately Anne became a scout, wearing buckskins and riding up and down the frontier carrying messages, spying on enemies and recruiting rebel soldiers.

Her actions were so reckless that local Indians thought her possessed by evil spirits and named her "Mad Anne." The name soon spread throughout the area and when her second husband died she returned to her lonely frontier life, this time as a peddlar.

Just before Anne died in 1825 at eighty three, a traveller who visited her reported: "She was fond of a dram. When I saw the poor creature, she was almost naked; she begged a dram, which I gave her, and also some other trifle."

The violence of frontier warfare did not diminish, even though the revolution was winding down in the east. In June of 1782, Col. William Crawford and a group of rebels were captured by Delaware and Shawnee near Ft. Pitt. The prisoners were marched to Sandusky, and according to one of the detainees, a Dr. Knight, the Delaware women were particularly proficient in torture:

> In the place where we were now made to sit down, there was a number of squaws and boys who fell on five prisoners and tomahawked them. There was a certain John McKinley amongst the prisoners, formerly an officer in the 13th Virginia Regiment, whose head an old squaw cut off, and the Indians kicked it about on the ground.

The women then attacked Col. Crawford, putting live coals upon his body:

> [Crawford] continued in all the extremities of pain for an hour and three quarters or two hours longer, as near as I

can judge, when at last being almost spent, he lay down on his belly: They then scalped him and repeatedly threw the scalp in my face, telling me "That was my great Captain." An old squaw (whose appearance everyway answered the ideas people entertain of the Devil) got a board, took a parcel of coals and ashes and laid them on his back and head after he had been scalped. . . .

Dr. Knight managed to escape as he was being transported to a Shawnee village. After hitting an Indian guard over the head with a stick, Knight lived for three weeks on berries, apples, herbs and blackbirds. Finally he reached safety at a whig fort.

While activities continued on the frontier, rebels in the east waited anxiously for the official end of hostilities with England. John Jay and John Adams had joined Benjamin Franklin in Paris for participation in diplomatic discussions.

In Philadelphia, the lull was filled by a great feast, given by the French minister to celebrate the birth of the Dauphin. The scene and preparations surpassed even those of the Meschianza which had scandalized the city only four years before.

Benjamin Rush recorded that the minister had constructed a special ballroom, decorated with elaborate paintings, to house the festivities. Gardens were planted and a veiled platform built so that Quaker ladies who chose not to participate in the dancing and drinking could discreetly view the gaiety. Thirty cooks were borrowed from the French Army to prepare the feast, for several thousand people had been invited to attend.

On the morning of the affair, many women had their "heads dressed," according to Rush. An estimated 10,000 uninvited citizens lined the approaches to the party and although the minister planned to distribute wine and money to the onlookers, city leaders suggested that the sum should be donated instead for the care of hospital patients and prisoners.

Rush saw the gathering as living proof that democracy had indeed been established by the revolution. He called the gathering "the world in minature," and proudly described the assortment of guests to Elizabeth Graeme Ferguson, one prominent Pennsylvanian who did not attend:

. . . Here were ladies and gentlemen of the most ancient as well as modern families. Here were lawyers, doctors and ministers of the gospel. Here were the learned faculty of the College and with them many who knew not whether Cicero plead in Latin or in Greek, or whether Horace was a Roman or a Scotchman. Here were painters and musicians, poets and philosophers, and men who were never moved by beauty or harmony or rhyme or reason. . . . Here were whigs and men who formerly bore the character of tories. . . .

Here were to be seen men who had opposed each other in the councils and parties of their country, forgetting all former resentments and exchanging civilities with each other. . . . Here were to be seen men of various countries and languages, such as Americans and Frenchmen, English- men and Scotchmen, Germans and Irishmen, conversing with each other like children of one father. And lastly, here were to be seen the extremes of the civilized and savage life. An Indian Chief in his savage habits and the Count Rocham- beau in his expensive and splendid uniform talked with each other as if they had been the subjects of the same govern- ment, generals in the same army, and the partakers of the same blessings of civilized life.

On April 19, 1783, the eighth anniversary of the battles at Lexington and Concord, the preliminary peace articles were at last announced to the American troops. The nation's indepen- dence was officially recognized by England. Rebel soldiers and their women could begin to return home. The British and Ger- man troops were free to cross the Atlantic for the final time. The long war was over, but years were still to be lived by many sur- viving women of the revolution. The post-war era would not be as amiable and unified as Benjamin Rush had envisoned it to be.

# *Epilogue*

AFTER THE WAR, the lives of many women fell back into the old pre-revolutionary pattern with little change. A small number of participants rose to new prominence. Others lost the temporary fame they had gained during the conflict and faded into obscurity. Most of those who left the country as loyalists began entirely new modes of living.

In the post-war years, Mary Baddeley fared best of the British generals' women. Sir Henry Clinton, who became Governor of Gibraltar, remained attached to the widow for the rest of his life. In England, Clinton maintained two separate homes, one supervised by his sister-in-law Elizabeth Carter for his legitimate family, and the other for Mary and his extracurricular children. The general chose to spend the greatest part of his final years with the woman who had befriended and supported him during the long American war, but marriage never legalized the affair.

In 1794, Clinton wrote a long explanation to his sons by Harriet Carter describing the entire relationship with Mary. The general was then in failing health and was concerned about the deep alienation which had developed over the matter. In addition, Clinton was attempting to quell any resentment his legitimate heirs might have over the liberal provisions included for Mary's children in his will. Clinton wrote:

> . . . I often wished to explain to you all the reasons why I should be under the necessity of taking something from you to give to them. They, poor souls, are alas left without a single friend to protect or support them, accustomed to my endearments and those of their poor, friendless mother, what will the difference be to them if my children don't give them some countenance? I trust they will and my sisters [will] be the first to show them the example.

General Gage's wife Margaret did not continue in the marriage which had seemed so satisfactory when she left her husband in defense of Boston. The general, whose reputation was permanently smeared by his conduct of the rebellion during the early months, returned to live with his wife in England, but in considerably reduced financial circumstances.

According to *Town and Country Magazine*, Gage ultimately became infatuated with the daughter of a clergyman, a "Mrs. F___g," whom he kept as a mistress. Gage died in 1787, but Margaret lived an ad___nal thirty-seven years.

Gentleman Johnny Burgoyne did not choose to extend his association with the champagne-drinking commissary's wife who he had feted on the road to Saratoga. Instead, he found a new love in singer Susan Caufield who shared his bed for ten years. Four children born of the union were raised by Lord Derby, for Burgoyne devoted much of his time to becoming well-known as a composer and playwright.

Lord Charles Cornwallis built an even greater reputation as Governor General of India and a member of the Cabinet. His subordinate during the revolution, Banastre Tarleton, was ultimately condemned for his action at Waxhaws. But Tarleton managed to partially clear his name, became both a baronet and a general and held a seat in Parliament for twenty-two years.

Francis, Lord Rawdon, and eight other British officers were

captured by the French late in the revolution while returning home. Also on board was Rawdon's reputed mistress, one Mme. Doyle. The lady, whose husband had been supposedly made a Lieutenant Colonel for his complicity in the Rawdon romance, was delighted to have been captured. According to several reports she claimed she actually preferred Frenchmen to the English.

Sir William Howe parted company with Elizabeth Loring who moved to England with Joshua and her children. Loring, who it is claimed made $30,000 a year in illegal profits while serving as commissary of prisoners in Manhattan, received an additional settlement of £850 from the loyalist claims commission. Elizabeth, soon left a widow, received a government pension for forty-one years, until 1830 when she presumably died. Howe may have assisted in promoting the careers of her children by Loring and by himself, for her son John Wentworth became a British Rear Admiral and another, Henry was made Archdeacon of Calcutta.

Sir William returned to his wife Frances Conolly, but died in 1814, without producing a legitimate male heir. His honors then went to his daughter Sophia-Charlotte, who became the Baroness Howe.

Because of her unorthodox behavior, Lady Sarah Lennox was divorced by horseman Bunbury. The separation was unusual for the era and for an English court woman of such high standing. But Lady Sarah's behavior would prove exemplary for the remainder of her life. She married a second time, to George Napier, a veteran of the American war whose wife and child had died in Manhattan during the British occupation. The family settled in Ireland where Napier became Collector of Accounts and eight children were born. Three of the Napier sons were knighted for bravery and Lady Sarah, like the British people at large, eventually mellowed in her feelings toward her former admirer the King.

After the rebellion she wrote: ". . . I *still* rejoice I was never Queen, and so I shall to my life's end. . . ." But Queen Charlotte would always regard George's past sweetheart with overt jealousy.

Increasingly, the King was subject to periods of irrationality and was widely considered to be growing mad. During these
spells, Lady Sarah did note some temporary regrets, but they
quickly passed. On receiving news of some new lapse she wrote:
"I did for a moment wish I was his wife. . . . I own I did almost
exclaim, 'Poor soul; if I was yours, I would never leave you an
instant; but try and calm your suffering mind!' But then I soon
forgot my pity, and rejoiced in the reflections on my own present
happy state, which no poverty can lessen."

Genteel poverty did fill Lady Sarah's last years, for despite a
pension from the King, her expenses were high and her accustomed life style became difficult to maintain. By 1820, the once
elegant belle of the court, the lover of the King and the scandal
of the aristocracy, was almost blind and was an invalid. She died
in 1826 at age eighty-one.

King George became increasingly more unstable after losing
his rebellious colonies. In 1788, he was rumored to have ordered
his carriage stopped in Windsor Park, where he wished to con-
verse with an oak tree he thought was his cousin Frederick the
Great of Prussia. Queen Charlotte, who had assured continuation
of the Hanoverian line by bearing fifteen children, was kept in almost total seclusion from the public. In 1811, George's oldest son
was made regent, for the last American king was considered to be
hopelessly insane. George III survived nine more years, becoming
increasingly farther removed from reality and in addition, totally
blind.

Patience Wright continued creating in wax and produced at
least one masque which was used by Josiah Wedgwood as the
model for his jasper medallions. Patience's son Joseph returned to
America as a sculptor and painter, but never achieved the fame of
his eccentric mother. Wright was responsible for designing some
of the first coins of the young American nation, for he was
appointed the First Draughtsman and Diesinker of the U.S.
Mint.

Not all Americans completely appreciated Patience's strange
ways. Abigail Adams called her the "Queen of Sluts" because of
the artist's habit of soundly kissing almost everyone to whom she
was introduced. In 1785, Patience wrote Thomas Jefferson that at

last she was planning to return home, but before she could begin the journey, the artist died in England.

Catharine Macaulay and her young husband did make the crossing to America. Here her reputation was perhaps even greater than it had been in England during her zenith. Throughout the colonies, the couple was entertained by leading figures, among them Mercy Warren who noted that "the world will not readily forgive" Catharine's "improper connection."

To John Adams, Mercy was more explicit. She explained that although the author was held in great esteem for her professional work, the liaison with Graham would overshadow the literary accomplishment because of severe moral condemnation: "[Catharine's] independency of spirit led her to suppose she might associate for the remainder of life, with an inoffensive, obliging youth, with the same impunity a gentleman of three score and ten might marry a damsel of fifteen."

Catharine's visit did stimulate sales of her books in the former colonies, but did not improve her reputation at home. Critics charged that she was a poor researcher and purposefully distorted historical facts she found unpleasing. Isaac Disraeli, father of the future Prime Minister, claimed that during her research in the British Museum, Catharine blatantly destroyed any documents she found which were contrary to her own hypotheses.

The Baroness von Riedesel never returned to the land where she had spent seven years of her young life. When the family finally left Canada in the summer of 1783, it was in distinctly grander style than the many months on the campaign trail and in confinement. Her ship was partially rebuilt to assure the greatest comfort, a small garden planted on deck and a cow and calf brought along for fresh meat.

Once home in Brunswick, the Baron continued his rise in the military and served for five years as commandant of the town of Brunswick. The Riedesel's lived in splendid elegance, partially because of the wealth they had accumulated during the revolution, when the Baron estimated that he had saved 15,000 thalers. In addition, Riedesel received a pension from the British crown and inherited a large estate from his father.

## M<sup>RS</sup>: WRIGHT.

*Publish'd as the Act directs Dec<sup>t</sup>. 1775.*

*Mrs. Wright* (Patience Lovell Wright), artist unknown. An
etching from *The London Magazine* of November, 1775. Photo
courtesy of the Library of Congress.

The Baroness lived until 1808. A century later, one of her descendants, Count Johann Heinrich, again returned to the new world. Just before World War I, Heinrich was appointed German ambassador to the United States.

Elsewhere in Brunswick, not all of the seventy-seven women camp followers who had sailed with the troops for the war returned home. Officially only sixty-four women arrived back, and many of these were probably Canadian or American females picked up along the way to replace German army wives who had died or deserted.

In nearby France, Marie Antoinette and Louis XVI continued to ignore the warnings which the American revolution had sounded to all monarchs. Instead of liberalizing and economizing the French court, royal expenditures were increased and the citizenry was even further deprived of the necessities of life. Marie's thirst for lavishness was constantly indulged and even larger amounts were required for her amusement. Unrest among the masses increased, fed in part by the libertarian philosophies introduced by the colonial conflict.

Within a decade of the American peace, revolution broke out in the city where Benjamin Franklin had planted its seeds. Aristocrats like the Marquise de Lafayette were imprisoned. Less fortunate ones like the Count d'Estaing who had become Admiral of France, were guillotined. On October 16, 1793, the once proud Queen of France was paraded through the streets of Paris to be executed.

Catherine the Great was not immediately affected by the American war. Many of the thirteen years left in her reign were dedicated to extending the boundaries of Russia at the expense of weaker nations. But in each passing year, Catherine became less sure of her throne. She felt threatened not only by her own son Paul I who she believed might attempt to overthrow her rule, but also by the growing ideas of democracy spawned by the American and French rebellions.

The excesses in Paris were particularly appalling to the Empress. She banned all French modes from her court and academy and when Marie and Louis were killed, became increasingly ruthless to even moderate critics at home. Her earlier goals of freedom and happiness for the masses were forgotten and her noble allies were allowed to mistreat their serfs even more severely. The Empress' acceptance of this exploitation of the masses may well have doomed the Romanoff line and created the basis for her nation's own violent revolution 125 years later.

Catherine's sexual appetite did not diminish with old age. Although she lost her teeth and became increasingly stout, the progression of paramours was continued. Just hours before her death from a stroke in 1796, Catherine enjoyed the company of her favorite, one Plato Zubov. The ruler's remains were interred in the Peter and Paul fortress, but in a grisly aftermath, Paul reportedly ordered the skeleton of his long dead father exhumed and placed on the throne for a short time. The idea was that the new monarch did not want to succeed directly his mother to the seat of power.

The eccentricities of royalty were of little concern to most women in America.

Ann Lee, after her disastrous tour of New England, returned to live at Niskeyuna where she also came under attack. Powerful enemies Valentine and Daniel Rathburn produced a constant barrage of criticism against the sect, usually based on supposed heresy or debauchery: "They meet together in the night," one critical blast declared, "They run about in the woods and elsewhere, hooting and tooting like owls; some of them have stripped naked in the woods, and thought they were angels and invisible. . . ."

Most prospective converts evidently believed the Rathburns' accusations, for the cult began a decided decline. After Mother Ann died in 1784, the attraction of new believers became more difficult.

According to legend, the Jackson Whites and Jackson Blacks met their greatest obstacles following the war. Because no provision was made for their return to England, the women and their small army reportedly were turned loose without any means of survival. An enraged citizenry supposedly drove the band out of Manhattan into neighboring New Jersey where they found refuge in an isolated area of the Ramapo Mountains. Here the women and children settled into comradeship with other outcasts of society such as British and Hessian deserters, escaped slaves, homeless free blacks and displaced Indians.

The Ramapo settlers were forgotten by the outside world until the early 20th century when they were "rediscovered" and became a popular anthropological phenomenon. According to various news reports, generations of close inbreeding had produced several unique characteristics such as a high incidence of albinism. In addition, it was claimed that the Jackson descendants showed a high incidence of polydactylism, the tendency to reproduce progeny with twelve toes and fingers, and syndactylism, a condition of webbed appendages.

The future problems of the Jackson women were far beyond the lifetime of James Otis, who lived to see the revolution won, but never again completely regained his sanity. Otis died in May of 1783, after being struck by lightning, soon after he had burned all of his speeches and writings in a giant bonfire.

Otis' sister, Mercy Warren, continued writing long after the war was over. One of her plays, "The Sack of Rome," met with little success. John Adams informed her that there was little hope of it being produced in London, as she had hoped, for he claimed that the British found it painful to dwell on the former colonies and rejected most things which reminded them of the bitter war.

Alexander Hamilton was more enthusiastic about the prospects of "Ladies of Castile," another new play. Hamilton informed her:

> It is certain that in "Ladies of Castile," the sex will find a new occasion of triumph. Not being a poet myself, I am in the less danger of feeling mortification at the idea that in the career of dramatic composition at least, female genius in the United States has out-stripped the male.

Mercy would have one more battle against what she considered to be oppression. During the debates on the ratification of the Constitution, she broke with most of her Federalist friends and strongly opposed adoption of the document which she considered to be potentially unjust to the common people.

Mercy's long friendship with John and Abigail Adams was

severed because of her anti-Federalist activities, and the President, who had grown increasingly more conservative, found additional ground of complaint in 1805 when Mercy published an extensive history of the American revolution. The history, based on twenty-five years of research and writing, was too "revolutionary" for Adams. Although democrats such as Thomas Jefferson proclaimed Mercy as a great writer, her reputation suffered from widespread accusations by Federalist critics that she was biased, inaccurate and partisan. The charges were partially correct, for just as Mercy had unhesitatingly propagandized against the British rule of the colonies, so she editorialized in her history against the defenders of the Constitution.

During the last years of her life, Mercy suffered increasing blindness and her writing days were ended. As tempers cooled, and the United States progressed forward under the central government, she was reconciled with John and Abigail. On October 19, 1814, Mercy Warren died.

In Philadelphia, Elizabeth Graeme Ferguson never regained that portion of her inheritance which had been attainted in her husband's name. Henry Ferguson never returned home, but instead applied for a British pension claiming that because of the war, his marriage was broken with irreconcilable difficulties.

Reverend Jacob Duché, who had been responsible for involving Elizabeth in the first mediation effort, returned to Philadelphia in 1792, in an unsuccessful attempt to resume the honored station he had held in pre-war days. In June, 1797, *Gentleman's Magazine* reported that Duché's wife had died in a freak accident. While opening a window, a sand bag fell on her head and she survived only a few hours. Duché died the following year.

Grace Galloway's husband also deserted family and country for a new life in England. When confiscation proceedings were initiated against the Galloway property, Grace barricaded herself inside her house and refused to admit government officials. Agents finally broke down the door and took such a complete inventory of her property that even the empty bottles and broken china were included. Although Galloway's estate was taken over by the rebels, Grace's private property was left untouched, but was sequestered during her husband's lifetime.

The handsome soldiers of the revolution never came back to claim the hand of young Sally Wister. The spinster spent many years in seclusion and devoted the last period of her life to intense religious study.

Charles Lee retired to his estate in the Shenandoah Valley, following his court martial after the Battle of Monmouth. Lee was filled with bitterness and resentment against the United States and like Benedict Arnold, felt that his contribution during the revolution had gone unrewarded. To his sister he wrote: "Great God, What a dupe and a victim have I been to the talismanic name of liberty."

By 1782, Lee's financial situation was critical and he was forced to sell his plantation. During a trip to Philadelphia, the general fell ill and died several days later in a third-rate inn. He was buried in Christ Churchyard, a location which would not have pleased the unorthodox Lee. In a will discovered later, the ex-general had stipulated that he was not to be interred: ". . . in any church, or churchyard, or within a mile of any Presbyterian or Anabaptish meeting-house; for since I have resided in this country, I have kept so much bad company when living, that I do not choose to continue it when dead."

Henry Knox and Lucy also experienced post war financial problems. Knox, who succeeded Washington as head of the army, served for a time as Secretary of War, a prestigious but lonely position, for the entire defense command at that time consisted of Knox, a secretary and a clerk.

Lucy continued her lavish entertaining, and although her reputation as a domineering gossip and meddler did not diminish, her parties were reportedly well attended. Lucy weighed nearly 250 pounds during this her prime, and according to one Dr. Manasseh Carter, she did not present a pleasing appearance. Carter wrote that she was:

> . . . very gross but her manners are easy and agreeable although with an affected singularity in dressing her hair. She seems to mimic the military style, very disgusting in a female. Her hair in front is craped up at least a foot high,

much in the form of a churn, bottom upward, and topped off with a wire skeleton in the same form, covered with black gauze, which hangs in streamers down her back. Her hair behind is a large braid, confined in a monsterous crooked comb.

After Knox retired from government, the family moved to Maine where Lucy had been awarded the vast tract of land which had formerly belonged to her loyalist mother. Here in the wilderness, the Knoxes built Montpelier, a four-story mansion with crystal chandeliers and twenty-four fireplaces.

The rural environment did little to change Lucy's aloofness and she refused to associate with locals. Much of her reserve may have stemmed from a series of tragedies that resulted in the death of ten of her thirteen children at relatively young ages. One cubicle in the house was used to lay out the dead children so frequently that it became known as the "Dead Room."

Some of the children died strange deaths. Caroline failed following a disease "common to children cutting teeth in summer." Son Marcus died from a "bruised" cheek he developed after a fall down a flight of stairs. Henry Knox, the general, choked to death on a chicken bone in 1806.

Lucy spent the remaining eighteen years of her life in quiet solitude at Montpelier and occasionally sold a plot of land to pay for her modest upkeep.

Nathanael Greene's circumstances were little better. One of the general's last letters was to Henry Knox, complaining of poor crops and growing miseries at Mulberry Grove, Greene's Georgia plantation. The hard life was also telling on Catharine, who he claimed had changed "from the gay lady to the sober housewife."

The Rhode Islander's services in the southern campaign of the revolution had been rewarded by four grateful states. North Carolina voted Greene a 25,000 acre tract on the frontier. South Carolina gave him a 7,000 acre estate worth 10,000 guineas. Virginia was less generous and sent only a pair of horses. But Greene chose to accept Mulberry Grove, a gift of Georgia.

The great plantation near Savannah included 2,000 acres of

the best rice land in the nation, and had been confiscated from Royal Governor John Graham. Greene threw himself into reclaiming the land which had been unworked for ten years. But in 1786, before it would be restored to full production, Greene died after a hard day's work in the fields. The death was attributed to sunstroke, but it may have been a heart attack. Sometime later, it would be rumored to have been caused by foul play, with Catharine as a major participant.

Immediately after the general's death, Catharine found herself deeply in debt, with several small children to support and a large plantation to be managed. Her husband's claims for personal services and expenses during the revolution had not been fully settled and much of his land had been heavily mortgaged to Robert Morris and the Marquis de Lafayette.

Jeremiah Wadsworth, Greene's old friend, served as executor of the legacy and attempted to untangle the confused finances, but almost immediately complications appeared when a romance sprang up between himself and Catharine. Unfortunately for both, Wadsworth was married to a much older and wealthier woman. Wadsworth and Catharine did plan an intimate and secret rendezvous in New York, but the meeting did not take place and they ended their series of love letters on an ambiguous note.

Catharine was not idle on her voyage back to South Carolina, for two new admirers had entered her life. One was Phineas Miller, an old employee of Wadsworth who had been hired to help manage Mulberry Grove. The other was Eli Whitney, a young graduate of Yale who was journeying to South Carolina as the prospective tutor for the children of a wealthy planter.

At Catharine's urging, Whitney ignored his teaching obligation and went instead to Mulberry Grove. Here the widow, Miller and Whitney forged a close triangular relationship which would last for many years. "I find myself in a new natural world," Whitney wrote during his stay at the plantation, "and as for the moral world, I believe it does not extend this far south."

Catharine's difficulties with cleaning the cotton harvested on her land prompted Whitney to develop the cotton gin during his sojourn. He immediately formed a partnership with Miller which was designed to perfect and market the device, but difficulties over patent rights resulted in only minor returns to the plantation manager.

About 1796, Catharine married Miller, but two years later her plantation was put up for sale because of their inability to pay General Greene's remaining debts. No buyers appeared and in 1800, the plantation was knocked down at public auction.

Miller died three years later, after the couple had moved to Cumberland Island off the Georgia coast. Kitty once again assumed control of a large plantation and regained much of the flamboyance of her youth. Her gaiety was partially marred by rumors, perhaps spread by her more conservative neighbors. According to one tale, Catharine had engineered her first husband's death by convincing her lover, "Mad" Anthony Wayne, to stab the general.

Kitty's relationship with Whitney grew even closer. She wrote him: "Your picture ornaments my toilet table—It is everyday looked at and sometimes kissed—that is to say when you are sick." In July of 1814, she notified him: "We have a party of Eighteen to eat Turtle with us tomorrow—I wish you were the nineteenth. . . ." Two months later Catharine was dead.

Peggy Arnold did not achieve the honored status accorded to other generals' wives such as Lucy Knox and Catharine Greene. Most British officers, as blue-blooded aristocrats, considered Arnold both an interloper and a peasant who had committed an unforgivable error during the revolution. When Arnold applied for a position with the British East India Company, he was notified: ". . . no power in theis country could suddenly place you in the situation you aim for. . . ."

In London, the pair was presented to the King who became captivated with Peggy's beauty. One tory in England agreed that she was lovely and noted:

> I saw Mrs. Arnold a few days after her arrival in town . . . and was really pleased she looked so well, as general expectation was raised so high by the incessant puffers of the newspapers and the declaration of Colonel Tarleton that she was the handsomest woman in England. . . . They have taken a house and set up a carriage and will, I suppose, be a good deal visited.

Arnold left England for Canada where he began a shipping business and probably fathered an illegitimate son named John Sage. For a while the general's fortunes improved. A particular bit of good luck came when one of his warehouses burned, shortly after he had taken out a large insurance policy. But the Canadian venture was abandoned when Arnold became involved in a series of court actions.

Peggy returned only once to visit her family in Philadelphia. The stay was unhappy, for few in the city had forgotten the events of the war and hatred for Arnold ran deeply. In 1801, the general died in relative obscurity; Peggy was soon struck with cancer. As the end neared in the summer of 1804, Peggy's old admirer Robert Livingston came to call. The once popular flirt of Howe's occupation was in great agony and in July wrote her father that she was ". . . constantly under the effects of opium, to relieve a pain which would otherwise be intolerable. . . ." She died on August 24.

Abigail Adams' life changed from a private to a public one following the war. In 1784, she joined John in London where he was serving as America's first minister. The Adams' returned to the United States in 1788 and almost immediately John was elected Vice-president. When he assumed the presidency in 1796, Abigail became the first President's wife to live in the newly constructed White House. Because the structure was still unfinished when they arrived, enterprising Abigail hung the family's wash to dry in the drafty East Room.

Abigail was ill during much of her husband's administration, but recovered when the Federalist was defeated for a second term. The Adams' returned to Quincy where they spent much of their last years in concern over the unhappy lives of their children. Daughter Abigail had married Col. William Stephens Smith, an ex-aide to Washington, but a financial failure. Son Charles, who wed Sally Smith, became an alcoholic and died at thirty. Thomas, the youngest boy frequently deserted his family, leaving no support.

Abigail Adams died in 1818. Unlike her "Dearest Friend," she did not live to see her first born son, John Quincy, become the second President Adams.

Elbridge Gerry became Governor of Massachusetts, there approving a controversial redistricting bill which resulted in his name being firmly incorporated into the English language in the term "Gerrymander." In 1812, he was elected vice-president under James Madison, but died almost penniless two years later. The once wealthy merchant was buried at public expense. Ann Gerry lived until 1849, thus becoming the last surviving widow of a signer of the Declaration of Independence.

John Hancock also served as Governor of Massachusetts, but began to drink heavily, perhaps because of his severe gout. In 1797, Hancock died intestate and his wife Dorothy received only a small portion of his fortune. She later created a public scandal by marrying a sea captain and lived until 1830.

Widow Annis Stockton badgered General Washington with her poetry for several years. For a time she was courted by the Reverend John Witherspoon, a sixty-seven-year-old signer who finally chose to marry instead twenty-four-year-old widow Dill of Philadelphia. Annis' daughter Julia gained a unique place in history by her marriage to Benjamin Rush. The ceremony, performed by Witherspoon, was the only wedding in America which included three signers of the Declaration of Independence in the wedding party—the groom, the minister and the father of the bride.

Annis' brother, Elias Boudinot, became close friends with Rush, but the association ended bitterly in a private quarrel. Ultimately Rush, as Treasurer of the U.S. Mint, charged Boudinot with irregularities in his office as Director of the organization. Specifically the charges were that Boudinot: ". . . has taken all the Dung of the Stable of the Mint, for his own use. . . ."

Sally Jay's life also became more public after the revolution. Her father served fourteen terms as governor of New Jersey and signed the U.S. Constitution. Her brother Henry Brockholst Livingston was captured by the British as he returned from Spain near the end of the revolution, but survived and became a Supreme Court justice. John Jay became Secretary of Foreign Affairs for the new nation, and was appointed the first Chief Justice of the Supreme Court. But Jay's long friendship with Sally's cousin Robert Livingston was severed in ill will. Livingston, who had administered the Presidential oath of office to George Washington, was defeated by Jay in a bitter fight for governor of New York. Livingston later was minister to France and played an integral role in the acquisition of the Louisiana Purchase.

Thomas Sumter's beloved Mary lived a long life, seeing her husband represent South Carolina as both a congressman and a senator. The frail woman, who had spent most of her life as an invalid, lived to be a hefty ninety-four years old, and succumbed only to yellow fever.

Eliza Lucas Pinckney, her vast fortune dissipated by the revolution, lived the rest of her life with her widowed daughter. One of Eliza's last personal appearances was in 1791 when Washington came to pay his respects to the once great businesswoman. Two years later, Eliza died in Philadelphia where she had journeyed for surgery. She was buried in St. Peter's Churchyard, with Washington reportedly serving as a pallbearer.

Eliza's son Charles C. Pinckney was one of the signers of the Constitution and became a leader in the Federalist party. He was an unsuccessful candidate for President in 1804 and 1808, but his most lasting fame resulted from an offhand statement concerning a proposed bribe for French leader Talleyrand. When asked his opinion of the gratuity, Charles C. replied "No, no, not a six pence." His answer was more poetically passed down as: "Millions for defense, but not one cent for tribute."

Eliza's son Thomas served as Governor of South Carolina, minister to London, and was made a Major General during the War of 1812.

Margaret Corbin, the cannoneer of Ft. Washington, settled near West Point where her unorthodox behavior continued to create difficulties for the garrison's commander. The foul-tempered heroine died about 1800, and more than a century later, her remains were discovered on an estate near the Hudson owned by J. P. Morgan. Her body was exhumed and reburied with honors in the West Point cemetery.

For many black women, the end of the war meant the beginning of a new life. Although the British did not completely honor their pledge to grant freedom to all slaves who joined their cause, thousands of blacks were transported out of the slave south. Not all of these, however, reached freedom, for southern tories were allowed to take their slaves with them to the British West Indies where human bondage was not condemned.

The revolution had more disastrous affects for Indian women. Many were forced to leave their homes and go into western territory because of the great whig stampede into Indian territory following the peace. Huge tracts of tribal property were distributed as bonuses to revolutionary veterans, and private speculators attempted blatant land grabs in the territory of the red peoples.

One such deal was engineered by Robert Morris and his son Thomas. In 1797, the Morrises offered to buy much of the Seneca land and called a great council meeting at Big Tree to discuss the scheme. The Morrises provided food, clothing and an abundant liquor supply which flowed throughout the deliberations.

According to Morris, the Seneca women were considered the key to acceptance of the deal. It was believed that if the squaws could be convinced that the land sale would be beneficial, then the braves would quickly fall into line. At the Women's Council, Morris distributed baubles and assured the women that with the income from the sale of their lands, each of their children could be adequately cared for. In addition, the women were promised that the tribe would be so wealthy that they would be able to hire white workers to till the remaining land. The women capitulated and almost immediately, pressured their men into accepting the deal.

Morris had originally offered $100,000 for the Seneca's land, but arranged payment so that the Tribe received only the interest on the sum, a total payment of about $4 per Indian per year. The figure proved scarcely sufficient for the life free of hunger and care that Morris had promised, and as a result, the Seneca lived in greater poverty than ever before. Their hunting lands were gone, their fields sold to white settlers.

Morris did not profit from the venture. His land purchases so diminished the profits he had made by speculating on war goods, that in February of 1798, he was arrested for debt. For more than three years he was confined at Prune Street, a Philadelphia prison. In 1806 he died a forgotten man.

Mary Jemison fared better than many of her Indian friends. Because of her status as a white woman, she retained a private plot near where she had settled after fleeing Sullivan's army. In 1810, she was "discovered" by a long lost cousin, who she later claimed hoodwinked her into deeding away much of her choicest land to him.

Mary Jemison had lived too long with Indians to be satisfied in the White world. She moved to the Buffalo Creek Reservation in 1831, and died there two years later at age ninety-one.

Nancy Ward remained the most honored of the Cherokee, but the revolution had crushed most of the power of the tribe. A smallpox epidemic which decimated the population in 1783, further added to the problems created by westward expanding whigs.

By 1817, Nancy was too feeble to attend the great council held at Amoah, but she once again attempted to help her people by warning them against accepting a land deal being offered for much of their property. In an impassioned message, Nancy spoke for the tribe's women and begged the council to hold firm and sign no agreement with the encroachers:

> Your mothers, your sisters ask and beg of you not to part with any more of our land. . . . but keep it for our growing children, for it was the good will of our creator to place us here and you know our father the great President will not allow his white children to take our country away. Only keep your hands off of paper. . . . take pity and listen to the talks of your sisters, although I am very old, yet cannot but pity the situation. . . . I have great many grandchildren which I wish them to do well on our land.

Nancy's grandchildren would not live in the traditional Cherokee territory. Sixteen years after she died in 1822, Andrew Jackson ordered the removal of the entire tribe to what is now Oklahoma. Thousands died on the long march westward in what became known as the "Trail of Tears." In the east, whigs rushed in immediately to settle the vacated land.

Other women were also forced from their homes following the war. Although the Treaty of Paris specified that Congress would recommend to the state governments that loyalists should not be persecuted, the suggestion was an empty one.

Some leaders such as John Jay recommended pardon for "all except the faithless and the cruel. . . . ," but in the majority of communities, the loyalists were treated little better after the peace than during the war. Citizens like Catharine Hubbard and Susannah Darrow of Stamford, Connecticut, were ordered to leave and to never again return.

One loyalist of Scottish descent fleeing from the Mohawk Valley described her sorrow on leaving the new world that her ancestors had sought for refuge:

> At last we are preparing to leave forever this land of my birth. . . . Our lands are confiscated and it is hard to raise money at forced sales. . . . We expect the journey to be long and hard and cannot tell how many weeks we will be on the road. . . .

> Our grandparents little thought when they sought this new land, after the rising of Prince Charlie, that a flitting would be our fate, but we must follow the old flag wherever it takes us. It is again "The March of the Cameron Men" and wives and children must tread the hard road.

The family of Hannah Ingraham met problems. Before he joined the British army, Benjamin Ingraham had been the owner of a prosperous farm near Albany. In his absence, the Ingraham family was subjected to constant abuses by local whigs and forced to pay rent on their own land. After the conflict, the Ingrahams were forced completely off their land and ultimately fled for Canada carrying only twenty barrels of wheat, a tub of butter, a keg of pickles and some potatoes.

The Canadian settlements into which refugee loyalists like the Ingrahams fled teemed with friction. Ill feelings broke out between the post-war arrivals and those who had left the colonies early in the conflict and established equity. Justice was severe for even minor infractions and for years, the primitive communities barely managed to survive each harsh winter.

In London, the claims commission was deluged with petitions from loyalist widows or single women urgently requiring immediate relief. Some of the settlements were as large as £17,000 granted for the confiscation of the lands inherited by Susannah Philipse. Other claims were more modest, such as one submitted by Elizabeth Gray which was discussed by the commission on June 11, 1783:

> Her husband lived in Philadelphia, he was a Master of a Ship and died in prison there, by the Cruelty of the Rebels. She kept a shop in Philadelphia with Drapery, linen, etc.— when the British left the Town, she was turned out of the Town and was obliged to go to New York. She says she does not want any allowance, she only wishes a little Money to go to France—and she thinks she could do it all for £10.

Since sixty-year-old Elizabeth's petition was for only a pittance, the commission quickly decided her fate. Unlike wealthy, influential loyalists, Elizabeth Gray was not welcome in London: "This person had very little property," the commission concluded, "but as it appears she will be content with a small sum, we think it will be worth while to pay her the sum of £10 to get rid of her."

Some claims were disallowed entirely. One was by eighty-six-year-old Rebecca Hallowell, a Boston widow who claimed that after fleeing Massachusetts, her house was given to Sam Adams who caused extensive damage to the structure. Rebecca Thompson, who claimed that £1,300 worth of bricks were taken from her during the war was also denied reimbursement.

Gradually the women of the revolution passed from the scene. Catherine Rankin, a Virginia tory who never acknowledged Britain's defeat, died in 1833 at 109. Esther O'Brien, a loyalist who originally fled to New Brunswick, but returned home to South Carolina, died in 1854 at 113. Only a few women of the conflict lived to see Americans once more fighting among themselves in a nationwide civil war.

As each year passed, pushing the rebellion more distant into history, the revolution's women began to be seen in a strange, new way. The energetic, active participants were gradually for-

gotten and a new breed of docile, prudishly proper females took
their place. While men were shown as busy on the battlefield,
women were increasingly portrayed as spending their days in the
home, making bandages, spinning, praying and generally keeping
the hearth warm.

This change in outlook was partially due to the scores of
Victorian chroniclers who began to write the history of a war
they had not witnessed. This new generation, born long after the
tragic memories of bloody battles had faded, saw the revolution's
women in the context of the staid and reticent ladies of their
own conservative 19th century.

In a perhaps subconscious but consistent selection, writers rejected the bold actions of women such as Dorothy Townsend
who, attempting to protect her newly harvested grain crop,
whacked a thieving calvaryman over the head with a bread
shovel. Instead, most chose to emphasize those women who were
in the demure mold of Martha Washington. Instead of Charles
Slocum's wife a convicted counterfeiter whose ears were cut off
and whose cheeks were branded before she was locked in stocks
and pelted with garbage, the typical American revolutionary
woman became a dainty maiden dressed in satin and holding a
lace handkerchief at her breast while she verbally berated an un-
couth British officer.

Peeking back through the pages of diaries and journals we
can find fragments of history showing different women: rowdy
Dorcas Griffiths, Crazy Queen Esther, Winifred McCowan stealing the town bull and the black poet Phillis Wheatley writing of
her will to be free. These are the real women of the revolution.

# Acknowledgments

GRATEFUL acknowledgment is made for permission to reprint quotes from the following:

*Poems of Phillis Wheatley*, Julian D. Mason, Jr., editor, the University of North Carolina Press, 1966; *Baroness von Riedesel and the American Revolution-Journal and Correspondence of a Tour of Duty 1776–1783*, Marvin L. Brown, Jr., translator, the University of North Carolina Press and the Institute of Early American History and Culture, 1965; *The Autobiography of Colonel John Trumbull*, Theodore Sizer, editor, Yale University Press, 1953; *Journal of a Lady of Quality*, by Janet Schaw, Evangeline W. and Charles M. Andrews, editors, Yale University Press, 1939; *Mr Franklin, a Selection from His Personal Letters*, Leonard W. Labaree and Whitfield J. Bell, Jr., editors, Yale University Press, 1956; *Chancellor Robert R. Livingston of New York*, by George Dangerfield, Harcourt, Brace, Jovanovich, Inc., 1960; *Mutiny in January*, by Carl Van Doren, Copyright 1943 by

Carl Van Doren, renewed © 1971 by Margaret Van Doren Bevans, Barbara Van Doren Klaw and Anne Van Doren Ross, reprinted by permission of The Viking Press, Inc.; *The Memoirs of Catherine the Great*, Dominique Maroger, editor, Moura Budberg, translator, The Macmillan Company, N.D.

*Revolution in America: Confidential Letters and Journals, 1776–1784 of Adj. Maj. Baurmeister of the Hessian Forces*, by Bernhard A. Uhlendorf, Rutgers University Press, New Brunswick, New Jersey, 1967; *The Green Dragoon*, by Robert Duncan Bass, copyright © 1957. First published by Henry Holt and Co., republished by Sandlapper Press, Inc., Columbia, S.C. 1973; *Admas Family Correspondence*, Vol. I & II, L. H. Butterfield, editor, Cambridge, Mass.: The Belknap Press of Harvard University Press, 1963; *The Diary of Frederick Mackenzie*, by Frederick MacKenzie, Cambridge, Mass.: Harvard University Press, 1930; *Report on the Manuscripts of the Late Reginald Rawdon Hastings*, Vol. III, London: H. M. Stationery Office, 1930–1947; *A Hessian Soldier in the American Revolution: The Diary of Stephan Popp*, Reinhart J. Pope, translator, private printing, 1953; *General Washington's Spies on Long Island and in New York*, by Morton Pennypacker, 1939, by permission of the Long Island Historical Society.

William B. Willcox's translations of materials from the Clinton Papers, Clements Library, the University of Michigan; *Margaret Morris: Her Journal*, John W. Jackson, editor, the George S. MacManus Co., 1949; material from the collections of The Historical Society of Pennsylvania; *Letters of Benjamin Rush*, 1761–1792, L. H. Butterfield, editor, Vol. II, (copyright 1951 by the American Philosophical Society), published by Princeton University Press, reprinted by permission of Princeton University Press; *The Baroness and the General*, by Louise Hall Tharp, Little, Brown and Company, 1962; "The Misfortunes of Dorcas Griffiths," by Frank W. C. Hersey, *Transactions*, by permission of the Colonial Society of Massachusetts; "Catharine Macaulay and Patience Wright-Patroness of the American Revolution," by Manfred S. Guttmacher, *The Johns Hopkins Alumni Magazine*, by permission of *Johns Hopkins Magazine*; *Broadsides and Bayonets: The Propaganda War of the American Revolution*, by Carl

Berger, the University of Pennsylvania Press, Philadelphia, 1961.
*General Charles Lee, Traitor or Patriot?* by John R. Alden,
Louisiana State University Press, 1951; *Colonial Women of Affairs*, by Elisabeth A. Dexter, copyright © 1924 and 1931 by Elisabeth Anthony Dexter. Reprinted by permission of Houghton Mifflin Company; "Extracts from the Journal of Mrs. Ann Manigault 1754–1781," by Mabel L. Webber, *The South Carolina Historical and Genealogical Magazine*, courtesy of the South Carolina Historical Society; "The Jay Papers" (*American Heritage*, 1968), from the forthcoming book *John Jay: The Making of a Revolutionary 1752–1782*, by Richard Morris, by permission of Harper & Row, Publishers, Inc.

*Franklin and His French Contemporaries*, by Alfred Owen Aldridge. Reprinted by permission of New York University Press. Copyright © 1957 by New York University; material from the Baldwin Papers by permission of the Harvard College Library: *Voices of 1776* by Richard Wheeler, copyright © 1972 by Richard Wheeler. With permission of the publishers, Thomas Y. Crowell Company, Inc.

# Bibliography

*Adams Family Correspondence.* Edited by L. H. Butterfield. Vol. I, and II. Cambridge: The Belknap Press of Harvard University Press, 1963.

Alden, John Richard. *General Charles Lee, Traitor or Patriot?* Baton Rouge: Louisiana State University Press, 1951.

———. *General Gage in America.* Baton Rouge: Louisiana State University Press, 1948.

———. *A History of the American Revolution.* New York: Alfred A. Knopf, 1969.

Aldrige, Alfred Owen. *Franklin and his French Contemporaries.* N.Y.: New York University Press, 1957.

*America Through Women's Eyes.* Edited by Mary R. Beard. N.Y.: The Macmillan Company, 1933; N.Y.: Greenwood Press, 1969.

*American Heritage Book of the Revolution, The.* Editor-in-charge Richard M. Ketchum. N.Y.: American Heritage Publishing Company, Inc. 1958.

*American Revolution, The; Sir Henry Clinton's Narrative of His Campaigns, 1775–1782.* Edited by William B. Willcox. New Haven: Yale University Press, 1954.

Andrews, Edward Deming. *The People Called Shakers: A Search for the Perfect Society.* N.Y.: Dover Publications, Inc., 1965.

Anthony, Katharine. *First Lady of the Revolution: The Life of Mercy Otis Warren.* Garden City: Doubleday and Company, Inc., 1958.

Ashmore, Otis. "Wilkes County, Its Place in Georgia History." *The Georgia Historical Quarterly.* Vol. I, No. 1. 1917.

Bakeless, John. *Turncoats, Traitors and Heroes.* Philadelphia: J. B. Lippincott Company, 1959.

Bakeless, Katherine and John. *Spies of the Revolution.* Philadelphia: J. B. Lippincott Company, 1962.

Barck, Oscar Theodore. *New York City During the War for Independence.* N.Y.: Columbia University Press, 1931; Port Washington, N.Y.: Ira J. Friedman, Inc., 1966.

*Baroness von Riedesel and the American Revolution-Journal and Correspondence of a Tour of Duty 1776–1783.* Translation by Marvin L. Brown, Jr. Published by the University of North Carolina Press for the Institute of Early American History and Culture. Chapel Hill: 1965.

Bartlett, Helen R. *Eighteenth Century Georgia Women.* Ph.D. Dissertation: The University of Maryland, 1939.

Bass, Robert D. *Gamecock: The Life and Campaigns of General Thomas Sumter.* N.Y.: Holt, Rinehart and Winston, 1961.
———. *The Green Dragoon: The Lives of Banastre Tarleton and Mary Robinson.* N.Y.: Henry Holt and Company, 1957.

Beauchamp, William M. *A History of the New York Iroquois.* Port Washington, N.Y.: Ira J. Friedman, Inc., 1962.

Beckwith, Mildred Chaffee. *Catharine Macaulay: Eighteenth Century Rebel.* Ph.D. Dissertation. Ohio State University, 1953.

Bellamy, Francis Rufus. *The Private Life of George Washington.* N.Y.: Thomas Y. Crowell Company, 1951.

Bemis, Samuel Flagg. *The Diplomacy of the American Revolution.* N.Y.: D. Appleton-Century Company, Inc., 1935; Bloomington: Indiana University Press, 1965.

Benson, Mary Sumner. *Women in Eighteenth-Century America.* N.Y.: Columbia University Press, 1935; Port Washington, N.Y.: Kennikat Press, Inc., 1966.

Berger, Carl. *Broadsides and Bayonets: The Propaganda War of the American Revolution.* Philadelphia: University of Pennsylvania Press, 1961.

Bill, Alfred Hoyt. *A House Called Morven.* Princeton: Princeton University Press, 1954.

————. *Valley Forge: The Making of an Army.* N.Y.: Harper and Brothers, 1952.

Billias, George. *General John Glover and his Marblehead Mariners.* N.Y.: Henry Holt and Company, 1960.

Bird, Harrison. *Attack on Quebec-The American Invasion of Canada, 1775.* N.Y.: Oxford University Press, 1968.

————. *March to Saratoga: General Burgoyne and the American Campaign 1777.* N.Y.: Oxford University Press, 1963.

Blumenthal, Walter Hart. *Women Camp Followers of the American Revolution.* Philadelphia: George S. MacManus Company, 1952.

Bobbé, Dorothie. *Abigail Adams-The Second First Lady.* N.Y.: Minton, Balch and Company, 1929.

*Boswell's Journal of A Tour to the Hebrides with Samuel Johnson, L.L.D., 1773.* Edited by Frederick A. Pottle and Charles H. Bennett. N.Y.: McGraw-Hill Book Company, Inc., 1961.

Boudinot, Elias. *Journal or Historical Recollections of American Events During the Revolutionary War.* Philadelphia: Frederick Bourquin, 1894; reprinted under the title *Journal of Events in the Revolution.* N.Y.: The New York Times and the Arno Press, Inc., 1968.

Bowen, Catherine Drinker. *John Adams and the American Revolution.* Boston: Little, Brown and Company, 1949.

Boyle, John. "Boyle's Journal of Occurrences in Boston, 1759–1778." *The New England Historical and Genealogical Register.* Vol. 84, 1930; Vol. 85, 1931.

Brown, Alice. *Mercy Warren.* N.Y.: Charles Scribner's Sons, 1896; Spartanburg: The Reprint Company, 1968.

Brown, John P. *Old Frontiers-The Story of the Cherokee Indians from Earliest Times to the Date of their Removal to the West, 1835.* Kingsport: Southern Publishers, Inc., 1938.

Brown, Wallace. *The Good Americans: The Loyalists in the American Revolution.* N.Y.: William Morrow and Company, Inc., 1969.

———. *The King's Friends: The Composition and Motives of the American Loyalist Claimants.* Providence: Brown University Press, 1965.

Bunce, Oliver Bell. *The Romance of the Revolution.* N.Y.: H. Dayton, 1858.

Butler, Caleb. *History of the Town of Groton.* Boston: Press of T. R. Marvin, 1848.

Callahan, North. *Flight from the Republic.* Indianapolis: The Bobbs-Merrill Company, Inc., 1967.

———. *Henry Knox: General Washington's General.* N.Y.: Rinehart and Company, Inc., 1958.

———. *Royal Raiders: The Tories of the American Revolution.* Indianapolis: The Bobbs-Merrill Company, Inc., 1963.

Chidsey, Donald Barr. *The American Privateers, A History.* N.Y.: Dodd, Mead and Company, 1962.

———. *The War in the North—An Informal History of the American Revolution in and near Canada.* N.Y.: Crown Publishers, Inc., 1967.

*Chronicles of the American Revolution.* Edited by Alden T. Vaughan. N.Y.: Grosset and Dunlap, 1965. Originally published as *Principles and Acts of the Revolution in America.* Compiled by Hezekiah Niles. Baltimore: 1822.

Clinton, Sir Henry. Unpublished *"Notebook L."* Transcribed by William B. Willcox. The Clinton Papers. William L. Clements Library, The University of Michigan.

Codman, John. *Arnold's Expedition to Quebec.* Special edition edited by William Abbatt. N.Y.: The Macmillan Company, 1903.

Cometti, Elizabeth. "Women in the American Revolution." *The New England Quarterly.* Vol. XX, No. 3. Sept., 1947.

Cook, Fred J. *What Manner of Men: Forgotten Heroes of the American Revolution.* N.Y.: William Morrow and Company, 1959.

Corkran, David H. *The Cherokee Frontier-Conflict and Survival.* Norman: University of Oklahoma Press, 1962.

Coulter, E. Merton. "Nancy Hart, Georgia Heroine of the Revolution: The Story of the Growth of A Tradition." *The Georgia Historical Quarterly.* Vol. XXXIX, No. 2. June, 1955.

Crankshaw, Edward. *Maria Theresa.* N.Y.: The Viking Press, 1969.

Crawford, Constance. *The Jackson Whites.* M. A. Thesis. New York University, 1940.

Dabney, William M. *After Saratoga: The Story of the Convention Army.* Albuquerque: The University of New Mexico Press, 1954.

Dangerfield, George. *Chancellor Robert R. Livingston of New York, 1746–1813.* N.Y.: Harcourt, Brace and Company, 1960.

*DEH-HE-WA-MIS or A Narrative of the Life of Mary Jemison.* Edited by James E. Seaver. Batavia, N.Y.: William Seaver and Son, 1844.

Dexter, Elisabeth Anthony. *Career Women of America, 1776–1840.* Francestown, N.H.: Marshall Jones Company, 1950.

———. *Colonial Woman of Affairs.* Boston: Houghton Mifflin Company, 1924.

Draper, Lyman C. *King's Mountain and its Heroes.* Cincinnati, Peter G. Thomson, 1881; N.Y.: Dauber and Pine Bookshops, 1929.

Duncan, Louis C. *Medical Men in the American Revolution, 1775–1783.* Carlisle Barracks, Pa.: Medical Field Service School, 1931.

Earle, Alice Morse. *Colonial Dames and Good Wives.* Boston: Houghton, Mifflin and Company, 1895.

Eddis, William. *Letters from America.* Edited by Aubrey C. Land. Cambridge: The Belknap Press of Harvard University Press, 1969.

Ellet, Elizabeth F. *Domestic History of the American Revolution.* Philadelphia: J. B. Lippincott Company, 1876.

———. *The Women of the American Revolution.* Vols. I, II, III. N.Y.: Baker and Scribner, 1848, 1850.

*Extracts from the Journal of Elizabeth Drinker, from 1759–1807 A.D.* Edited by Henry D. Biddle. Philadelphia: J. B. Lippincott Company, 1889.

Fleming, Thomas. *The Man Who Dared the Lightning.* N.Y.: William Morrow and Company, Inc., 1971.

Flexner, James Thomas. "Benedict Arnold: How the Traitor was Unmasked." *American Heritage.* Vol. XVIII, No. 6. October, 1967.

———. *The Traitor and the Spy: Benedict Arnold and John André.* N.Y.: Harcourt, Brace and Company, 1935.

Forbes, Esther. *Paul Revere & The World He Lived In.* Boston: Houghton, Mifflin Company, 1942.

Forbes-Robertson, Diana. "Lady Knox." *American Heritage.* Vol. XVII, No. 3. April, 1966.

Force, Peter. *American Archives.* Vols. I, II, III, IV, V. Fourth Series. Washington: M. St. Clair Clarke and Peter Force, 1837.

Ford, Corey. *A Peculiar Service.* Boston: Little, Brown and Company, 1965.

Foreman, Carolyn Thomas. *Indian Women Chiefs.* Muskogee, Okla: The Star Printery, Inc., 1954.

Fowler, William W. *Women on the American Frontier.* Hartford: S. S. Scranton & Company, 1878; Ann Arbor: Plutarch Press, 1971.

Garden, Alexander. *Anecdotes of the American Revolution.* Vol. II. Reprinted Brooklyn: 1865.

Golder, Frank A. "Catherine II and The American Revolution." *The American Historical Review.* Vol. XXI, No. 1. October, 1915.

Gottlieb, Theodore. *The Origin and Evolution of the Betsy Ross Flag Legend or Tradition.* Newark: 1938.

Gratz, Simon. "Some Material for a Bibliography of Mrs. Elizabeth Ferguson, nee Graeme." *The Pennsylvania Magazine of History and Biography.* Vols. 39, 41. 1915, 1917.

Greene, George Washington. *The Life of Nathanael Greene.* Vols. I, II, III. Vol. I, N.Y.: G. P. Putnam and Son, 1867; Vols II and III, Hurd and Houghton, 1871.

Grey, Ian. *Catherine the Great, Autocrat and Empress of All Russia.* Philadelphia: J. P. Lippincott Company, 1962.

Griswold, Rufus. *The Female Poets of America.* N.Y.: James Miller, Publisher, 1874.

Guttmacher, Manfred S. "Catharine Macaulay and Patience Wright-Patronesses of the American Revolution." *The Johns Hopkins Alumni Magazine.* Vol. XXIV. 1936.

Hall, Edward Hagaman. *Margaret Corbin: Heroine of the Battle of Ft. Washington 16 November 1776.* N.Y.: The American Scenic and Historic Preservation Society, 1932.

Halliday, Mark. "An Agreable Voyage." *American Heritage.* Vol. XXI, No. 4. June, 1970.

Hargreaves, Reginald. *The Bloodybacks: The British Serviceman in North America and the Caribbean 1655–1783.* N.Y.: Walker and Company, 1968.

Hersey, Frank W. C. "The Misfortunes of Dorcas Griffiths." Publications of the Colonial Society of Massachusetts. Vol. XXXIV. *Transactions,* 1937–1942.

Hess, Stephen. *America's Political Dynasties, From Adams to Kennedy.* Garden City: Doubleday and Company, Inc., 1966.

*Hessian Soldier in the American Revolution, A; The Diary of Stephan Popp.* Translated by Rinehart J. Pope. Private Printing, 1953.

*Historical Anecdotes, Civil and Military: in a Series of Letters, written from America in the years 1777 and 1778.* London: Printed for J. Bew, 1779.

Hoehling, A. A. *Women Who Spied.* N.Y.: Dodd, Mead and Company, 1967.

Holliday, Carl. *Woman's Life in Colonial Days.* Boston: The Cornhill Publishing Company, 1922; Williamstown, Mass: Corner House Publishers, 1968.

Hutcheson, Maud M. "Mercy Warren, 1728–1814." *The William and Mary Quarterly.* Third Series. Vol. X. July, 1953.

Jones, E. Alfred. *The Loyalists of Massachusetts-their Memorials, Petitions & Claims.* London: The Saint Catherine Press, 1930.

Jones, Thomas. *History of New York During the Revolutionary War*. Vol. I, II. N.Y.: The New York Historical Society, 1879; N.Y.: The New York Times and the Arno Press Inc., 1968.

*Journal and Letters of the Late Samuel Curwen*. Edited by George Atkinson Ward. N.Y.: Leavitt, Trow and Company, 1845.

*Journal of James Melvin, The; Private Soldier in Arnold's Expedition Against Quebec in the year 1775*. Notes by Andrew A. Melvin. Portland: H. W. Bryant, 1902.

*Journal of Nicholas, Cresswell, 1774–1777, The*. Edited by Lincoln MacVeagh. N.Y.: The Dial Press, 1924.

*Journals of the Military Expedition of Major General John Sullivan*. Edited by Frederick Cook. Auburn, N.Y.: Knapp, Peck and Thomson, Printers, 1887.

Laffin, John. *Women in Battle*. London: Abelard-Schuman, 1967.

Lamb, R. *An Original and Authentic Journal of Occurrences During the Late American War from its Commencement to the Year 1783*. Dublin: Wilkinson and Courtney, 1809; N.Y.: The New York Times and the Arno Press, Inc., 1968.

Leonard, Eugenie Andruss. *The Dear-Bought Heritage*. Philadelphia: University of Pennsylvania Press, 1965.

*Letters From America 1776–1779: Being. Letters of Brunswick, Hessian, and Waldeck Officers with the British Armies During the Revolution*. Boston: Houghton Mifflin Company, 1924; Port Washington, N.Y.: Kennikat Press, Inc., 1964.

*Letters of a Loyalist Lady: Being the Letters of Ann Hulton, sister of Henry Hulton, Commissioner of Customs at Boston, 1767–1776*. Cambridge: Harvard University Press, 1927.

*Letters of Benjamin Rush*. Vol. I. Edited by L. H. Butterfield. Princeton: Princeton University Press, 1951.

*Letters of Eliza Wilkinson*. Arranged by Caroline Gilman. N.Y.: Samuel Colman, 1839; N.Y.: The New York Times and the Arno Press, Inc., 1969.

*Life and Letters of Lady Sarah Lennox 1745–1826, The*. Vols. I, II. Edited by The Countess of Ilchester and Lord Stavordale. London: John Murry, 1901.

Loggins, Vernon. *The Negro Author, His Development in America to 1900.* N.Y.: Columbia University Press, 1931; Port Washington, N.Y.: Kennikat Press, Inc., 1964.

Lomask, Milton. "The Aftermath of Treason." *American Heritage.* Vol. XVIII, No. 6. October, 1967.

*London Magazine, The.* November, 1775, pp. 555, 556.

Long, J.C. *George III.* Boston: Little, Brown and Company, 1960.

————. "Patience Wright of Bordentown." *Proceedings of the New Jersey Historical Society.* Vol. LXXIX, No. 2, April, 1961.

Lopez, Claude-Anne. *Mon Cher Papa Franklin and the Ladies of Paris.* New Haven: Yale University Press, 1966.

Lossing, Benson. *The Pictorial Field Book of the Revolution.* Vol. I, II. N.Y.: Harper and Brothers, Publishers, 1860.

Loudon, Archibald. *A Selection of Some of the Most Interesting Narratives of Outrages, Committed by the Indians in their Wars with the White People.* Vol. I, II. Carlisle, Pa: A. Loudon, 1808.

Lutnick, Soloman. *The American Revolution and the British Press-1775–1783.* Columbia: University of Missouri Press, 1967.

Lyman, Susan E. "Three New York Women of the Revolution." *New York Historical Society Bulletin.* Vol. XXIX, No. 2. April, 1945.

MacKenzie, Frederick. *The Diary of Frederick MacKenzie.* Cambridge: Harvard University Press, 1930; N.Y.: The New York Times and the Arno Press, Inc., 1968.

MacLean, J. P. *Flora MacDonald in America.* Lumberton, N.C.: by the author, 1909.

Malone, Dumas. *The Story of the Declaration of Independence.* N.Y.: Oxford University Press, 1954.

Malone, Henry Thompson. *Cherokees of the Old South-A People in Transition.* Athens: The University of Georgia Press, 1956.

*March to Quebec-Journals of the Members of Arnold's Expedition.* Compiled and annotated by Kenneth Roberts. N.Y.: Doubleday, Doran and Company, Inc., 1938.

*Margaret Morris: Her Journal.* Edited by John W. Jackson. Philadelphia: George S. MacManus Company, 1949.

Martin, Joseph Plumb. *A Narrative of Some of the Adventures, Dangers and Sufferings of a Revolutionary Soldier.* Hallowell: Glazier, Masters and Company, 1830.

May, Caroline. *The American Female Poets.* Philadelphia: Lindsay and Blakiston, 1848.

Mayer, Dorothy Moulton. *Marie Antoinette: The Tragic Queen.* N.Y.: Coward-McCann, Inc., 1968.

*Memoirs of Aaron Burr.* Vol. I. Edited by Matthew L. Davis. N.Y.: Harper and Brothers, 1836.

*Memoirs of Catherine the Great, The.* Edited by Dominique Maroger. Translated by Moura Budberg. N.Y.: The MacMillan Company, N.D.

*Men and Times of the Revolution; or Memoirs of Elkanah Watson.* Edited by Winslow C. Watson. N.Y.: Dana and Company, Publishers, 1856.

Miller, William C. "The Betsy Ross Legend." *The Social Studies.* Vol. XXXVII, No. 7. November, 1946.

Miner, Charles. *History of Wyoming.* Philadelphia: J. Crissy, 1845.

*Minutes of the Commissioners for Detecting and Defeating Conspiracies in the State of New York.* Vol. II. Albany County Sessions, 1778–1781.

Mirsky, Jeannette and Nevins, Allan. *The World of Eli Whitney.* N.Y.: The MacMillan Company, 1952.

Moore, Frank. *Sons and Ballads of the American Revolution.* N.Y.: D. Appleton and Company, 1856; N.Y.: The New York Times and the Arno Press, Inc., 1969.

Morris, Richard B. "The Jay Papers I: Mission to Spain." *American Heritage.* Vol. XIX, No. 2. February, 1968.

———. *The Peacemakers: The Great Powers and American Independence.* N.Y.: Harper and Row, Publishers, 1965.

*Mr Franklin, A Selection from his Personal Letters.* Edited by Leonard W. Labaree and Whitfield J. Bell, Jr. New Haven: Yale University Press, 1956.

"Mulberry Grove from the Revolution to the Present Time." Savannah Unit of the Georgia Writers Project of the WPA.

*The Georgia Historical Quarterly.* Vol. XXIII, No. 4. December 1939.

*Narrative of a Late Expedition Against the Indians.* Edited by Hugh Henry Brackenridge. Andover: Ames and Parker, 1798 (?).

Neill, Edward Duffield. "Reverend Jacob Duché, The First Chaplain of Congress." *The Pennsylvania Magazine of History and Biography.* Vol. II, No. 1. 1878.

*Noble Deeds of American Women.* Edited by J. Clement. Buffalo: George H. Derby and Company, 1851.

*Notable Women of Pennsylvania.* Edited by Gertrude Bosler Biddle and Sarah Dickinson Lowrie. Philadelphia: University of Pennsylvania Press, 1942.

O'Meara, Walter. *Daughters of the Country: The Women of the Fur Traders and Mountain Men.* N.Y.: Harcourt, Brace and World, Inc., 1968.

*On the Threshold of Liberty: Journal of a Frenchman's Tour of the American Colonies in 1777.* Translated by Edward D. Seeber. Bloomington: Indiana University Press, 1959.

Partridge, Bellamy. *Sir Billy Howe.* N.Y.: Longmans, Green and Company, 1932.

Pennypacker, Morton. *General Washington's Spies on Long Island and in New York.* Brooklyn: The Long Island Historical Society, 1939.

*Poems of Phillis Wheatley.* Edited by Julian D. Mason, Jr. Chapel Hill: The University of North Carolina Press, 1966.

Priest, Josiah. *Stories of the Revolution.* Albany: Hoffman and White, 1836.

Quarles, Benjamin. *The Negro in the American Revolution.* Published for the Institute of Early American History and Culture by the University of North Carolina Press, Chapel Hill, 1961.

Ravenel, Harriott Horry. *Eliza Pinckney.* N.Y.: Charles Scribner's Sons, 1896.

*Recollections of the Jersey Prison-Ship From the Original Manuscripts of Captain Thomas Dring one of the Prisoners.* Edited by Henry B. Dawson. Morrisania, N.Y.: 1865.

Reid, John Phillip. *A Law of Blood: The Primitive Law of the Cherokee Nation.* N.Y.: New York University Press, 1970.

*Reminiscences of An American Loyalist 1738–1789.* Edited by Jonathan Bouchier. Boston: Houghton Mifflin Company, 1925: Port Washington, N.Y.: Kennikat Press Inc., 1967.

*Revolution in America: Confidential Letters and Journals 1776–1784 of Adjutant General Major Baurmeister of the Hessian Forces.* Translated by Bernhard A. Uhlendorf. New Brunswick: Rutgers University Press, 1957.

*Revolutionary Journal of Baron Ludwig Von Closen, 1780–1783, The.* Translated by Evelyn M. Acomb. Published by the University of North Carolina Press for the Institute of Early American History and Culture. Chapel Hill: 1958.

*The Royal Commission on the Losses and Services of American Loyalists 1783–1785.* Notes of Mr. Daniel Parker Coke, M.P. One of the Commissioners. Edited by Hugh Edward Egerton. Oxford: Printed for presentation to the members of The Roxburghe Club, 1915.

Sabine, Lorenzo. *Biographical Sketches of Loyalists of the American Revolution.* Vol. I, II. Boston: Little, Brown and Company, 1864.

*Sally Wister's Journal.* Edited by Albert Cook Meyers. Philadelphia: Ferris and Leach, Publishers, 1902; N.Y.: The New York Times and the Arno Press, Inc., 1969.

Schaw, Janet. *Journal of a Lady of Quality.* Edited by Evangeline W. and Charles M. Andrews. New Haven: Yale University Press, 1939.

Scheer, George F. and Rankin, Hugh F. *Rebels and Redcoats. The Living Story of the American Revolution.* Cleveland: The World Publishing Company, 1957.

Sinclair, Andrew. *The Better Half-The Emancipation of the American Woman.* N.Y.: Harper and Row Publishers, 1965.

Sosin, Jack M. *The Revolutionary Frontier 1763–1783.* N.Y.: Holt, Rinehart and Winston, 1967.

*Spirit of 'Seventy-Six, The.* Edited by Henry Steele Commager and Richard B. Morris. Vol. I. Indianapolis: The Bobbs-Merrill Company, Inc., 1958.

Spruill, Julia Cherry. *Women's Life and Work in the Southern Colonies*. N.Y.: Russell and Russell, 1938.

Stark, James H. *The Loyalists of Massachusetts and the Other Side of the American Revolution*. Boston: J. H. Stark, 1910.

Stickley, Julia Ward. "The Records of Deborah Sampson Gannett, Woman Soldier of the Revolution." *Prologue*. Winter 1972. Vol. 4, No. 4.

Storms, J. C. *Origin of the Jackson-Whites of the Ramapo Mountains*. Park Ridge, N.J.: By the Author, 1958.

Swiggett, Howard. *The Forgotten Leaders of the Revolution*. Garden City: Doubleday and Company, Inc., 1955.

*Testimonies of the Life, Character, Revelations and Doctrines of our ever Blessed Mother Ann Lee*. Hancock: J. Tallcott and J. Deming, Jr., 1816.

Thacher, James. *A Military Journal During the American Revolutionary War from 1775–1783*. Boston: Richardson and Lord, 1823.

Thane, Elswyth. *Washington's Lady*. N.Y.: The Curtis Publishing Company, 1954; N.Y.: Dodd, Mead and Company, 1960.

Tharp, Louise Hall. *The Baroness and the General*. Boston: Little, Brown and Company, 1962.

Thayer, Theodore. *Nathanael Greene, Strategist of the American Revolution*. N.Y.: Twayne Publishers, 1960.

Thomas, Isaiah. *The History of Printing in America*. Vol. I, II. Albany: J. Munsell, Printer, 1874; N.Y.: Burt Franklin, 1967.

*Transcripts of the Manuscript Books and Papers of the Commission of Enquiry into the Losses and Services of America Loyalists*. Audit Office Records in the Public Record Office of England, 1783–1790. Library of Congress microfilm of the 1899 transcription for the New York Public Library.

Trumbull, John. *The Autobiography of Col. John Trumbull*. Edited by Theodore Sizer. New Haven, Yale University Press, 1953.

Tyler, Moses Coit. *The Literary History of the American Revolution*. Vol. II. N.Y.: G. P. Putnam's Sons, 1897; N.Y.: Frederick Ungar Publishing Company, 1967.

Van Doren, Carl. *Mutiny in January*. N.Y.: The Viking Press, 1943.

Van Doren, Carl. *Secret History of the American Revolution.* N.Y.: The Viking Press, 1941.

Van Every, Dale. *A Company of Heroes: The American Frontier 1775–1783.* N.Y.: William Morrow and Company, 1962.

Van Tyne, Claude Halstead. *The Loyalists in the American Revolution.* N.Y.: The MacMillan Company, 1902; Gloucester, Mass: Peter Smith, 1959.

Vining, Elizabeth Gray. *Flora, A Biography.* Philadelphia: J. B. Lippincott Company, 1966.

Wallace, Anthony F. C. *The Death and Rebirth of the Seneca.* N.Y.: Alfred A. Knopf, 1970.

Ward, Christopher. *The War of the Revolution.* Edited by John R. Alden. N.Y.: The MacMillan Company, 1952. Vol. I and II.

Washington, George and Kitman, Marvin. *George Washington's Expense Account.* N.Y.: Simon and Schuster, 1970.

Watson, J. Steven. *The Reign of George III, 1760–1815.* Oxford: Oxford University Press, 1960.

Webber, Mabel L. "Extracts from the Journal of Mrs. Ann Manigault 1754–1781." *The South Carolina Historical and Genealogical Magazine.* Vol. XX, XXI. 1919, 1920.

Weller, George. "The Jackson Whites." *The New Yorker.* September 17, 1938.

Wharton, Anne Hollingsworth. *Through Colonial Doorways.* Philadelphia: J. B. Lippincott Company, 1893.

Wheatley, Phillis. (Phillis Peters) *Poems and Letters.* Edited by Charles Fred Heartman. N.Y.: Printed by Charles Fred Heartman.

Wheeler, Richard. "Voices of Lexington and Concord." *American Heritage.* Vol. XXII, No. 3. April, 1971.

Whitton, Mary Ormsbee. *These were the Women, U.S.A. 1776–1860.* N.Y.: Hastings House, 1954.

Willcox, William B. *Portrait of a General: Sir Henry Clinton in the War of Independence.* N.Y.: Alfred A. Knopf, 1962.

Withers, Alexander Scott. *Chronicles of Border Warfare.* Cincinnati: The Robert Clarke Company, 1895.

Wroth, Lawrence C. *A History of Printing in Colonial Maryland 1686–1776.* Baltimore: The Typothetae of Baltimore, 1922.

# Index

Acland, Lady Christian Harriot, *139*, 140-141

Adams, Abigail Smith, 7, *9*, 10, 15, 36, 86-90, 107-108, 115-116, 118, 160, 163, 287, 292, 293, 298

Adams, John, 8, 10, 11, 36, 46, 62, 86-90, 160, 266, 282, 292, 293, 298

Adams, John Quincy, 298

Adams, Samuel, 10, 17, 304

Agent 355, 239, 240, 242, 243

Alexander, Sarah Livingston, 159, 215

Allen, Ethan, 20-21, 149

André, John, 167, 225, 228-230

Armed Neutrality, league of, 221-222

Arnold, Benedict, 20; march to Québec, 49-54, 75; 108, 135, 161-162, 167; West Point plot, 224-225, 227-232; 238, 272, 294, 297-298

Arnold, Hannah, 228

Arnold, Peggy Shippen, 167, *168*, 224-225, 227-232, 297-298

attainder, of women, 66


Bache, Richard, 144

Bache, Sarah Franklin, 265-266

Baddeley, Mary O'Callaghan, 188-190, 273, 284-285

Baddeley, Thomas, 188-190, 273

Bailey, Anne, 281

Baldwin, Loammi, 86

banishment, of women, 303

Bates, Ann, 243-244

Baurmeister, Major Carl, 95-96, 245-247

Bean, Mrs. William, 80-81

Belcher, Elizabeth, 67-68

Bennington, battle of, 134, 135, 137

Black Americans, 32, 38-43, 63, 75, 186-187, 188, 200-201, 255-256, 291-292, 300-301, 305

Bland, Martha Dangerfield, 273-274

Bleecker, Anne Eliza, 130-131

"blood clause," 124, 125

Bluestocking Movement, 89

Boone, Daniel, 77, 204

Boone, Jemina, 77

Boston Massacre, 58, 278

Boston, siege of, 33-35, 49, 54, 55, 57-58, 252

Boston Tea Party, 10

Boudinot, Elias, 101, 151-152, 166, 274-275, 299

Boucher, Eleanor Addison, 64

boycotts, 12

Bozarth, Experience, 193-194

Brandywine, battle of, 144, 183

Brant, Joseph, 74, 76, 190, 200

Brant, Molly, 74, 190

bribery, 149, 150-151, 223, 224

Brillon de Jouy, Mme., 115

British East India Company, 85, 297

Bunker Hill, battle of, 23, 29, 47, 48, 75, 92

Burgoyne, Lady Charlotte Stanley, 125-126, 127

Burgoyne, General John, 21, 47; Saratoga campaign, 125-144, 167, 193, 224; 247, 285

Burr, Aaron, 50, 93, 231

Butler, Colonel John, 199, 200


Camden, battle of, 247, 248, 249

campfollowers, 35, 50-52, 54, 84, 121, 122, 127, 142, 144, 159, 166, 171, 181-188, 250-251, 263-264, 271-272, 283, 290; see also Mar-

campfollowers (*continued*)
garet Corbin, Molly Hays, Baroness von Riedesel, etc.
captivity of women, Indian, 77, 80-81, 98, 131, 195, 198-199; see also Mary Jemison, Francis Slocum.
Carleton, Governor Guy, 53, 126
Carroll, Charles, 244
Carroll, Mary Darnall, 244
Catherine II, Empress of Russia, 122, *218*, 217-223, 290-291
Champion, Deborah, 55-57
Charleston, South Carolina, 91, 202, 207-211, 256, 257, 258, 259, 261, 262, 273
Charlotte, Queen of England, 27, *28*, 117-118, 122, 126, 286, 287
Cherokee War, 77, 80-82
Cherry Valley Massacre, 191, 193
Church, Dr. Benjamin, 36-38, 49
Church, Sarah, 37
Clinton, Sir Henry, 21, 23; Charleston campaign, 91, 208, 211; 108, 122; Saratoga campaign, 134, 138-139; 167, 171, 175, 183; and Mary Baddeley, 188-190, 272-273, 284-285; 191; Arnold plot, 224, 227-230; 243, 263-264
Clinton, General James, 195, 196
Committees of Correspondence, 8
Concord, Massachusetts, 17, 21, 22, 25, 160, 202, 251, 283
Continental Congress, 7, 21, 44, 45, 48, 86, 87, 89, 90, 100, 113, 125, 144, 148, 149, 150, 151, 178, 227
Corbin, Margaret Cochran, 98-99, 174, 300
Cornbury, Lord Viscount, 102-103
Cornwallis, Lord Charles, 111, 113, 211, 247, 251, 253, 254, 271, 272, 285
Cowpens, battle of, 253
Cresswell, Nicholas, 184-185
Cromer, Jane, 129, 134
Crouch, Mary Timothy, 210
Cruger, Anne De Lancey, 257-258

Curwen, Abigail Russell, 64, 65
Curwen, Samuel, 63-65

Dana, Francis, 151, 222
Darragh, Lydia, 153-155, 163
Dartmouth, Earl of, 31, 40, 41
Daughters of Liberty, 11-12, 22
Deane, Silas, 149
De Blois, Elizabeth, 161-162, 227
Declaration of Independence, 90-91, 100, 113
d'Estaing, Count, 175, 258, 290
defense, women's, 18-19, 193-194, 206, 276, 277, 280, 305
Dibblee, Polly Jarvis, 68
Dickinson, John, 46, 152
domestic activity and war, 164-165, 264-266, 277, 278, 305
Draper, Margaret Green, 43, 44-46, 62, 109
Drinker, Elizabeth, 145, 157, 170, 231
Duché, Reverend Jacob, 149, 150, 151, 293

Easson, Mary, 32-33
East Chester, skirmish of, 267, 269
Edenton, North Carolina, 12-14; *A Society of Patriotic Ladies, 13*
Elizabeth, Empress of Russia, 220
Esther, Queen, 191, 192, 305

Ferguson, Elizabeth Graeme, *148*, 147-152, 172, 282, 293
Ferguson, Patrick, 250
Flucker, Thomas, 48, 61-62, 160
folk heroines, 12, 203-207, 275-280
Fort Anne, battle of, 129
Fort Lee, 97, 99
Fort Motte, 256-257
Fort Stanwix, battle of, 135, 137, 190
Fort Ticonderoga, 20-21, 49, 57, 110, 127, 128, 161, 268
Fort Washington, battle of, 97, 98, 99
Franklin, Lady Agnes, 48-49

Franklin, Benjamin, 41, 65, 88, 90, 114-117, 119, 120, 149, 165, 191, 216, 217, 251, 256, 265-266, 282, 290
Franklin, Elizabeth Downes, 65
Franklin, William, 65, 111, 147
Franks, Rebecca, 157-158, 226-227
Fraser, General Simon, 131, 139-140, 193
Frederick the Great of Prussia, 124, 223, 287
Freeman's Farm, battle of, 138
Freneau, Philip, 242
French alliance, 114, 116, 165, 167, 171, 175, 207, 217, 222, 223, 258, 272, 282-283
French Revolution, 290
fund raising, by women, 264-266

Gage, Lady Margaret Kemble, 21-22, 24, 285
Gage, General Thomas, 17, 18, 21-23, 24, 60, 247, 285
Galloway, Grace Crowden, 172, 293
Gannett, Benjamin, 268, 269, 270
Gannett, Deborah Sampson, 266-270
Gates, Elizabeth, 252
Gates, General Horatio, 132, 133, 138, 139, 141, 142, 247-248, 251
George III, King of England, 26-29, 91, 117, 122, 124, 126, 179, 191, 217, 219-220, 223, 286-287, 297
Germantown, battle of, 146
German mercenaries, 109, 110, 121-125, 127, 136, 143, 173, 175, 176, 178, 181, 182, 245-247, 292
German women, 122, 181, 182, 187, 245-247, 290; see also Baroness von Riedesel
Gerry, Ann Thompson, 89, 299
Gerry, Elbridge, 88-89, 299
Glover, General John, 92, 109, 143, 175
Goddard, Mary Katherine, 113-114

Goldwait, Hannah, 35
Gray, Elizabeth, 304
Greene, Anne Catherine, 44, 114
Greene, Catharine Littlefield, 160, 166, 251-253, 295-297
Greene, General Nathanael, 94, 146, 159-160, 165, 166, 251-253, 254, 258, 295, 296, 297
Griffiths, Dorcas Pringle, 47-48, 60-62, 66, 160, 305
Guilford Courthouse, battle of, 254, 271, 277

Hamilton, Alexander, 144, 230, 292
Hancock, John, 16, 38, 48, 84, 91, 175, 299
Hart, Benjamin, 204, 205, 206, 207
Hart, Nancy Morgan, *203*, 203-207
Hays, Molly Ludwig, 173-174
Helvétius, Mme. Anne-Catherine, 115-116
Hill, Margaret Francis, 76-77
Howe, Admiral Richard, Lord, 92, 146, 175, 178
Howe, General William, 21, 24, 58, 60, 83, 92, 94; campaign of 1776, 83, 92-94, 96-97, 99-100, 102; and Elizabeth Loring, 103-105, 155-157, 188, 286; 127, 134, 144, 146, 153, 166-167, 168, 169, 183, 231, 247, 257
Huntington, Faith Trumbull, 23

Indian women, 50, 54, 74, 75-76, 77-81, 137, 190, 191-193, 195, 196-199, 281-282, 301-302; see also Mary Jemison, Francis Slocum
inflation, 177, 245, 263, 265
Ingraham, Hannah, 303

Jacataqua, 50, 54
Jackson, Andrew, 302
Jackson whites and blacks, 187-188, 291-292
Jay, John, 213-217, 222, 282, 299-300, 303

Jay, Sally Livingston, *214*, 213-216,
    228, 299
Jefferson, Thomas, 10, 43, 62, 90,
    108, 180, 263, 287, 293
Jemison, Mary, 136-137, 200-201,
    302
*Jersey*, 239-241, 242, 243
Johnson, John, 76
Johnson, Lady Mary Watts, 76, 257
Johnson, Sir William, 74, 75, 76,
    133
Jones, Judge Thomas, 103, 105, 257
Joseph II, Hapsburg Emperor, 223,
    224

Kettle Creek, battle of, 202, 203,
    204
kidnapping, 108, 162, 255
Kings Mountain, battle of, 250,
    251
Knox, General Henry, 10, 57-58,
    160-161, 166, 225, 294-295
Knox, Lucy Flucker, 160-162, 178,
    181, 225, 227, 252, 294-295, 297

Lafayette, Marquis de, 166, 173,
    179, 272, 290, 296
Lee, Mother Ann, 202, 232-237, 291
Lee, General Charles, 29, 33, 42,
    45, 75-76, 106-109, 166, 173, 226-
    227, 294
Lennox, Lady Sarah, *26*, 26-29, 128,
    140, 212, 286-287
Lewis, Elizabeth Annesley, 97
Lexington, Massachusetts, 17-18,
    25, 160, 202, 251, 283
Lincoln, General Benjamin, 207-
    208
Livingston, Margaret Beekman, 83,
    91, 138-139
Livingston, Robert, 90, 91, 138,
    214, 228, 298, 299-300
Livingston, Governor William,
    102, 213-214, 216, 299
Long Island, battle of, 92-93, 98
looting, 19, 34-35, 37, 67, 113, 130,
    138, 158, 172, 181, 182, 256, 258-
    259, 261, 271-272, 277, 280

Loring, Elizabeth Lloyd, 103-105,
    155-157, 170, 188, 257, 286
Loring, Joshua, 103, 104, 274, 286
Louis XVI, King of France, 116,
    171, 223-224, 290
loyalist legions, 68-69, 71, 127, 203,
    248-249, 250-251, 267, 303
loyalists, persecution of, 30-31, 32-
    33, 37, 59, 60, 62, 64-68, 72, 76-
    77, 172, 176, 195, 204, 209, 236,
    257-258, 276, 277-278, 293, 302-
    304
Lynch, Elizabeth Shubrick, 211

Macaulay, Catharine Sawbridge,
    7, 14-16, 25, 109, 114, 118, 212-
    213, 288
MacDonald, Flora, 69-72
Madison, James, 299
male impersonators, 18-19, 267-268,
    276, 277, 280
Manhattan, 1776 fire, 94-96, 102
Manigault, Ann, 207
Maria Theresa, Empress, 116, 217,
    223-224
Marie Antoinette, Queen of France,
    116, 223, 290
Marion, Francis, 249, 256, 258
Marshall, Susannah, 66-67
McCowan, Winifred, 182, 305
McCrea, Jane, 131-132, *133*, 134,
    137
medical care, 240, 248, 273-275
merchants, women, 48, 66-67, 96-
    97, 112, 209, 278
meschianza, 167-170, 225
messengers, women, 36, 53, 55-57,
    243, 275-276, 281
Minutewomen, 18-19
mistresses, 27, 36, 47, 84, 127-128,
    156, 187, 250-251, 285, 286; see
    also Elizabeth Loring, Mary
    Baddeley.
mobs, 7, 37, 59, 65, 68, 73, 91, 176,
    212, 231, 236, 277
Monmouth Courthouse, battle of,
    170, 173-175

Montgomery, General Richard, 53,
    54, 138
Montour, Catharine, 192, 197-198
Montour, Margaret, 192
Montreal, 49, 53, 127, 138
Morgan, Daniel, 50, 138, 204, 253,
    254
Morris, Margaret, 111-112
Morris, Robert, 151, 152, 228, 296,
    301
Motte, Rebecca Brewton, 256-257,
    261
Moulton, Martha, 17-18
Mulligan, Hercules, 239, 241
Murray, Mary Lindley, 93-94, 95
mutiny, 84, 263-264

narratives, soldiers', John Trum-
    bull, 23; Isaac Senter, 51; John
    Joseph Henry, 51, 52; Abner
    Stocking, 52; Caleb Haskell, 54;
    Loami Baldwin, 86; John Wood-
    hill, 93-94; James Thacher, 94,
    233-234; Carl Baurmeister, 95-
    96; Frederick Mackenzie, 96;
    Joseph Martin, 97, 174; Frances,
    Lord Rawdon, 105; Stephan
    Popp, 124-125, 175; Roger Lamb,
    134; Elias Boudinot, 152-153,
    274-275; Lt. Du Roi, 176-177;
    Sir Henry Clinton, 189; Adam
    Hubley, 197, 198, 199; William
    Barton, 197-198; Alexander
    Hamilton, 230; Aaron Burr,
    231; Thomas Dring, 240-241;
    Henry Lee, 257; Baron Ludwig
    von Closen, 271
Newport campaign, 175-176, 195
Ninety-Six, siege of, 257
nurses, women, 34, 171, 211, 248,
    249, 274, 275

Otis, James, 8, 10, 292

Paca, Anne Harrison, 157-158, 226
pacifism, 154, 155, 232, 234-236
Paddock, Lydia, 35-36
Paine, Thomas, 41, 100

Partherton, Mary, 235
pensions, loyalist women, 37, 47,
    60-62, 72, 209, 244, 286, 303-
    304
pensions, rebel women, 18, 98-99,
    174, 268-270
Peter, Grand Duke of Russia, 217,
    220, 291
Pinckney, Charles Cotesworth,
    261, 300
Pinckney, Eliza Lucas, 238, 259-
    263, 300
Pinckney, Thomas, 238, 261, 300
Prescott, General Richard, 108
press comment, 24, 25, 45, 84, 91,
    191, 212
Prevost, Theodosia, 231
Princeton, battle of, 111, 112, 113
prisoners, treatment of, 103-104,
    113, 239-243, 273, 274-275
privateers, 34, 221, 222
prostitutes, 34, 47, 61, 85-86, 182,
    187-188, 226
publishers, women, 43-46, 62, 113-
    114, 210
Putnam, General Israel, 20, 33, 93,
    94, 149

Quakers, 111, 145, 154, 155, 282
Québec, 49, 50, 53-55, 75, 138, 224
Quincy, Dorothy, 48, 299

rape, 105-106, 181, 187, 196, 208
Rawdon, Frances, Lord, 105, 187,
    256, 285-286
Reed, Esther De Berdt, 265
Reed, General Joseph, 150, 151,
    264-265
Revere, Paul, 17, 21, 36, 38, 55,
    57, 175, 268-269
Revere, Rachel, 38
Ross, Betsy Griscom, 206, 278-279
rumors, 16, 55, 83-85, 162, 164, 192,
    273, 275
Rush, Benjamin, 38-39, 100, 151-
    152, 266, 282-283, 299
Rush, Julia Stockton, 148, 266, 299

Saratoga, battle of, 137-142, 167, 190, 193, 212, 224, 228
Schaw, Janet, 30-32
Schuyler, Catherine Rensselaer, 137
Schuyler, General Philip, 49, 53, 57, 76, 129, 137, 149
Shakers; see Ann Lee
Sherman, Roger, 90
Signers, Declaration of Independence, 90-91, 100, 157-158, 210, 211, 244, 261, 299
Simpson, Sarah, 96
Six Nations expedition, 195-201
Slaves, see Black Americans
Slocum, Mrs. Charles, 305
Slocum, Francis, 194-195
smallpox, 34, 55, 161, 240, 273-274, 302
Smallwood, General William, 147, 186
smuggling, by women, 209
Spanish alliance, 215-217, 222, 224
spies, women, 21-22, 117, 119, 152-155, 204, 232, 234, 239-240, 243-244, 253, 276, 277-278, 281
Stockton, Annis Boudinot, 100-102, *101*, 113, 148, 299
Stockton, Richard, 100-102, 113
St. Clair, General Arthur, 128
St. Leger, Barry, 127, 135, 136, 137
Sullivan, General John, 146, 149, 175, 195, 196, 199
Sumter, Mary Cantey, 254-255, 300
Sumter, John, 249, 254-255, 258, 300

Tappan Bay, skirmish of, 267
tar and feathers, 30-31, 66, 68, 176
Tarleton, Banastre, 108, 211, 250, 253, 285
Thompson, Elizabeth, 209
Timothy, Peter, 210
Tories: see loyalists, persecution of; loyalist legions; pensions, loyalist women
torture, 136, 190-193, 281-282
Townsend, Robert, 239

Treaty of Paris, 283, 302
Trenton, battle of, 109-110, 154, 161, 245
Trumbull, John, 23
Trumbull, Governor Jonathan, 23, 75
Tryon, Margaret Wake, 102
Tryon, Governor William, 94, 102, 245
Tucker, Frances Bland, 254

Valley Forge, 57, 155, 157, 159, 160, 162, 164-166, 170, 171, 173, 226, 252
von Riedesel, Baron Friedrich, 121-122, 126, 127, 129, 135, 176, 180, 208, 245, 288
von Riedesel, Baroness Frederika, 121, 122, *123*, 126-127; Saratoga campaign, 129, 135, 139-143; Convention Army, 176, 177, 178-181; 244-245, 288, 290
von Steuben, Baron, 165

Wadsworth, Jeremiah, 252, 296
Ward, Nancy, 79-81, 302
Warner, Jemima, 50, 51-52, 54
Warren, James, 8, 10, 11, 86
Warren, Mercy Otis, 6, 7-11, 15, 19, 25, 40, 47, 86, 88, 107, 144, 162, 177, 288, 292-293
Washington, General George, 10, 22; at Cambridge, 33, 34, 38, 41, 44, 55, 58; 76, 83-85; New York campaign, 91, 92, 94, 96, 97, 99, 100; 106, 107, 108; at Trenton, 109-110, 112; 113; 148-149, 154; and Martha Washington, 160, 162, 163, 164, 165, 159, 166, 171, 173, 182-183, 211, 215, 229-230, 251, 263, 299, 300
Washington, Martha, 83, 160, 162-165, *163*, 181, 183, 305
Watson, Elkanah, 119-120
Waxhaws, battle of, 108, 211, 250
Wayne, "Mad" Anthony, 148, 170, 263, 297

West Point, 224, 228, 229, 232, 300
Wheatley, Phillis, 38-43, *39*, 300
White Marsh, battle of, 155
Whitney, Eli, 296-297
Widow Moore's Creek Bridge, battle of, 69, 71-72
Wilkinson, Eliza, 258-259
Wilkinson, Jemima, 237
Winthrop, Hannah, 19-20, 144, 177-178
Wister, Sally, 145-147, 186, 294

women's rights, 14, 89-90, 212-213
Wright, Patience Lovell, 117-120, 212, 287-288, *289*
Wright, Prudence, 18
Wyoming Valley Massacre, 190, 191, 193

Yorktown, battle of, 268, 272

Zane, Elizabeth, 279